THE

COLUMBIAN ORATOR

Containing A Variety of Original
and Selected Pieces together with Rules
Calculated to Improve Youth and Others
in the Ornamental and Useful
Art of Eloquence

(1811)

Caleb Bingham

ISBN 0-7661-0821-X

THE

COLUMBIAN ORATOR:

CONTAINING

A variety of Original and Selected Pieces;

TOGETHER WITH

RULES,

CALCULATED TO IMPROVE YOUTH AND OTHERS

IN THE

ORNAMENTAL AND USEFUL

Art of Eloquence.

BY CALEB BINGHAM, A. M.

Author of The American Preceptor, Young Lady's Accidence, &c.

" Cato cultivated Eloquence as a necessary mean for defending the rights of the people, and for enforcing good counsels."
ROLLIN.

Published according to Act of Congress.

TENTH EDITION.

ALBANY:

PUBLISHED BY D. FARRAND AND GREEN.
1811.

PREFACE.

NOTWITHSTANDING the multiplicity of School-Books now in use, it has been often suggested, that a Selection calculated particularly for Dialogue and Declamation, would be of extensive utility in our seminaries.

The art of Oratory needs no encomium. To cultivate its rudiments, and diffuse its spirit among the Youth of America, is the design of this Book.

Of the many pieces which this volume contains, three only are to be found in any publication of the kind. A large proportion is entirely original. To those, who have assisted him in this part, the author returns his warmest acknowledgments.

The COLUMBIAN ORATOR is designed for a Second Part to the AMERICAN PRECEPTOR; for this reason, no pieces are inserted from that book.

As no advantage could arise from a methodical arrangement, the Author has preferred variety to system. In his choice of materials, it has been his object to select such as should inspire the pupil with the ardour of eloquence, and the love of virtue. He has spared no pains to render the Work, in every respect, worthy of the generous patronage, which a liberal public have bestowed on his former publications.

Boston, May 17, 1797.

CONTENTS.

A

CONTENTS.

THE

COLUMBIAN ORATOR.

INTRODUCTION.

GENERAL DIRECTIONS FOR SPEAKING; EXTRACTED
FROM VARIOUS AUTHORS.

OF PRONUNCIATION IN GENERAL.

THE best judges among the ancients have represented Pronunciation, which they likewise called
Action, as the principal part of an orator's province;
from whence he is chiefly to expect success in the art
of persuasion. When Cicero, in the person of Crassus,
has largely and elegantly discoursed upon all the other
parts of oratory, coming at last to speak of this, he says,
" All the former have their effect as they are pronounced. It is the action alone which governs in speaking;
without which the best orator is of no value; and is
often defeated by one, in other respects much his inferior." And he lets us know, that Demosthenes was
of the same opinion; who, when he was asked what
was the principal thing in oratory, he replied, Action;
and being asked again a second and third time, what
was next considerable, he still made the same answer.

And, indeed, if he had not judged this highly necessary for an orator, he would scarcely have taken so much pains in correcting those natural defects, under which he laboured at first, in order to acquire it. For he had both a weak voice, and likewise an impediment in his speech, so that he could not pronounce distinctly some particular letters. The former of which defects he conquered, partly by speaking as loud as he could upon the shore, when the sea roared and was boisterous; and partly by pronouncing long periods as he walked up hill; both of which methods contributed to strengthen his voice. And he found means to render his pronunciation more clear and articulate, by the help of some little stones put under his tongue. Nor was he less careful in endeavouring to gain the habit of a becoming and decent gesture; for which purpose he used to pronounce his discourses alone before a large glass. And because he had an ill custom of drawing up his shoulders when he spoke, to amend that, he used to place them under a sword, which hung over him with the point downward.

Such pains did this prince of the Grecian orators take to remove those difficulties, which would have been sufficient to discourage an inferior, and less aspiring genius. And to how great a perfection he arrived in his action under all these disadvantages, by his indefatigable diligence and application, is evident from the confession of his great adversary and rival in oratory, Eschines; who, when he could not bear the disgrace of being worsted by Demosthenes in the cause of Ctesiphon, retired to Rhodes. And being desired by the inhabitants, he recited to them his own oration upon that occasion; the next day they requested of him to let them hear that of Demosthenes; which, having pronounced in a most graceful manner, to the admiration of all who were present, " How much more (says he) would you have wondered, if you had heard him speak it himself!"

We might add to these authorities the judgment of Quintilian; who says, that " It is not of so much moment what our compositions are, as how they are pronounced; since it is the manner of the delivery, by which the audience is moved."

The truth of this sentiment of the ancients, concerning the power and efficacy of pronunciation, might be proved from many instances; but one or two may here suffice. Hortensius a cotemporary with Cicero, and while living, next to him in reputation as an orator, was highly applauded for his action. But his orations after his death, as Quintilian tells us, did not appear answerable to his character; from whence he justly concludes, there must have been something pleasing when he spoke, by which he gained his character, which was lost in reading them.

But perhaps there is scarcely a more considerable instance of this than in Cicero himself. After the death of Pompey, when Cesar had gotten the government into his own hands, many of his acquaintance interceded with him in behalf of their relations and friends, who had been of the contrary party in the late wars. Among others, Cicero solicited for his friend Ligarius; which, Tubero understanding, who owed Ligarius a grudge, opposed; and undertook to represent him to Cesar as unworthy of his mercy. Cesar himself was prejudiced against Ligarius; and therefore, when the cause was to come before him, he said, "We may venture to hear Cicero display his eloquence; for I know the person he pleads for to be an ill man, and my enemy."

But however in the course of his oration, Cicero so wrought upon his passions, that by the frequent alteration in his countenance, the emotions of his mind were very conspicuous. And when he came to touch upon the battle of Pharsalia, which had given Cesar the empire of the world, he represented it in such a moving and lively manner, that Cesar could no longer contain himself, but was thrown into such a fit of shivering, that he dropped the papers which he held in his hand. That was the more remarkable, because Cesar was himself one of the greatest orators of that age; knew all the arts of address, and avenues to the passions; and consequently was better prepared to guard against them.

But neither his skill, nor resolution of mind, was of sufficient force against the power of oratory; but the conqueror of the world became a conquest to the charms of Cicero's eloquence; so that, contrary to his intention, he pardoned Ligarius. Now that oration is still extant, and appears exceedingly well calculated to touch the soft and tender passions and springs of the soul; but we believe it can scarcely be discernible to any, in reading it, how it should have had so surprising an effect; which must therefore have been chiefly owing to the wonderful address of the speaker.

The more natural the pronunciation is, the more moving it will be; since the perfection of art consists in its nearest resemblance to nature. And therefore it is not without good reason, that the ancients make it one qualification of an orator, that he be a *good* man; because a person of this character will make the cause he espouses his own; and the more sensibly he is touched with it himself, the more natural will be his action; and, of course, the more easily will he affect others. Cicero says, " It is certain that truth (by which he means nature) in every thing excels imitation; but if that were sufficient of itself in action, we should have no occasion for art."

In his opinion therefore (and who was ever a better judge?) art, in this case, as well as in many others, if well managed, will assist and improve nature. But this is not all; for sometimes we find the force of it so great and powerful, that, where it is wholly counterfeit, it will for the time work the same effect as if it were founded in truth. This is well known to those who have been conversant with the representations of the theatre: In tragedies, though we are sensible that every thing we see and hear is counterfeit, yet such is the power of action, that we are oftentimes affected by it in the same manner as if it were all reality.

Anger and resentment at the appearance of cruelty, concern and solicitude for distressed virtue, rise in our breasts; and tears are extorted from us for oppressed innocence: though at the same time, perhaps, we are ready to laugh at ourselves for being thus decoyed. If art then has so great an influence upon us, when supported by fancy and imagination only, how powerful must be the effect of a just and lively representation of what we know to be true.

How agreeable it is, both to nature and reason, that a warmth of expression and vehemency of motion should rise in proportion to the importance of the subject and concern of the speaker, will further appear by looking back a little into the more early and simple ages of the world. For the higher we go, the more we shall find of both. The Romans had a very great talent this way, and the Greeks a greater. The eastern nations excelled in it, and particularly the Hebrews.

Nothing can equal the strength and vivacity of the figures they employed in their discourse, and the very actions they used to express their sentiments; such as putting ashes on their heads, and tearing their garments, and covering themselves with sackcloth under any deep distress and sorrow of mind. And hence, no doubt, arose those surprising effects of eloquence which we never experience now.

And what is said here, with respect to the action of the eastern nations, was in a good measure customary among the Greeks and Romans; if not entirely of the same kind, yet perhaps as vehement and expressive.

They did not think language of itself sufficient to express the height of their passions, unless enforced by uncommon motions and gestures. Thus, when Achilles had driven the Trojans into their city with the greatest precipitation and terror, and only Hector ventured to tarry without the gates to engage him, Homer represents both king Priam and his queen under highest consternation for the danger of their son. And therefore, in order to prevail with him to come into city and not fight with Achilles, they not only entreat him from the walls in the most tender and moving language imaginable; but they tear off their gray locks with their hands, and adjure him to comply with their request.

The poet knew very well that no words of themselves could represent those agonies of mind he endeavoured to convey, unless heightened by the idea of such actions as were expressive of the deepest sorrow. In one of Cicero's orations, he does not stick to argue in this manner with his adversary. " Would you talk thus (says he) if you were serious? Would you, who are wont to display your eloquence so warmly in the danger of others, act so coldly in your own? Where is that concern, that ardour which used to extort pity even from children? Here is no emotion either of mind or body; neither the forehead struck, nor the thigh; nor so much as a stamp of the foot. Therefore, you have been so far from inflaming our minds, that you have scarcely kept us awake."

The ancients had persons, whose proper business it was to teach them how to regulate and manage their voice; and others, who instructed them in the whole art of pronunciation, both as to their voice and gestures. These latter were generally taken from the theatre, being some eminent experienced actors. But tho' they made use of actors to instruct their youth in forming their speech and gestures, yet the action of an orator was very different from that of the theatre.

Cicero very plainly represents this distinction, in the words of Crassus; when speaking of orators, he says, " The motions of the body ought to be suited to the expressions, not in a theatrical way, mimicking the words by particular gesticulations; but in a manner expressive of the general sense; with a sedate and manly inflection of the sides; not taken from the stage and actors, but from the exercise of arms and the palestra."

And Quintilian says to the same purpose, " Every gesture and motion of the comedians is not to be imi-

tated, nor to the same degree." They thought the
action of the theatre too light and extravagant for the
imitation of an orator; and therefore, though they
employed actors to inform young persons in the first
rudiments, yet they were afterwards sent to schools,
designed on purpose to teach them a decent and
graceful management of their bodies.

Being thus far prepared, they were afterwards sent
to the schools of the rhetoricians. And here, as their
business was to cultivate their style, and gain the whole
art of eloquence, so particularly to acquire a just and
accurate pronunciation by those exercises, in which for
that end they were constantly employed. Nor, after
all this pains and industry, did they yet think themselves sufficiently qualified to take upon them the character of orators. But it was their constant custom to
get together some of their friends and acquaintance,
who were proper judges of such performances, and
declaim before them in private.

The business of these persons was to make observations both on their language and pronunciation. And
they were allowed the greatest freedom to take notice
of any thing thought to be amiss, either as to inaccuracy
of method, impropriety of style, or indecency of their
voice or actions. This gave them an opportunity to
correct any such defects at first, before they became
habitual. What effects might not justly be expected
from such an institution? Persons trained up in this
manner, with all those advantages, joined to a good
natural genius, could not fail of making very complete
orators. Though even after they came to appear in
public they did not lay aside the custom of declaiming.

The influence of sounds, either to raise or allay our
passions, is evident from music. And certainly the
harmony of a fine discourse, well and gracefully pronounced, is as capable of moving us, if not in a way
so violent and ecstatic, yet not less powerful, and more
agreeable to our rational faculties. As persons are differently affected when they speak, so they naturally

B

alter the tone of their voice, though they do not attend to it. It rises, sinks, and has various inflections given it, according to the present state and disposition of the mind. When the mind is calm and sedate, the voice is moderate and even; when the former is dejected with sorrow, the latter is languid; and when that is inflamed by passion, this is elevated.

It is the orator's business, therefore, to follow nature, and to endeavour that the tone of his voice appear natural and unaffected. And for this end, he must take care to suit it to the nature of the subject; but still so as to be always grave and decent. Some persons continue a discourse in such a low and drawling manner, that they can scarcely be heard by their audience. Others again hurry on in so loud and boisterous a manner, as if they imagined their hearers were deaf. But all the music and harmony of voice lie between these extremes. Perhaps nothing is of more importance to a speaker, than a proper attention to accent, emphasis, and cadence. Every word in our language, of more than one syllable, has, at least, one accented syllable. This syllable ought to be rightly known, and the word should be pronounced by the speaker in the same manner as he would pronounce it in ordinary conversation. By emphasis, we distinguish those words in a sentence which we esteem the most important, by laying a greater stress of voice upon them than we do upon the others. And it is surprising to observe how the sense of a phrase may be altered by varying the emphasis. The following example will serve as an illustration.

This short question, "Will you ride to town to-day?" may be understood in four different ways, and, consequently, may receive four different answers, according to the placing of the emphasis.

If it be pronounced thus: Will *you* ride to town to-day? the answer may properly be; No; I shall send my son. If thus; Will you *ride* to town to-day? Answer, No; I intend to walk. Will you ride to *town* to-day? No; I shall ride into the country. Will you ride to town *to-day?* No, but I shall to-morrow.

This shows how necessary it is that a speaker should know how to place his emphasis. And the only rule for this is, that he study to attain a just conception of the force and spirit of the sentiments which he delivers. There is as great a difference between one who lays his emphasis properly, and one who pays no regard to it, or places it wrong, as there is between one who plays on an instrument with a masterly hand, and the most bungling performer.

Cadence is the reverse of emphasis. It is a depression or lowering of the voice; and commonly falls upon the last syllable in a sentence. It is varied, however, according to the sense. When a question is asked, it seldom falls upon the last word; and many sentences require no cadence at all.

Every person who speaks in public, should endeavour, if he can, to fill the place where he speaks. But still he ought to be careful not to exceed the natural key of his voice. If he does, it will neither be soft nor agreeable, but either harsh and rough, or too shrill and squeaking. Besides, he will not be able to give every syllable its full and distinct sound; which will render what he says obscure, and difficult to be understood. He should therefore take care to keep his voice within reach, so as to have it under management, that he may raise or sink it, or give it any inflection he thinks proper; which it will not be in his power to do, if he put a force upon it, and strain it beyond its natural tone.

The like caution is to be used against the contrary extreme, that the voice be not suffered to sink too low. This will give the speaker pain in raising it again to its proper pitch, and be no less offensive to the hearers. The medium between these two is a moderate and even voice. But this is not the same in all; that which is moderate in one would be high in another. Every person therefore must regulate it by the natural key of his own voice. A calm and sedate voice is generally best;

as a moderate sound is most pleasing to the ear, if
it be clear and distinct. But this equality of the voice
must also be accompanied with a variety: otherwise
there can be no harmony; since all harmony consists
in variety.

Nothing is less pleasing than a discourse pronounced
throughout in one continued tone of the voice, without any alteration. The equality, therefore, we are
here speaking of, admits a variety of inflections and
changes within the same pitch. And when that is altered, the gradations, whether higher or lower, should
be so gentle and regular as to preserve a due proportion of the parts, and harmony of the whole; which
cannot be done when the voice is suddenly varied with
too great a distinction. And therefore it should move
from one key to another, so as rather to glide like a
gentle stream, than to pour down like a rapid torrent,
as an ingenious writer has well expressed it.

But an affected variety, ill placed, is as disagreeable
to a judicious audience, as the want of it where the
subject requires it. We may find some persons, in pronouncing a grave and plain discourse, affect as many
different tones, and variations of their voice, as if they
were acting a comedy; which is doubtless a very great
impropriety. But the orator's province is not barely
to apply to the mind, but likewise to the passions;
which require a great variety of the voice, high or
low, vehement or languid, according to the nature of
the passions he designs to affect. So that for an orator
always to use the same tone or degree of his voice, and
expect to answer all his views by it, would be much the
same thing as if a physician should propose to cure all
distempers by one medicine. And, as a perfect monotony is always unpleasant, so it can never be necessary
in any discourse.

That some sentences ought to be pronounced faster
than others is very manifest. Gay and sprightly ideas
should not only be expressed louder, but also quicker
than such as are melancholy. And when we press an

opponent, the voice should be brisk. But to hurry on in a precipitant manner without pausing, till stopped for want of breath, is certainly a very great fault. This destroys not only the necessary distinction between sentence and sentence, but likewise between the several words of the same sentence; by which mean all the grace of speaking is lost, and in a great measure, the advantage of hearing.

Young persons are very liable to this, especially at first setting out. And it often arises from diffidence. They are jealous of their performances, and the success they may have in speaking, which gives them a pain till it is over; and this puts them into a hurry of mind, which incapacitates them from governing their voice, and keeping it under that due regulation which perhaps they proposed to themselves before they began to speak.

And as a precipitant and hasty pronunciation is culpable, so likewise on the other hand, it is a fault to speak too slow. This seems to argue a heaviness in the speaker. And as he appears cool himself, he can never expect to warm his hearers, and excite their affections. When not only every word, but every syllable is drawn out to too great a length, the ideas do not come fast enough to keep up the attention without much uneasiness. Now, to avoid either of the two extremes last mentioned, the voice ought to be sedate and distinct. And in order to render it distinct, it is necessary, not only that each word and syllable should have its just and full sound, both as to time and accent, but likewise that every sentence, and part of a sentence, should be separated by its proper pause.

This is more easy to be done in reading, from the assistance of the points; but it is no less to be attended to in speaking, if we would pronounce in a distinct and graceful manner. For every one should speak in the same manner as he ought to read, if he could arrive at that exactness. Now the common rule given in pausing is, that we stop our voice at a comma till we can tell one, at a semicolon two, at a colon three, and at a full period four. And as these points are either accommodated to the several parts of the same sentence, as the first three; or different sentences, as the last, this occasions the different length of the pause, by which either the dependence of what precedes upon that which follows, or its distinction from it, is represented.

It is not in our power to give ourselves what qualities of the voice we please; but only to make the best use we can of what nature has bestowed upon us. However, several defects of the voice are capable of being helped by care and proper means; as, on the other hand, the best voice may be greatly hurt by ill management and indiscretion. Temperance is a great preservative of the voice, and all excess is highly prejudicial to it. The voice must necessarily suffer, if the organs of speech have not their proper tone. A strong voice is very serviceable to an orator, because, if he want some other advantages, he is, however, capable to make himself heard. And if at any time he is forced to strain it, he is in less danger of its failing him before he has finished his discourse.

But he, who has a weak voice, should be very careful not to strain it, especially at first. He ought to begin slow, and rise gradually to such a pitch as the key of his voice will well carry him, without being obliged to sink again afterwards. Frequent inflections of the voice will likewise be some assistance to him. But especially he should take care to speak deliberately, and ease his voice, by allowing due time for respiration at all the proper pauses. It is an extreme much less inconvenient for such a person rather to speak too slow, than too fast. But this defect of a weak voice is sometimes capable of being helped by the use of proper methods; as is evident from the instance of Demosthenes, before mentioned.

Some persons either from want of due care in their education at first, or from inadvertency and negligence afterwards, run into a very irregular and confused manner of expressing their words; either by misplacing the accent, confounding the sound of the letters, or huddling the syllables one upon another, so as to render what they say often unintelligible. Indeed, sometimes this arises from a natural defect, as in the case of Demosthenes; who found a method to rectify that, as well as the weakness of his voice. But in faults of this kind, which proceed from habit, doubtless the most likely way to mend them is to speak deliberately.

OF GESTURE.

By this is meant, a suitable conformity of the motions of the countenance, and several parts of the body in speaking, to the subject-matter of the discourse. It is not agreed among the learned, whether voice or gesture has the greater influence upon us. But as the latter affects us by the eye as the former does by the ear, gesture in the nature of it seems to have this advantage, that it conveys the impression more speedily to the mind; for the sight is the quickest of all our senses. Nor is its influence less upon our passions; nay, in some instances, it appears to act more powerfully. A cast of the eye will express desire in as moving a manner as the softest language; and a different motion of it, resentment.

To wring the hands, tear the hair, or strike the breast, are all strong indications of sorrow. And he, who claps his hand to his sword, throws us into a greater panic than one who only threatens to kill us. Nor is it in some respects less various and extensive than language. Cicero tells us he often diverted himself by trying this with Roscius the comedian; who could express a sentence as many ways by his gestures, as he himself could by words. And some dramas, called pantomimes, have been carried on wholly by mutes, who have performed every part by gestures only, without words, in a way very intelligible.

But with respect to oratory, gesture may very properly be called the second part of pronunciation; in which, as the voice should be suited to the impressions it receives from the mind, so the several motions of the body ought to be accommodated to the various tones and inflections of the voice. When the voice is even and moderate, little gesture is required; and nothing is more unnatural than violent motion, in discoursing upon ordinary and familiar subjects. The motions of the body should rise therefore in proportion to the vehemence and energy of the expression, as the natural and genuine effect of it.

But as gesture is very different and various as to the manner of it, which depends upon the decent conduct of several parts of the body, it will not be amiss to consider more particularly the proper management of each of those parts. Now all gesture is either natural, or from imitation. By natural gesture, we mean such actions and motions of the body, as naturally accompany our words, as these do the impressions of our mind. And these either respect the whole body or some particular part of it.

The speaker should not long continue standing in the same position, like a statue, but be constantly changing, though the motion be very moderate. There ought to be no appearance of stiffness, but a certain ease and pliableness, naturally suiting itself to every expression; by which means, when a greater degree of motion is necessary, it will appear less sudden and vehement: for as the raising, sinking, and various inflections of the voice must be gradual, so likewise should the motions of the body. It is only on some particular occasions that a hasty vehemence and impetuosity is proper in either case.

As to the several parts of the body, the head is the most considerable. To lift it up too high has the air of arrogance and pride; and to stretch it out too far or throw it back, looks clownish and unmannerly; to hang it downwards on the breast, shows an unmanly bashfulness and want of spirit; and to suffer it to lean on either shoulder, argues both sloth and indolence. Wherefore, in calm and sedate discourse, it ought to keep its natural state, and upright posture. However, it should not be long without motion, nor yet always moving; but gently turn sometimes on one side, and sometimes on the other, as occasion requires, that the voice may be heard by all who are present; and then return again to its natural position. It should always accompany the other actions of the body, and turn on the same side with them; except when aversion to any thing is expressed, which is done by stretching out the right hand, and turning the head to the left.

But it is the countenance, that chiefly represents both the passions and dispositions of the mind. By this we express love, hatred, joy, sorrow, modesty, and confidence: by this we supplicate, threaten, soothe, invite, forbid, consent, or refuse; and all this without speaking. Nay, from hence we form a judgment not only of a person's present temper, but of his capacity and natural disposition. And therefore it is common to say, such a one has a "promising countenance," or that "he promises little by his countenance." It is true, this is no certain rule of judging; nor is it in the power of any one to alter the natural make of his countenance.

But the several parts of the face bear their part, and contribute to the proper and decent motion of the whole. In a calm and sedate discourse, all the features retain their natural state and situation. In sorrow, the forehead and eyebrows lower, and the cheeks hang down. But in expressions of joy and cheerfulness, the forehead and eyebrows are expanded, the cheeks contracted, and the corners of the mouth drawn upwards. Anger and resentment contract the forehead, draw the brows together, and thrust out the lips. And terror elevates both the brows and forehead. As these are the natural signs of such passions, the orator should endeavour to conform to them.

But as the eyes are most active and significant, it is the advice of Cicero that the greatest care should be taken in their management. And he gives this reason for it. " Because other parts of the countenance have but few motions; whereas all the passions of the soul are expressed in the eyes, by so many different actions which cannot possibly be represented by any gestures of the body, if the eyes are kept in a fixed posture." Common experience does in a great measure confirm the truth of this observation. We readily guess at a person's intention, or how he is affected to us by his eyes. And any sudden change or emotion of the mind is presently followed by an alteration in the look.

In speaking, therefore, upon pleasant and delightful subjects, the eyes are brisk and cheerful; as, on the contrary, they sink and are languid in delivering any thing melancholy and sorrowful. This is so agreeable to nature, that before a person speaks, we are prepared with the expectation of one or the other from his different aspect. So likewise in anger, a certain vehemence and intenseness appears in the eyes, which, for want of proper words to express it by, we endeavour to represent by metaphors taken from fire, the most violent and rapid element; and say in such cases, the eyes sparkle, burn, or are inflamed. In expressions of hatred or detestation, it is natural to alter the looks, either by turning the eyes aside, or downwards.

Indeed the eyes are sometimes turned downwards upon other occasions, as to express modesty. And if at any time a particular object be addressed, whatever it be, the eyes should be turned that way. And therefore Philostratus very deservedly ridicules a certain rhetorician as guilty of a solecism in gesture, who, upon saying, O Jupiter! turned his eyes downwards; and when he said, O earth! looked upward. A staring look has the appearance of giddiness and want of thought: and to contract the eyes gives suspicion of craft and design. A fixed look may be occasioned from intenseness of thought; but at the same time shows a disregard to the audience; and a too quick and wandering motion of the eyes denotes levity and wantonness. A gentle and moderate motion of the eyes is, therefore, in common, most suitable; always directed to some of the audience, and gradually turning from side to side with an air of respect and modesty, and looking them decently in the face, as in common discourse. Such a behaviour will of course draw an attention.

As to the other parts of the body distinct from the head, the shoulders ought not to be elevated; for this is not only in itself indecent; but it likewise contracts the neck, and hinders the proper motion of the head. Nor, on the other hand, should they be drawn down and depressed; because this occasions a stiffness both to the neck and the whole body. Their natural posture therefore is best, as being most easy and graceful. To shrug the shoulders has an abject and servile air; and frequently to heave them upwards and downwards is a very disagreeable sight. A continued motion of the arms any way, is by all means to be avoided. Their action should generally be very moderate, and follow that of the hands; unless in very pathetic expressions, where it may be proper to give them a more lively spring.

Now, all bodily motion is either upward or downward, to the right or left, forward or backward, or else circular. The hands are employed by the orator in all these, except the last. And as they ought to correspond with our expressions, so they ought to begin and end with them. In admiration, and addresses to Heaven, they must be elevated, but never raised above the eyes; and in speaking of things below us, they are directed downwards. Side motion should generally begin from the left, and terminate gently on the right. In demonstrating, addressing, and on several other occasions, they are moved forward; and in threatening, sometimes thrown back. But when the orator speaks of himself his right hand should be gently laid on his breast.

The left hand should seldom move alone, but accommodate itself to the motions of the right. In motions to the left side, the right hand should not be carried beyond the left shoulder. In promises, and expressions of compliment, the motion of the hands should be gentle and slow; but in exhortations and applause, more swift. The hands should generally be open; but in expressions of compunction and anger, they may be closed. All finical and trifling actions of the fingers ought to be avoided; nor should they be stretched out and expanded in a stiff and rigid posture, but kept easy and pliable.

The gestures we have hitherto discoursed of, are such as naturally accompany our expressions. And we believe those we have mentioned, if duly attended to, will be found sufficient to answer all the purposes of our modern pronunciation. The other sort of gestures above mentioned are such as arise from imitation; as where the orator describes some action or personates another speaking. But here great care is to be taken not to overact his part by running into any ludicrous or theatrical mimicry. It is sufficient for him to represent things of this nature, as may best convey the image of them in a lively manner to the minds of the hearers, without any such changes either of his actions or voice as are not suitable to his own character.

Some PARTICULAR RULES for the VOICE and GESTURE.

We shall begin with the parts of a discourse, and treat of them in their natural order. And here the view and design of the speaker in each of them will easily help us to see the proper manner of pronunciation. Let us suppose then a person presenting himself before an assembly, in order to make a discourse to them. It cannot be decent immediately to begin to speak so soon as ever he makes his appearance. He will first settle himself, compose his countenance, and take a respectful view of his audience. This prepares them for silence and attention.

Persons commonly form some opinion of a speaker from their first view of him, which prejudices them either in his favour or otherwise, as to what he says afterwards. A grave and sedate aspect inclines them to think him serious; that he had considered his subject, and may have something to offer worth their attention. A haughty and forbidding air occasions distaste, as it looks like disrespect. A wandering giddy countenance argues levity. A dejected drooping appearance is apt to raise contempt, unless where the subject is melancholy; and a cheerful aspect is a proper prelude to a pleasant and agreeable argument.

To speak low at first has the appearance of modesty, and is best for the voice; which, by rising gradually, will with more ease be carried to any pitch that may be afterwards necessary, without straining it. However, some variation of the voice is always proper to give it harmony. Nay, and sometimes it is not improper for an orator to set out with a considerable degree of warmth. We have some few instances of this in Cicero; as in his oration for Roscius Amerinus, where the heinousness of the charge could not but excite his indignation against the accusers. And so likewise, in that against Piso, and the two first against Catiline, which begin in the same manner, from the resentment he had conceived against their persons and conduct.

In the narration the voice ought to be raised to somewhat a higher pitch. Matters of fact should be related in a very plain and distinct manner, with a proper stress and emphasis laid upon each circumstance, accompanied with a suitable address and motions of the body to engage the attention of the hearers. For there

C

is a certain grace in telling a story, by which those who are masters of it seldom fail to recommend themselves in conversation.

The proposition, or subject of the discourse, should be delivered with a very clear and audible voice. For if this be not plainly heard, all that follows in proof of it cannot be well understood. And for the same reason, if it be divided into several parts or branches, they should each be expressed very deliberately and distinctly. But as the design here is only information, there can be little room for gesture.

The confirmation admits of great variety both of the voice and gesture. In reasoning, the voice is quick and pungent, and should be enforced with suitable actions. And as descriptions likewise have often a place here, in painting out the images of things, the orator should so endeavour to adapt both his voice, and the motions of his body, particularly the turn of his eyes, and action of his hands, as may best help the imagination of his hearers. Where he introduces another person speaking, or addresses an absent person, it should be with some degree of imitation. And in dialogue, the voice should alter with the parts. When he diverts from his subject by any digression, his voice should be lively and cheerful; since that is rather designed for entertainment than instruction.

In confutation, the arguments of the adverse party ought first to be repeated in a plain and distinct manner that the speaker may not seem to conceal, or avoid the force of them, unless they appear trifling and unworthy a serious answer, and then a facetious manner, both of expression and gesture, may be the most proper way to confute them. For, to attempt to answer in a grave and serious manner, what is in itself empty and ludicrous, is apt to create a suspicion of its having more in it than it really has.

But caution should be used not to represent any argument of weight in a ludicrous way, least by so doing the speaker should more expose himself than his adversary. In the conclusion, both the voice and gesture should be brisk and sprightly; which may seem to arise from a sense of the speaker's opinion of the goodness of his cause, and that he has offered nothing but what is agreeable to reason and truth; as likewise from his assurance that the audience agree with him in the same sentiment. If an enumeration of the principal arguments of the discourse be convenient, as it sometimes is, where they are pretty numerous, or the discourse is long, they ought to be expressed in the most clear and forcible manner. And if there be an address to the passions both the voice and gesture must be suited to the nature of them.

We proceed now to the consideration of particular expressions. And what we shall offer here, will be in relation to the single words, sentences, and the passions. Even in those sentences which are expressed in the most even and sedate manner, there is often one or more words which require an emphasis and distinction of the voice. Pronouns are often of this kind; as, *this* is the man. And such are many words that denote the circumstances and qualities of things. Such as heighten or magnify the idea of the thing to which they are joined, elevate the voice; as *noble*, *admirable*, *majestic*, *greatly*, and the like. On the contrary, those which lessen the idea, or debase it, depress the voice, or at least protract the tone: of which sort are the words, *little*, *mean*, *poorly*, *contemptible*, with many others.

Some tropes, likewise, as metaphors and verbal figures, which consist in the repetition of a single word, should have a particular emphasis. As when Virgil says of the river Araxes, " It *disdained* a bridge." And Nisus of himself, in the same poet, "I, *I* am the man;" where the repeated word is loudest. This distinction of words, and giving them their proper emphasis, does not only render the expression more clear and intelligible, but very much contributes to the variation of the voice and the preventing of a monotony.

In sentences, regard should be had to their length, and the number of their parts, in order to distinguish them by proper pauses. The frame and structure of the period ought likewise to be considered, that the voice may be so managed as to give it the most musical accent. Unless there be some special reason for the contrary, it should end louder than it begins. And this difference of tone between the end of the former sentence and the beginning of the next, not only helps to distinguish the sense, but adds to the harmony of the voice.

In an antithesis, or a sentence consisting of opposite parts, one contrary must be louder than the other. As, " He is gone, but by a *gainful* remove, from *painful labour* to *quiet rest; from unquiet desire* to *happy contentment;* from *sorrow* to *joy;* and from *transitory time* to *immortality*." In a climax or gradation, the voice should generally rise with it. Thus, " There is no enjoyment of property without government; no government without a magistrate; no magistrate without obedience; no obedience where every one acts as he pleases." And so in other gradations of a different form; as, " Since concord was lost, friendship was lost, fidelity was lost, liberty was lost, all was lost."

That the passions have each of them both a different voice and action, is evident from hence, that we know in what manner a person is affected, by the tone of his voice, though we do not understand the sense of what he says, or many times so much as see him; and we can often make the same judgment from his countenance and gestures. Love and esteem are expressed in a smooth and cheerful tone; but anger and resentment, with a rough, harsh, and interrupted voice; for when the spirits are ruffled, the organs are moved unequally. Joy raises and dilates the voice, as sorrow sinks and contracts it. Cicero takes notice of a passage in an oration of Gracchus, wherein he bewails the death of his brother, who was killed by Scipio, which in his time was thought very moving: "Unhappy man (says he,) whither shall I betake myself? Where shall I go? Into the capitol? that flows with my brother's blood. Shall I go home and behold my unhappy mother all in tears and despair?"

Though Gracchus had a very ill design in that speech, and his view was to excite the populace against their governors, yet (as Cicero tells us) when he came to this passage, he expressed himself in such moving accents and gestures, that he extorted tears even from his enemies. Fear occasions a tremor and hesitation of the voice, and assurance gives it strength and firmness. Admiration elevates the voice, and should be expressed with pomp and magnificence. "O surprising clemency, worthy of the highest praise and greatest encomiums, and fit to be perpetuated in lasting monuments!" This is Cicero's compliment to Cesar when he thought it for his purpose. And oftentimes this passion is accompanied with an elevation both of the eyes and hands. On the contrary contempt sinks and protracts the voice.

All exclamations should be violent. When we address inanimate things, the voice should be higher than when animated beings; and appeals to Heaven must be made in a loftier tone than those to men. These few hints for expressing the principal passions, may if duly attended to, suffice to direct our practice in others. Though, after all, it is impossible to gain a just and decent pronunciation of voice and gesture merely from rules without practice and an imitation of the best examples: which shows the wisdom of the ancients, in training up their youth to it, by the assistance of masters, to form both their speech and actions. But here, as has been before observed, great caution should be used in directing our choice of an example. An affected imitation of others, in pronunciation or gesture, especially of stage-players, whose pretensions to literature are seldom considerable, and who are generally too fond of *singularity*, ought to be carefully avoided. For nothing can appear more disgusting to persons of discernment than affectation.

PRACTICAL PIECES for SPEAKING;

CONSISTING OF

ORATIONS, ADDRESSES, EXHORTA-
TIONS FROM THE PULPIT, PLEADINGS
AT THE BAR, SUBLIME DESCRIPTIONS,
DEBATES, DECLAMATIONS, GRAVE
AND HUMOROUS DIALOGUES, POETRY,
&c. VARIOUSLY INTERSPERSED.

EXTRACT FROM AN ORATION ON ELOQUENCE, PRONOUNCED AT HARVARD UNIVERSITY, ON COMMENCEMENT DAY, 1794.

THE excellence, utility, and importance of ELOQUENCE; its origin, progress, and present state; and its superior claim to the particular attention of Columbia's freeborn sons, will exercise for a few moments the patience of this learned, polite, and respected assembly.

Speech and reason are the characteristics, the glory, and the happiness of man. These are the pillars which support the fair fabric of eloquence; the foundation, upon which is erected the most magnificent edifice, that genius could design, or art construct. To cultivate eloquence, then, is to improve the noblest faculties of our nature, the richest talents with which we are entrusted. A more convincing proof of the dignity and importance of our subject need not, cannot be advanced.

The benevolent design and the beneficial effects of eloquence, evince its great superiority over every other art, which ever exercised the ingenuity of man. To instruct, to persuade, to please; these are its objects.

To scatter the clouds of ignorance and error from the atmosphere of reason; to remove the film of prejudice from the mental eye; and thus to eradiate the benighted mind with the cheering beams of truth, is at once the business and the glory of eloquence.

To promote the innocent and refined pleasures of the fancy and intellect; to strip the monster vice of all his borrowed charms, and expose to view his native deformity; to display the resistless attractions of virtue; and in one word, to rouse to action all the latent energies of man, in the proper and ardent pursuit of the great end of his existence, is the orator's pleasing, benevolent, sublime employment.

Nor let it be objected, that eloquence sometimes impedes the course of justice and screens the guilty from the punishment due to their crimes. Is there any thing which is not obnoxious to abuse? Even the benign religion of the Prince of Peace has been made the unwilling instrument of the greatest calamities ever experienced by man. The greater the benefits which naturally result from any thing, the more pernicious are its effects, when diverted from its proper course. This objection to eloquence is therefore its highest eulogium.

The orator does not succeed, as some would insinuate, by dazzling the eye of reason with the illusive glare of rhetorical art, nor, by silencing her still small voice in the thunder of his declamation; for to her impartial tribunal he refers the truth and propriety of whatever he asserts or proposes. After fairly convincing the understanding, he may, without the imputation of disingenuousness, proceed to address the fancy and the passions. In this way he will more effectually transfuse into his hearers his own sentiments, and make every spring in the human machine cooperate in the production of the desired effect.

The astonishing powers of eloquence are well known, at least to those who are conversant in ancient history. Like a resistless torrent, it bears down every obstacle, and turns even the current of opposing ignorance and prejudice into the desired channel of active and zealous compliance. It is indisputably the most potent art within the compass of human acquirement. An Alexander and a Cesar could conquer a world; but to overcome the passions, to subdue the wills, and to command at pleasure the inclinations of men, can be effected only by the all-powerful charm of enrapturing eloquence.

Though it be more than probable, that oratory was known and cultivated in some degree in those eastern nations, where science first began to dawn upon the world; yet it was not till Greece became civilized and formed into distinct governments, that it made its appearance in its native peerless majesty. Here we may fix the era of eloquence; here was its morn; here its meridian too; for here it shone with splendor never since surpassed.

It is a common and a just remark, that eloquence can flourish only in the soil of liberty. Athens was a republic, where the affairs of state were transacted in the assembly of the whole people. This afforded to eloquence a field too fertile to remain long uncultivated by the ingenious Athenians. Orators soon made their appearance, who did honour to language, to Greece, to humanity.

But though the names of many have been transmitted to us, whose genius and eloquence demand our veneration and applause; yet, like stars when the sun appears, they are lost in the superior blaze of the incomparable Demosthenes. His story is well known; and his example affords the greatest encouragement to students in eloquence; as it proves, that, by art, almost in defiance of nature, a man may attain such excellence in oratory as shall stamp his name with the seal of immortality. Demosthenes and the liberty of Greece together expired; and from this period we hear very little more of Grecian eloquence.

Let us now direct our attention to that other garden of eloquence, the Roman commonwealth. Here, as in Greece, a free government opened the list to such as wished to dispute the palm in oratory. Numbers advance, and contend manfully for the prize. But their glory is soon faded; for Cicero appears; Cicero, another name for eloquence itself. It is needless to enlarge on his character as an orator. Suffice it to say, that if we ransack the histories of the world to find a rival for Demosthenes, Cicero alone can be found capable of supporting a claim to that distinguished honour.

And when did Greece or Rome present a fairer field for eloquence, than that which now invites the culture of the enlightened citizens of Columbia? We live in a republic, the orator's natal soil; we enjoy as much liberty, as is consistent with the nature of man; we possess as a nation all the advantages which climate, soil, and situation can bestow; and nothing but *real merit* is here required as a qualification for the most dignified offices of state. Never had eloquence more ample scope.

And shall we rest satisfied with only admiring, or at most with following at an awful distance the most illustrious orators of Greece and Rome? Shall every other useful and ornamental art speed swiftly towards perfection, while oratory, that most sublime of all arts; that art, which could render one man more dreadful to a tyrant, than hostile fleets and armies, is almost forgotten? It must not, cannot be. That refinement of taste, that laudable ambition to excel in every thing which does honour to humanity, which distinguishes the Americans, and their free and popular government, are so many springs, which, though not instantaneous in their operation, cannot fail in time to raise Columbian eloquence "above all Greek, above all Roman fame."

With pleasure we descry the dawning of that bright day of eloquence, which we have anticipated. The grand council of our nation has already evinced, that in this respect, as in all others, our republic acknowledges no existing superior. And we trust, that, as our sacred teachers make it their constant endea-

vour to imitate the great learning, the exemplary virtue, the exalted piety, and the extensive usefulness,
of the great apostle of the Gentiles; they will not fail
to resemble him in that commanding, that heavenly
eloquence, which made an avaricious, and unbelieving
Felix tremble.

May Columbia always afford more than one Demosthenes, to support the sacred cause of Freedom,
and to thunder terror into the ears of every transatlantic Philip. May more than Ciceronean eloquence
be ever ready to plead for injured innocence, and
suffering virtue. Warned by the fate of her prede-
cessors, may she escape those quicksands of vice,
which have ever proved the bane of empire. May her
glory and her felicity increase with each revolving
year, till the last trump shall announce the catastrophe
of nature, and time shall immerge in the ocean of
eternity.

EXTRACT FROM PRESIDENT WASHINGTON'S FIRST SPEECH IN CONGRESS, 1789.

Fellow-Citizens of the Senate,
and of the House of Representatives.

AMONG the vicissitudes incident to life, no event
could have filled me with greater anxieties than
that of which the notification was transmitted by your
order, and received on the 14th day of the present
month. On the one hand, I was summoned by my
country, whose voice I can never hear but with veneration and love, from a retreat which I had chosen
with the fondest predilection, and, in my flattering
hopes, with an immutable decision, as the asylum of
my declining years. A retreat which was rendered
every day more necessary as well as more dear to me,
by the addition of habit to inclination, and of frequent
interruptions in my health to the gradual waste committed on it by time.

On the other hand, the magnitude and difficulty of the trust, to which the voice of my country called me, being sufficient to awaken in the wisest and most experienced of her citizens, a distrustful scrutiny into his qualifications, could not but overwhelm with despondence one, who inheriting inferior endowments from nature, and unpractised in the duties of civil administration, ought to be peculiarly conscious of his own deficiencies.

In this conflict of emotions, all I dare aver is, that it has been my faithful study to collect my duty from a just appreciation of every circumstance by which it might be affected. All I dare hope is, that if, in executing this task, I have been too much swayed by a grateful remembrance of former instances, or by an affectionate sensibility to this transcendent proof of the confidence of my fellow-citizens, and have thence too little consulted my incapacity as well as disinclination for the weighty and untried cares before me, my error will be palliated by the motives which misled me; and its consequences be judged by my country, with some share of the partiality in which they originated.

Such being the impressions under which I have, in obedience to the public summons, repaired to the present station, it would be peculiarly improper to omit in this first official act, my fervent supplications to that Almighty Being, who rules over the universe, who presides in the councils of nations, and whose providential aids can supply every human defect, that his benediction may consecrate to the liberties and happiness of the people of the United States, a government instituted by themselves for these essential purposes; and may enable every instrument employed in its administration, to execute with success, the functions allotted to his charge. In tendering this homage to the great Author of every public and private good, I assure myself that it expresses your sentiments not less than my own; nor those of my fellow-citizens at large, less than either.

No people can be bound to acknowledge and adore the invisible Hand, which conducts the affairs of men, more than the people of the United States. Every step, by which we have advanced to the character of an independent nation, seems to have been distinguished by some token of providential agency. And in the important revolution just accomplished in the system of their united government, the tranquil deliberations and voluntary consent of so many distinct communities, from which the event has resulted, cannot be compared with the means by which most governments have been established, without some return of pious gratitude, with a humble anticipation of the future blessing which the past seems to presage. These reflections, arising out of the present crisis, have forced themselves too strongly on my mind to be suppressed. You will join with me, I trust, in thinking that there are none, under the influence of which, the proceedings of a new and free government can more auspiciously commence.

SPEECH OF PAULUS EMILIUS TO THE ROMAN PEOPLE, AS HE WAS ABOUT TAKING THE COMMAND OF THEIR ARMY.

YOU seem to me, Romans, to have expressed more joy when Macedonia fell to my lot, than when I was elected consul, or entered upon that office. And to me your joy seemed to be occasioned by the hopes you conceived, that I should put an end, worthy of the grandeur and reputation of the Roman people, to a war, which in your opinion, has already been of too long continuance. I have reason to believe, that the same gods, who have occasioned Macedonia to fall to my lot, will also assist me with their protection in conducting and terminating this war successfully. But of this, I may venture to assure you, that I shall do my utmost not to fall short of your expectations.

The senate has wisely regulated every thing necessary in the expedition I am charged with; and, as I am ordered to set out immediately, I shall make no delay; and I know that my colleague Caius Licinius, out of his great zeal for the public service, will raise and march off the troops appointed for me, with as much order and expedition, as if they were for himself. I shall take care to transmit to you, as well as to the senate, an exact account of all that passes; and you may rely upon the certainty and truth of my letters. But I beg of you, as a great favour, that you will not give credit to, or lay any weight, out of credulity, upon the light reports, which are frequently spread abroad without any author.

I perceive well, that in this war, more than in any other, whatever resolution people may form to obviate these rumors, they will not fail to make impression, and inspire I know not what discouragement. There are those, who in company, and even at table, command armies, make dispositions, and prescribe all the operations of the campaign. They know better than we, where we should encamp, and what posts it is necessary for us to seize; at what time, and by what defile we ought to enter Macedonia; where it is proper to have magazines; from whence, either by sea or land, we are to bring provisions; when we are to fight the enemy, and when lie still.

They not only prescribe what is best to do; but for deviating ever so little from their plans, they make it a crime in their consul, and cite him before their tribunal. But know, Romans, this is of very bad effect with your generals. All have not the resolution and constancy of Fabius, to despise impertinent reports. He could choose rather to suffer the people, upon such unhappy rumors, to invade his authority, than to ruin affairs in order to preserve their opinion, and an empty name.

D.

I am far from believing, that generals stand in no need of advice: I think, on the contrary, that whoever would conduct every thing alone, upon his own opinion, and without counsel, shows more presumption than prudence. But some may ask, How then shall we act reasonably? I answer, by not suffering any persons to obtrude their advice upon your generals, but such as are, in the first place, versed in the art of war, and have learned from experience what it is to command; and in the second place, who are upon the spot; who know the enemy; are witnesses in person to all that passes; and sharers with us in all dangers.

If there be any one, who conceives himself capable of assisting me with his counsels in the war you have charged me with, let him not refuse to do the republic that service; but let him go with me into Macedonia. Ships, horses, tents, provisions, shall all be provided for him at my charge. But if he will not take so much trouble, and prefers the tranquillity of the city to the dangers and fatigues of the field, let him not take upon him to hold the helm, and continue idle in the port. The city of itself supplies sufficient matter of discourse on other subjects; but as for these, let it be silent upon them; and know, that we shall pay no regard to any counsels, but such as shall be given us in the camp itself.

EXHORTATION ON TEMPERANCE IN PLEASURE.

LET me particularly exhort youth to temperance in pleasure. Let me admonish them, to beware of that rock on which thousands, from race to race, continue to split. The love of pleasure, natural to man in every period of his life, glows at this age with excessive ardor. Novelty adds fresh charms, as yet, to every gratification. The world appears to spread a continual feast; and health, vigor, and high spirits, invite them to partake of it without restraint. In vain we warn them of latent dangers. Religion is accused of insufferable severity, in prohibiting enjoyment: and the old, when they offer their admonitions, are upbraided with having forgotten that they once were young.

And yet, my friends, to what do the restraints of religion, and the counsels of age, with respect to pleasure, amount? They may all be comprised in few words,—not to hurt yourselves, and not to hurt others, by your pursuit of pleasure. Within these bounds, pleasure is lawful; beyond them, it becomes criminal, because it is ruinous. Are these restraints any other, than what a wise man would choose to impose on himself? We call you not to renounce pleasure, but to enjoy it in safety. Instead of abridging it, we exhort you to pursue it on an extensive plan. We propose measures for securing its possession, and for prolonging its duration.

Consult your whole nature. Consider yourselves not only as sensitive, but as rational beings; not only as rational, but social; not only as social, but immortal. Whatever violates your nature, in any of these respects, cannot afford true pleasure, any more than that which undermines an essential part of the vital system can promote health. For the truth of this conclusion, we appeal not merely to the authority of religion, nor to the testimony of the aged, but to yourselves and your own experience. We ask, whether you have not found, that in a course of criminal excess, your pleasure was more than compensated by succeeding pain? Whether, if not from every particular instance, yet from every habit, at least, of unlawful gratification, there did not spring some thorn to wound you; there did not arise some consequence to make you repent of it in the issue?

" How long then, ye simple ones, will ye love simplicity?" How long repeat the same round of pernicious folly, and tamely expose yourselves to be caught in the same snare? If you have any consideration, or any firmness left, avoid temptations, for which you have found yourselves unequal, with as much care as you would shun pestilential infection. Break off all connexions with the loose and profligate. " When sinners entice thee, consent thou not. Look not on the wine when it is red, when it giveth its colour in the cup; for at the last, it biteth like a serpent, and stingeth like an adder. Remove thy way from the strange woman, and come not near the door of her house. Let not thy heart decline to her ways; for her house is the way to hell. Thou goest after her as a bird hasteneth to the snare, and knoweth not that it is for his life."

By these unhappy excesses of irregular pleasure in youth, how many amiable dispositions are corrupted or destroyed! How many rising capacities and powers are suppressed! How many flattering hopes of parents and friends are totally extinguished! Who but must drop a tear over human nature, when he beholds that morning, which arose so bright, overcast with such untimely darkness; that good humor which once captivated all hearts; that vivacity which sparkled in every company; those abilities which were fitted for adorning the highest station, all sacrificed at the shrine of low sensuality; and one, who was formed for running the fair career of life in the midst of public esteem, cut off by his vices at the beginning of his course, or sunk, for the whole of it, into insignificancy and contempt! These, O sinful pleasure! are thy trophies. It is thus, that cooperating with the foe of God and man, thou degradest human nature, and blastest the opening prospects of human felicity.

Judah's Plea for his brother Benjamin, before Joseph in Egypt.

WHEN we appeared before you, Sir, the first time, we answered without reserve, and according to the strictest truth, all the questions which you were pleased to put to us concerning our family. We acquainted you, that we had a father, heavily laden with years, but still more heavily with misfortunes; a father, whose whole life had been one continued struggle with adversity. We added that we had a brother peculiarly dear to him, as the children born towards the end of their life generally are to old men, and who is the only one remaining of his mother; his brother having come in early youth to a most tragical end.

You commanded us, as the proof of our veracity and innocence to bring that brother unto you; and your command was delivered with such threatenings, that the terror of them accompanied us all the way back to our country, and embittered the remainder of our journey. We reported every thing minutely to our father, as you directed us. Resolutely and long, he refused to intrust us with the care of that child. Love suggested a thousand causes of apprehension upon his account. He loaded us with the bitterest reproaches for having declared that we had another brother.

Subdued by the famine, he at length reluctantly consented; and putting his beloved son, this unhappy youth, into our hands, conjured us by every dear, every awful name, to guard with tenderness his precious life; and as we would not see him expire before our eyes in anguish and despair, to bring him back in safety. He parted with him as with a limb torn from his own body; and in an agony of grief inexpressible, deplored the dreadful necessity which separated him from a son, on whom all the happiness of his life depended.

D 2

How then can we appear before a father of such delicate sensibility? With what eyes shall we dare to look upon him, unless we carry back with us this son of his right hand, this staff of his old age, whom, alas! you have condemned to slavery? The good old man will expire in horrors dreadful to nature, as soon as he shall find that his son is not with us. Our enemies will insult over us under these misfortunes, and treat us as the most infamous of parricides.

I must appear to the world, and to myself, as the perpetrator of the most horrid of crimes, the murder of a father; for it was I who most urgently pressed my father to yield. I engaged by the most solemn promises, and the most sacred pledges, to bring the child back. Me he intrusted with the sacred deposit, and of my hand he will require it. Have pity I beseech you, on the deplorable condition of an old man, stripped of his last comfort; and whose misery will be aggravated by reflecting that he foresaw its approach, and yet wanted resolution to prevent it.

If your just indignation must needs have a sacrifice, here I am ready, at the price of my liberty or of my life, to expiate this young man's guilt, and to purchase his release! Grant this request, not so much for the sake of the youth himself, as of his absent father, who never offended you, but who venerates your person and esteems your virtues.

Suffer us not to plead in vain for a shelter under your right hand, to which we flee, as to an holy altar, consecrated as a refuge to the miserable. Pity an old man, who during the whole course of a long life, has cultivated arts becoming a man of wisdom and probity, and who, on account of his amiable qualities, is almost adored by the inhabitants of Syria and Canaan, though he professes a religion, and follows a mode of living totally different from theirs.

EXTRACT FROM THE PLEA OF THOMAS MUIR, ESQ. AT HIS CELEBRATED TRIAL IN SCOTLAND.

Gentlemen of the Jury,

THIS is now perhaps the last time that I shall address my country. I have explored the tenor of my past life. Nothing shall tear from me the record of my departed days. The enemies of reform have scrutinized, in a manner hitherto unexampled in Scotland, every action I may have performed, every word I may have uttered. Of crimes, most foul and horrible, have I been accused: of attempting to rear the standard of civil war; to plunge this land in blood, and to cover it with desolation. At every step, as the evidence of the crown advanced, my innocency has brightened. So far from inflaming the minds of men to sedition and outrage, all the witnesses have concurred, that my only anxiety was, to impress upon them the necessity of peace, of good order, and of good morals.

What then has been my crime? Not the lending to a relation a copy of Mr. Paine's Works; not the giving away to another a few numbers of an innocent and constitutional publication; but for having dared to be, according to the measure of my feeble abilities, a strenuous and active advocate for an equal representation of the PEOPLE, in the HOUSE OF THE PEOPLE; for having dared to attempt to accomplish a measure, by legal means, which was to diminish the weight of their taxes, and put an end to the profusion of their blood.

From my infancy to this moment, I have devoted myself to the cause of the PEOPLE. It is a good cause. It will ultimately prevail. It will finally triumph. Say then openly, in your verdict, if you do condemn me, which I presume you will not, that it is for my attachment to this cause alone, and not for those vain and wretched pretexts stated in the indictment, intended only to color and disguise the real motives of my accusation. The time will come, when men must stand or fall by their actions; when all human pageantry shall cease; when the hearts of all shall be laid open to view.

If you regard your most important interests; if you wish that your consciences should whisper to you the words of consolation, rather than speak to you in the terrible language of remorse, weigh well the verdict you are to pronounce.

As for me, I am careless and indifferent to my fate. I can look danger, and I can look death in the face; for I am shielded by the consciousness of my own rectitude. I may be condemned to languish in the recesses of a dungeon: I may be doomed to ascend the scaffold. Nothing can deprive me of the recollection of the past; nothing can destroy my inward peace of mind, arising from the remembrance of having discharged my duty.

———

On the starry Heavens.

TO us who dwell on its surface, the earth is by far the most extensive orb that our eyes can any where behold. It is also clothed with verdure; distinguished by trees; and adorned with a variety of beautiful decorations. Whereas, to a spectator placed on one of the planets, it wears a uniform aspect; looks all luminous, and no larger than a spot. To beings who dwell at still greater distances, it entirely disappears.

That which we call, alternately, the morning and evening star; as in one part of her orbit, she rides foremost in the procession of night; in the other, ushers in, and anticipates the dawn, is a planetary world; which with the five others, that so wonderfully vary their mystic dance, are in themselves dark bodies, and shine only by reflection; have fields, and seas, and skies of their own; are furnished with all accom-

modations for animal subsistence, and are supposed to
be abodes of intellectual life. All which together
with this our earthly habitation, are dependent on that
grand dispenser of divine munificence, the sun; receive their light from the distribution of his rays;
derive their comfort from his divine agency.

The sun is the great axle of heaven, about which,
the globe we inhabit, and other more spacious orbs,
wheel their stated courses. The sun, though seemingly smaller than the dial it illuminates, is abundantly
larger than this whole earth; on which so many lofty
mountains rise, and such vast oceans roll. A line, extending through the centre of that resplendent orb,
would measure more than eight hundred thousand
miles. A girdle, formed to surround it, would require
a length of millions. Were its solid contents to be es-
timated the account would overpower our understanding, and be almost beyond the power of language
to express.

Are we startled at these reports of astronomy? Are
we ready to cry out in a transport of surprise, How
mighty is the Being, who kindled such a prodigious
fire, and who keeps alive, from age to age, such an
enormous mass of flame! Let us attend our philosophic
guides, and we shall be brought acquainted with spec-
ulations more enlarged, and more amazing.

This sun, with all attendant planets, is but a very
little part of the grand machine of the universe. Every star, though in appearance no bigger than the dia-
mond that glitters on a lady's ring, is really a mighty
globe; like the sun in size, and in glory; no less spacious; no less luminous than the radiant source of our
day. So that every star is not barely a world, but the
centre of a magnificent system; has a retinue of worlds,
irradiated by its beams, and revolving round its at-
tractive influence. All which are lost to our sight in
unmeasurable wilds of ether.

That the stars appear like so many diminutive, and
scarcely distinguishable points, is owing to their im-

mense, and inconceivable distance. Such a distance, that a cannon ball, could it continue its impetuous flight, with unabating rapidity, would not reach the nearest of those twinkling luminaries for more than five hundred thousand years!

Can any thing be more wonderful than these observations? Yes; there are truths far more stupendous; there are scenes far more extensive. As there is no end of the Almighty Maker's greatness, so no imagination can set limits to his creating hand. Could you soar beyond the moon, and pass through all the planetary choir; could you wing your way to the highest apparent star, and take your stand on one of those lofty pinnacles of heaven, you would there see other skies expanded; another sun, distributing his inexhaustible beams by day; other stars which gild the horrors of the alternate night; and other, perhaps nobler systems, established in unknown profusion through the boundless dimensions of space. Nor do the dominions of the universal Sovereign terminate there. Even at the end of this vast tour, you would find yourself advanced no further than the suburbs of creation; arrived only at the frontiers of the great JEHOVAH'S kingdom.

PAPER, A POEM.

SOME wit of old; such wits of old there were,
Whose hints show'd meaning, whose allusions, care,
By one brave stroke, to mark all human kind,
Call'd clear *blank paper* every infant mind;
When still, as opening sense her dictates wrote,
Fair virtue put a seal, or vice a blot.

The thought was happy, pertinent, and true,
Methinks a genius might the plan pursue.
I, (can you pardon my presumption?) I,
No wit, no genius, yet for once will try.

Various the papers, various wants produce,
The wants of fashion, elegance, and use.
Men are as various: and, if right I scan,
Each sort of *paper* represents some *man*.

Pray note the fop; half powder and half lace;
Nice, as a band-box were, his dwelling place;
He's the *gilt paper*, which apart you store,
And lock from vulgar hands in the scrutoire.

Mechanics, servants, farmers, and so forth,
Are *copy paper* of inferior worth;
Less priz'd, more useful, for your desk decreed,
Free to all pens, and prompt at ev'ry need.

The wretch, whom av'rice bids to pinch and spare,
Starve, cheat, and pilfer, to enrich an heir,
Is coarse *brown paper*, such as pedlars choose
To wrap up wares, which better men will use.

Take next the miser's contrast, who destroys
Health, fame, and fortune, in a round of joys.
Will any paper match him? Yes, throughout,
He's a true *sinking paper*, past all doubt.

The retail politician's anxious thought
Deems this side always right, and that stark naught;
He foams with censure, with applause he raves,
A dupe to rumors, and a tool of knaves;
He'll want no type his weakness to proclaim,
While such a thing as *fools-cap* has a name.

The hasty gentleman, whose blood runs high,
Who picks a quarrel if you step awry,
Who can't a jest, or hint, or look endure:
What's he? What? *Touch-paper* to be sure.

What are our poets, take them as they fall,
Good, bad, rich, poor, much read, not read at all?
Them, and their works in the same class you'll find;
They are the mere *waste-paper* of mankind.

Observe the maiden, innocently sweet,
She's fair *white paper*, an unsullied sheet;
On which the happy man, whom fate ordains,
May write his name, and take her for his pains.

One instance more, and only one I'll bring;
'Tis the great man whe scorns a little thing;
Whose thoughts, whose deeds, whose maxims are his
     own,
Form'd on the feelings of his heart alone:
True genuine *royal paper* is his breast;
Of all the kinds most precious, purest, best.

EXTRACT FROM CATO'S SPEECH BEFORE THE ROMAN SENATE, AFTER THE CONSPIRACY OF CATILINE.

I HAVE often spoken before you, Fathers, with some extent, to complain of luxury and the greediness for money, the twin vices of our corrupt citizens; and have thereby drawn upon myself abundance of enemies. As I never spared any fault in myself, I was not easily inclined to favor the criminal excesses of others.

But though you paid little regard to my remonstrances, the Commonwealth has still subsisted by its own strength; has borne itself up, notwithstanding your neglect. It is not now the same. Our manners, good or bad, are not the question; nor to preserve the greatness and lustre of the Roman empire; but to resolve whether all we possess and govern, well or ill, shall continue ours, or be transferred with ourselves to enemies.

At such a time, in such a state, some talk to us of lenity and compassion. It is long that we have lost the right names of things. The Commonwealth is in this deplorable situation, only because we call bestowing other people's estates, liberality, and audaciousness in perpetrating crimes, courage.

Let such men, since they will have it so, and it is become the established mode, value themselves upon their liberality at the expense of the allies of the empire, and of their lenity to the robbers of the public treasury; but let them not make a largess of our blood; and, to spare a small number of vile wretches, expose all good men to destruction.

Do not imagine, Fathers, that it was by arms our ancestors rendered this Commonwealth so great, from so small a beginning. If it had been so, we should now see it much more flourishing, as we have more allies and citizens, more horse and foot, than they had. But they had other things, that made them great, of which no traces remain amongst us: at home, labor and industry; abroad, just and equitable government; a constancy of soul, and an innocence of manners, that kept them perfectly free in their councils; unrestrained either by the remembrance of past crimes, or by craving appetites to satisfy.

For these virtues, we have luxury and avarice, or madness to squander, joined with no less, to gain; the State is poor, and private men are rich. We admire nothing but riches; we give ourselves up to sloth and effeminacy; we make no distinction between the good and the bad; whilst ambition engrosses all the rewards of virtue. Do you wonder, then, that dangerous conspiracies should be formed? Whilst you regard nothing but your private interest; whilst voluptuousness solely employs you at home, and avidity or favor governs you here, the commonwealth, without defence, is exposed to the devices of any one who thinks fit to attack it.

E

DIALOGUE BETWEEN THE GHOSTS OF AN ENGLISH DUELLIST, A NORTH-AMERICAN SAVAGE, AND MERCURY.

Duellist. MERCURY, Charon's boat is on the other side of the water. Allow me, before it returns, to have some conversation with the North-American savage, whom you brought hither with me. I never before saw one of that species. He looks very grim. Pray, Sir, what is your name? I understand you speak English.

Savage. Yes, I learned it in my childhood, having been bred for some years among the English of New-York. But, before I was a man, I returned to my valiant countrymen, the Mohawks; and having been villanously cheated by one of yours in the sale of some rum, I never cared to have any thing to do with them afterwards. Yet I took up the hatchet for them with the rest of my tribe in the late war against France, and was killed while I was out upon a scalping party. But I died very well satisfied: for my brethren were victorious; and before I was shot, I had gloriously scalped seven men, and five women and children. In a former war, I had performed still greater exploits. My name is the Bloody Bear: it was given me to express my fierceness and valor.

Duel. Bloody Bear, I respect you, and am much your humble servant. My name is Tom Pushwell, very well known at Arthur's. I am a gentleman by my birth, and by profession a gamester and man of honor. I have killed men in fair fighting, in honorable single combat; but don't understand cutting the throats of women and children.

Sav. Sir, that is our way of making war. Every nation has its customs. But by the grimness of your countenance, and that hole in your breast, I presume you were killed as I was, in some scalping party. How happened it that your enemy did not take off your scalp?

Duel. Sir, I was killed in a duel. A friend of mine had lent me a sum of money; and after two or three years, being in great want himself, he asked me to pay him. I thought his demand, which was somewhat peremptory, an affront to my honor, and sent him a challenge. We met in Hyde Park. The fellow could not fence: but I was absolutely the adroitest swordsman in England. So I gave him three or four wounds; but at last he ran upon me with such impetuosity, that he put me out of my play, and I could not prevent him from whipping me through the lungs. I died the next day, as a man of honor should; without any snivelling signs of contrition or repentance: and he will follow me soon; for his surgeon has declared his wounds to be mortal. It is said that his wife is dead of grief, and that his family of seven children will be undone by his death. So I am well revenged, and that is a comfort. For my part, I had no wife. I always hated marriage: my mistress will take good care of herself, and my children are provided for at the foundling hospital.

Sav. Mercury I won't go in the boat with that fellow. He has murdered his countryman: he has murdered his friend: I say positively, I won't go in the boat with that fellow. I will swim over the river: I can swim like a duck.

Mer. Swim over the Styx! it must not be done: it is against the laws of Pluto's empire. You must go in the boat and be quiet.

Sav. Don't tell me of laws: I am a savage: I value no laws. Talk of laws to the Englishman: there are laws in his country; and yet you see he did not regard them. For they could never allow him to kill his fellow-subject, in time of peace, because he asked him to pay an honest debt. I know, indeed, that the English are a barbarous nation: but they can't possibly be so brutal as to make such things lawful.

Mer. You reason well against him. But how comes it that you are so offended with murder; you, who have frequently massacred women in their sleep, and children in their cradle?

Sav. I killed none but my enemies: I never killed my own countrymen: I never killed my friend. Here, take my blanket, and let it come over in the boat; but see that the murderer does not sit upon it, or touch it. If he does, I will burn it instantly in the fire I see yonder. Farewel. I am determined to swim over the water.

Mer. By this touch of my wand, I deprive thee of all thy strength. Swim now if thou canst.

Sav. This is a potent enchanter. Restore me my strength, and I promise to obey thee.

Mer. I restore it; but be orderly, and do as I bid you; otherwise worse will befal you.

Duel. Mercury, leave him to me. I'll tutor him for you. Sirrah Savage, dost thou pretend to be ashamed of my company? Dost thou not know that I have kept the best company in England?

Sav. I know thou art a scoundrel. Not pay thy debts! kill thy friend who lent thee money for asking thee for it! Get out of my sight. I will drive thee into the Styx.

Mer. Stop. I command thee. No violence. Talk to him calmly.

Sav. I must obey thee. Well, Sir, let me know what merit you had to introduce you into good company? What could you do?

Duel. Sir, I gamed, as I told you. Besides, I kept a good table. I eat as well as any man either in England or France.

Sav. Eat! did you ever eat the liver of a Frenchman, or his leg, or his shoulder? There is fine eating for you! I have eat twenty. My table was always well served. My wife was esteemed the best cook for the dressing of man's flesh in all North America. You will not pretend to compare your eating with mine?

Duel. I dance very finely.

Sav. I'll dance with thee for thy ears. I can dance all day long. I can dance the war dance with more spirit than any man in my nation. Let us see thee begin it. How thou standest like a post! Has Mercury struck thee with his enfeebling rod? Or art thou ashamed to let us see how awkward thou art? If he would permit me, I would teach thee to dance in a way that thou hast never yet learned. But what else canst thou do, thou bragging rascal?

Duel. O misery! must I bear all this! What can I do with this fellow? I have neither sword nor pistol; and his shade seems to be twice as strong as mine.

Mer. You must answer his questions. It was your own desire to have a conversation with him. He is not well-bred; but he will tell you some truths which you must necessarily hear, when you come before Rhadamanthus. He asked you what you could do beside eating and dancing.

Duel. I sang very agreeably.

Sav. Let me hear you sing your death song, or the warhoop. I challenge you to sing. Come, begin. The fellow is mute. Mercury, this is a liar. He has told us nothing but lies. Let me put out his tongue.

Duel. The lie given me! and alas! I dare not resent it! What an indelible disgrace to the family of the Bushwells! This is indeed tormenting.

Mer. Here, Charon, take these two savages to your care. How far the barbarism of the Mohawk will excuse his horrid acts, I leave Minos to judge. But what can be said for the Englishman? Can we plead the custom of Duelling! A bad excuse at the best! but here it cannot avail. The spirit that urged him to draw his sword against his friend is not that of honor, it is the spirit of the furies; and to them he must go.

Sav. If he is to be punished for his wickedness, turn him over to me. I perfectly understand the art of tormenting. Sirrah, I begin my work with this box on

2 E

your ears, and will soon teach you better manners than you have yet learned.

Duel. Oh my honor, my honor, to what infamy art thou fallen!

———

SPEECH OF AN INDIAN CHIEF, OF THE STOCKBRIDGE TRIBE, TO THE MASSACHUSETTS CONGRESS, IN THE YEAR 1775.

Brothers!

YOU remember, when you first came over the great waters, I was great and, you were little; very small. I then took you in for a friend, and kept you under my arms, so that no one might injure you. Since that time we have ever been true friends: there has never been any quarrel between us. But now our conditions are changed. You are become great and tall. You reach to the clouds. You are seen all round the world. I am become small; very little. I am not so high as your knee. Now you take care of me; and I look to you for protection.

Brothers! I am sorry to hear of this great quarrel between you and Old England. It appears that blood must soon be shed to end this quarrel. We never till this day understood the foundation of this quarrel between you and the country you came from. Brothers! Whenever I see your blood running, you will soon find me about you to revenge my brothers' blood. Although I am low and very small, I will gripe hold of your enemy's heel, that he cannot run so fast, and so light, as if he had nothing at his heels.

Brothers! You know I am not so wise as you are, therefore I ask your advice in what I am now going to say. I have been thinking, before you come to action, to take a run to the westward, and feel the mind of my Indian brethren, the Six Nations, and know how they stand; whether they are on your side, or for your enemies. If I find they are against you. I will try to turn their minds. I think they will listen to me; for they have always looked this way for advice, concerning all important news that comes from the rising sun. If they hearken to me, you will not be afraid of any danger from behind you. However their minds are affected, you shall soon know by me. Now I think I can do you more service in this way than by marching off immediately to Boston, and staying there. It may be a great while before blood runs. Now, as I said, you are wiser than I, I leave this for your consideration, whether I come down immediately, or wait till I hear some blood is spilled.

Brothers! I would not have you think by this, that we are falling back from our engagements. We are ready to do any thing for your relief, and shall be guided by your counsel.

Brothers! one thing I ask of you, if you send for me to fight, that you will let me fight my own Indian way. I am not used to fight English fashion; therefore you must not expect I can train like your men. Only point out to me where your enemies keep, and that is all I shall want to know.

ON THE CREATION OF THE WORLD.

TO the ancient philosophers, creation from nothing appeared an unintelligible idea. They maintained the eternal existence of matter, which they supposed to be modelled by the sovereign mind of the universe, into the form which the earth now exhibits. But there is nothing in this opinion which gives it any title to be opposed to the authority of revelation. The doctrine of two self-existent, independent principles, God and matter, the one active, the other passive, is a hypothesis which presents difficulties to human reason, at least as great as the creation of matter from nothing. Adhering then to the testimony of scripture we believe that " in the beginning, God created," or from nonexistence brought into being, " the heavens and the earth."

But though there was a period when this globe, with all that we see upon it, did not exist, we have no reason to think, that the wisdom and power of the Almighty were then without exercise or employment. Boundless is the extent of his dominion. Other globes and worlds, enlightened by other suns, may then have occupied, they still appear to occupy, the immense regions of space. Numberless orders of beings, to us unknown, people the wide extent of the universe, and afford an endless variety of objects to the ruling care of the great Father of all. At length, in the course and progress of his government there arrived a period, when this earth was to be called into existence. When the signal moment, predestinated from all eternity, was come, the Deity arose in his might, and with a word created the world.

What an illustrious moment was that, when, from nonexistence, there sprang at once into being this mighty globe, on which so many millions of creatures now dwell! No preparatory measures were required. No long circuit of means was employed. " He spake; and it was done: He commanded, and it stood fast." The earth was, at first, without form, and void; and darkness was on the face of the deep." The Almighty surveyed the dark abyss; and fixed bounds to the several divisions of nature. He said, " Let there be light, and there was light."

Then appeared the sea, and the dry land. The mountains rose; and the rivers flowed, The sun and moon began their course in the skies. Herbs and plants clothed the ground. The air, the earth, and the waters, were stored with their respective inhabitants. At last, man was made after the image of God. He appeared, walking with countenance erect; and received his Creator's benediction, as the lord of this new world. The Almighty beheld his work when it was finished, and pronounced it good. Superior beings saw with wonder this new accession to existence. "The morning stars sang together; and all the sons of God shouted for joy."

But, on this great work of creation, let us not merely gaze with astonishment. Let us consider how it should affect our conduct, by presenting the divine perfections in a light which is at once edifying and comforting to man. It displays the Creator as supreme in power, in wisdom, and in goodness. Let us look around, and survey this stupendous edifice, which we have been admitted to inhabit. Let us think of the extent of the different climates and regions of the earth; of the magnitude of the mountains, and of the expanse of the ocean. Let us conceive that immense globe which contains them, launched at once from the hand of the Almighty; made to revolve incessantly on its axis, that it might produce the vicissitudes of day and night; thrown forth, at the same time, to run its annual course in perpetual circuit through the heavens.

After such a meditation, where is the greatness, where is the pride of man? Into what total annihilation do we sink, before an omnipotent Being? Reverence, and humble adoration ought spontaneously to arise. He, who feels no propensity to worship and adore, is dead to all sense of grandeur and majesty; has extinguished one of the most natural feelings of the human heart.

LINES SPOKEN AT A SCHOOL-EXHIBITION, BY A LITTLE BOY SEVEN YEARS OLD.

YOU'D scarce expect one of my age,
　To speak in public, on the stage;
And if I chance to fall below
Demosthenes or Cicero,
Don't view me with a critic's eye,
But pass my imperfections by.

Large streams from little fountains flow;
Tall oaks from little acorns grow:
And though I now am small and young,
Of judgment weak, and feeble tongue;
Yet all great learned men, like me,
Once learn'd to read their A, B, C.
But why may not Columbia's soil
Rear men as great as Britain's isle;
Exceed what Greece and Rome have done,
Or any land beneath the sun?
Mayn't Massachusetts boast as great
As any other sister State?
Or, where's the town, go far and near,
That does not find a rival here?
Or where's the boy, but three feet high,
Who's made improvements more than I?
These thoughts inspire my youthful mind
To be the greatest of mankind;
Great, not like Cesar, stain'd with blood;
But only great, as I am good.

EXTRACT FROM MR. PITT'S SPEECH IN THE BRITISH PARLIAMENT, IN THE YEAR 1766, ON THE SUBJECT OF THE STAMP-ACT.

IT is a long time, Mr. Speaker, since I have attended in Parliament. When the resolution was taken in the House to tax America, I was ill in bed. If I could have endured to have been carried in my bed, so great was the agitation of my mind for the consequences, that I would have solicited some kind hand to have laid me down on this floor, to have borne my testimony against it. It is now an act that has passed. I would speak with decency of every act of this House; but I must beg the indulgence of the House to speak of it with freedom.

I hope a day may be soon appointed to consider the state of the nation with respect to America. I hope gentlemen will come to this debate with all the temper and impartiality that his Majesty recommends, and the importance of the subject requires. A subject of greater importance than ever engaged the attention of this House! That subject only excepted, when, nearly a century ago, it was the question whether you yourselves were to be bond or free. In the mean time, as I cannot depend upon health for any future day, such is the nature of my infirmities, I will beg to say a few words at present, leaving the justice, the equity, the policy, the expediency of the act to another time.

I will only speak to one point, which seems not to have been generally understood. Some gentlemen seem to have considered it as a point of *honor*. If gentlemen consider it in that light, they leave all measures of right and wrong, to follow a delusion that may lead to destruction. It is my opinion that this kingdom has no right to lay a tax upon the Colonies. When in this House we give and grant, we give and grant what is our own. But in an American tax, what do we do? We, your Majesty's Commons of Great-Britain, give and grant to your Majesty, what? our own property? No. We give and grant to your Majesty, the property of your Majesty's Commons of America. It is an absurdity in terms.

There is an idea in some, that the colonies are virtually represented in this House. I would fain know by whom an American is represented here? Is he represented by any knight of the shire, in any county in this kingdom? Or will you tell him that he is represented by any representative of a borough; a borough, which perhaps no man ever saw? This is what is called the *rotten part* of the Constitution. It cannot continue a century. If it does not drop, it must be amputated. The idea of a virtual representation of America, in this House, is the most contemptible idea that ever entered into the head of a man. It does not deserve a serious refutation.

The Commons of America, represented in their several assemblies, have ever been in possession of the exercise of this, their constitutional right of giving and granting their own money. They would have been slaves if they had not enjoyed it.

A great deal has been said without doors, of the power, of the strength of America. It is a topic which ought to be cautiously meddled with. In a good cause, on a sound bottom, the force of this country can crush America to atoms. I know the valor of your troops. I know the skill of your officers. There is not a company of foot that has served in America, out of which you may not pick a man of sufficient knowledge and experience, to make a governor of a colony there. But on this ground, on the Stamp-Act, when so many here will think it a crying injustice, I am one who will lift up my hands against it.

In such a cause your success would be hazardous. America, if she fell, would fall like the strong man. She would embrace the pillars of the State, and pull down the constitution along with her. Is this your boasted peace? Not to sheath the sword in its scabbard, but to sheath it in the bowels of your countrymen? Will you quarrel with yourselves, now the whole House of Bourbon is united against you?

The Americans have been wronged. They have been driven to madness by injustice. Will you punish them for the madness you have occasioned? Rather let prudence and temper come first from this side. I will undertake for America, that she will follow the example.

Upon the whole, I will beg leave to tell the House what is really my opinion. It is that the Stamp-Act be repealed absolutely, totally, and immediately.

Scene from the Farce of Lethe.

Enter Mr. and Mrs. Tatoo, and Æsop.

Mrs. Tat. WHY don't you come along, Mr. Tatoo? what the deuce are you afraid of?

Æs. Don't be angry young lady; the gentleman is your husband, I suppose.

Mrs. Tat. How do you know that, Sir? What, you an't all conjurers in this world, are you?

Æs. Your behaviour to him is a sufficient proof of his condition, without the gift of conjuration.

Mrs. Tat. Why, I was as free with him before marriage as I am now; I never was coy or prudish in my life.

Æs. I believe you, madam; pray, how long have you been married? You seem to be very young, madam.

Mrs. Tat. I am old enough for a husband, and have been married long enough to be tired of one.

Æs. How long pray?

Mrs. Tat. Why, above three months: I married Mr. Tatoo without my guardian's consent.

Æs. If you married him with your own consent, I think you might continue your affection a little longer.

Mrs. Tat. What signifies what you think, if I don't think so? We are quite tired of one another, and are come to drink some of your le—lethaly—le-lethily, I think they call it, to forget one another, and be un-married again.

Æs. The waters can't divorce you, madam; and you may easily forget him without the assistance of Lethe.

Mrs. Tat. Ay! how so?

Æs. By remembering continually he is your husband: there are several ladies have no other receipt. But what does the gentleman say to this?

F

Mrs. Tat. What signifies what he says? I an't so young and so foolish as that comes to, to be directed by my husband, or to care what either he says, or you say.

Mr. Tat. Sir, I was a drummer in a marching regiment when I ran away with that young lady. I immediately bought out of the corps, and thought myself made forever; little imagining that a poor vain fellow was purchasing fortune at the expense of his happiness.

Æs. 'Tis even so, friend; fortune and felicity are as often at variance as man and wife.

Mr. Tat. I found it so, Sir. This high life (as I thought it) did not agree with me; I have not laugh'd, and scarcely slept since my advancement; and unless your worship can alter her notions, I must e'en quit the blessings of a fine lady and her portion, and, for content, have recourse to eight pence a day and my drum again.

Æs. Pray, who has advised you to a separation?

Mrs. Tat. Several young ladies of my acquaintance; who tell me, they are not angry at me for marrying him; but for being fond of him since I have married him: and they say I should be as complete a fine lady as any of them, if I would but procure a separate divorcement.

Æs. Pray, madam, will you let me know what you call a fine lady?

Mrs. Tat. Why, a fine lady, and a fine gentleman, are two of the finest things upon earth.

Æs. I have just now had the honor of knowing what a fine gentleman is; so, pray confine yourself to the lady.

Mrs. Tat. A fine lady, before marriage, lives with her papa and mamma, who breed her up till she learns to despise them, and resolve to do nothing they bid her; this makes her such a prodigious favorite, that she wants for nothing. And when once she is her own mistress, then comes the pleasure!

Æs. Pray let us hear.

Mrs. Tat. She lies in bed all the morning, rattles about all day, and sits up all night; she goes every where, and sees every thing; knows every body, and loves no body; ridicules her friends, coquets with her lovers, sets them together by the ears, tells fibs, makes mischief, buys china, cheats at cards, keeps a lapdog, and hates the parson; she laughs much, talks loud, never blushes, says what she will, does what she will, goes where she will, marries whom she pleases, hates her husband in a month, breaks his heart in four, becomes a widow, slips from her gallants, and begins the world again. There's a life for you; what do you think of a fine lady now?

Æs. As I expected. You are very young, madam, and, if you are not very careful, your natural propensity to noise and affectation will run you headlong into folly, extravagance, and repentance.

Mrs. Tat. What would you have me do?

Æs. Drink a large quantity of Lethe to the loss of your acquaintance; and do you, Sir, drink another, to forget this false step of your wife; for whilst you remember her folly, you can never thoroughly regard her; and whilst you keep good company, madam, as you call it, and follow their example, you can never have a just regard for your husband; so both drink and be happy.

Mrs. Tat. Well, give it me whilst I am in humor, or I shall certainly change my mind again.

Æs. Be patient till the rest of the company drink, and divert yourself in the mean time with walking in the grove.

Mrs. Tat. Well, come along husband, and keep me in humor, or I shall beat you such an alarum as you never beat in all your life.

EXTRACT FROM THE EULOGY ON DR. FRANKLIN, PRONOUNCED BY THE ABBE FAUCHET, IN THE NAME OF THE COMMONS OF PARIS, 1790.

A SECOND creation has taken place; the elements of society begin to combine together; the moral universe is now seen issuing from chaos; the genius of Liberty is awakened, and springs up; she sheds her divine light and creative powers upon the two hemispheres. A great nation, astonished at seeing herself free, stretches her arms from one extremity of the earth to the other, and embraces the first nation that became so: the foundations of a new city are created in the two worlds; brother nations hasten to inhabit it. It is the city of mankind!

One of the first founders of this universal city was the immortal FRANKLIN, the deliverer of America. The second founders who accelerated this great work, made it worthy of Europe. The legislators of France have rendered the most solemn homage to his memory. They have said, " A friend of humanity is dead; mankind ought to be overwhelmed with sorrow! Nations have hitherto only worn mourning for Kings; let us assume it for a Man, and let the tears of Frenchmen mingle with those of Americans, in order to do honor to the memory of one of the Fathers of Liberty!"

The city of Paris, which once contained this philosopher within its walls, which was intoxicated with the pleasure of hearing, admiring, and loving him; of gathering from his lips the maxims of a moral legislator, and of imbibing from the effusions of his heart a passion for the public welfare, rivals Boston and Philadelphia, his two native cities (for in one he was born as it were a man, and in the other a legislator) in its profound attachment to his merit and his glory.

It has commanded this funeral solemnity, in order to perpetuate the gratitude and the grief of this third country, which, by the courage and activity with which it has profited of his lessons, has shown itself worthy of having him at once for an instructor and a model.

In selecting me for the interpreter of its wishes, it has declared, that it is less to the talents of an orator, than to the patriotism of a citizen, the zeal of a preacher of liberty, and the sensibility of a friend of men, that it hath confided this solemn function. In this point of view, I may speak with firm confidence; for I have the public opinion, and the testimony of my own conscience, to second my wishes. Since nothing else is wanting than freedom, and sensibility, for that species of eloquence which this eulogium requires, I am satisfied; for I already possess them.

My voice shall extend to France, to America, to posterity. I am now to do justice to a great man, the founder of transatlantic freedom; I am to praise him in the name of the mother city of French liberty. I myself also am a man; I am a freeman; I possess the suffrages of my fellow-citizens: this is enough; my discourse shall be immortal.

The academies, the philosophical societies, the learned associations which have done themselves honor by inscribing the name of Franklin in their records, can best appreciate the debt due to his genius, for having extended the power of man over nature, and presented new and sublime ideas, in a style simple as truth, and pure as light.

It is not the naturalist and the philosopher that the orator of the Commons of Paris ought to describe; it is the *man*, who hath accelerated the progress of social order; it is the *legislator*, who hath prepared the liberty of nations!

Franklin, in his periodical works, which had prodigious circulation on the continent of America, laid the sacred foundations of social morality. He was no less inimitable in the developments of the same morality, when applied to the duties of friendship, general charity, the employment of one's time, the happiness attendant upon good works, the necessary combination of private with public welfare, the propriety and necessity of industry; and to that happy state which puts us at ease with society and with ourselves. The proverbs of " Old Henry," and " Poor Richard," are in the hands both of the learned and of the ignorant; they contain the most sublime morality, reduced to popular language and common comprehension; and form the catechism of happiness for all mankind.

Franklin was too great a moralist, and too well acquainted with human affairs, not to perceive that women were the arbiters of manners. He strove to perfect their empire; and accordingly engaged them to adorn the sceptre of virtue with their graces. It is in their power to excite courage; to overthrow vice, by means of their disdain; to kindle civism, and to light up in every heart the holy love of our country.

His daughter, who was opulent and honored with the public esteem, helped to manufacture and to make up the clothing for the army with her own hands; and spread abroad a noble emulation among the female citizens, who became eager to assist those by means of the needle and the spindle, who were serving the state with their swords and their guns.

With the charm ever attendant upon true wisdom and the grace ever flowing from true sentiment, this grave philosopher knew how to converse with the other sex; to inspire them with a taste for domestic occupations; to hold out to them the prize attendant upon honor unaccompanied by reproach, and instil the duty of cultivating the first precepts of education, in order to teach them to their children; and thus to acquit the debt due to nature, and fulfil the hope of society. It must be acknowledged, that, in his own country, he addressed himself to minds capable of comprehending him.

Immortal females of America! I will tell it to the daughters of France, and they only are fit to applaud you! You have attained the utmost of what your sex is capable; you possess the beauty, the simplicity, the manners, at once natural and pure; the primitive graces of the golden age. It was among you that liberty was first to have its origin. But the empire of freedom, which is extended to France, is about to carry your manners along with it, and produce a revolution in morals as well as in politics.

Already our female citizens, (for they have lately become such) are not any longer occupied with those frivolous ornaments, and vain pleasures, which were nothing more than the amusements of slavery; they have awakened the love of liberty in the bosoms of fathers, of brothers, and of husbands; they have encouraged them to make the most generous sacrifices; their delicate hands have removed the earth, dragged it along, and helped to elevate the immense amphitheatre of the grand confederation. It is no longer the love of voluptuous softness that attracts their regard; it is the sacred fire of patriotism.

The laws which are to reform education, and with it the national manners, are already prepared; they will advance, they will fortify the cause of liberty by means of their happy influence, and become the second saviors of their country!

Franklin did not omit any of the means of being useful to men, or serviceable to society. He spoke to all conditions, to both sexes, to every age. This amiable moralist descended, in his writings to the most artless details; to the most ingenuous familiarities; to the first ideas of a rural, a commercial, and civil life; to the dialogues of old men and children; full at once of all the verdure and all the maturity of wisdom. In short, the prudent lessons arising from the exposition of those obscure, happy, easy virtues, which form so many links in the chain of a good man's life, derived immense weight from that reputation for genius which he had acquired, by being one of the first naturalists and greatest philosophers in the universe.

At one and the same time he governed nature in the heavens and in the hearts of men. Amidst the tempests of the atmosphere, he directed the thunder; amidst the storms of society, he directed the passions. Think, gentlemen, with what attentive docility, with what religious respect, one must hear the voice of a simple man who preached up human happiness, when it was recollected that it was the powerful voice of the same man who regulated the lightning.

He electrified the consciences, in order to extract the destructive fire of vice, exactly in the same manner as he electrified the heavens, in order peaceably to invite from them the terrible fire of the elements.

Venerable old man! august philosopher! legislator of the felicity of thy country, prophet of the fraternity of the human race, what ecstatic happiness embellished the end of thy career! From thy fortunate asylum, and in the midst of thy brothers who enjoyed in tranquillity the fruit of thy virtues, and the success of thy genius, thou hast sung songs of deliverance. The last looks, which thou didst cast around thee, beheld America happy; France on the other side of the ocean, free, and a sure indication of the approaching freedom and happiness of the world.

The United States, looking upon themselves as thy children, have bewailed the death of the father of their republic. France, thy family by adoption, has honored thee as the founder of her laws; and the human race has revered thee as the universal patriarch who has formed the alliance of nature with society. Thy remembrance belongs to all ages; thy memory to all nations; thy glory to eternity!

EPILOGUE TO ADDISON'S CATO.

YOU see mankind the same in every age:
   Heroic fortitude, tyrannic rage,
Boundless ambition, patriotic truth,
And hoary treason, and untainted youth,
Have deeply mark'd all periods and all climes,
The noblest virtues, and the blackest crimes.
Did Cesar, drunk with power, and madly brave,
Insatiate burn, his country to enslave?
Did he for this, lead forth a servile host
To spill the choicest blood that Rome could boast?
The British Cesar too hath done the same,
And doom'd this age to everlasting fame.
Columbia's crimson'd fields still smoke with gore;
Her bravest heroes cover all the shore:
The flower of Britain, in full martial bloom,
In this sad war, sent headlong to the tomb.
Did Rome's brave senate nobly dare t' oppose
The mighty torrent, stand confess'd their foes,
And boldly arm the virtuous few, and dare
The desp'rate horrors of unequal war?
Our senate too the same bold deed have done,
And for a Cato, arm'd a Washington;
A chief, in all the ways of battle skill'd,
Great in the council, mighty in the field.
His martial arm, and steady soul alone,   ⎫
Have made thy legions shake, thy navy groan, ⎬
And thy proud empire totter to the throne. ⎭
O, what thou art, may'st thou forever be,
And death the lot of any chief but thee!
We've had our Decius too; and Howe could say,
Health, pardon, peace, George sends America;
Yet brought destruction for the olive wreath;
For health, contagion, and for pardon, death.
Rise! then, my countrymen, for fight prepare;
Gird on your swords, and fearless rush to war:

'Tis your bold task the gen'rous strife to try;
For your griev'd country 'nobly dare to die!
No pent-up Utica contracts your pow'rs;
For the whole boundless continent is ours!

SELF-CONCEIT.

An Address, spoken by a very small Boy.

WHEN boys are exhibiting in public, the polite-
ness or curiosity of the hearers frequently
induces them to inquire the names of the performers.
To save the trouble of answers, so far as relates to
myself, my name is Charles Chatterbox. I was born
in this town; and have grown to my present enormous stature, without any artificial help. It is true,
I eat, drink, and sleep, and take as much care of my
noble self, as any young man about; but I am a monstrous great student. There is no telling the half of
what I have read.

. Why, what do you think of the Arabian Tales?
Truth! every word truth! There's the story of the
lamp, and of rook's eggs as big as a meeting-house.
And there is the history of Sinbad the Sailor. I have
read every word of them. And I have read Tom
Thumb's Folio through, Winter Evening Tales, and
Seven Champions, and Parismus, and Parismenus,
and Valentine and Orson, and Mother Bunch, and
Seven Wise Masters, and a curious book, entitled,
Think well on't.

Then there is another wonderful book, containing
fifty reasons why an old bachelor was not married.
The first was, that nobody would have him; and the
second was, he declared to every body, that he would
not marry; and so it went on stronger and stronger.
Then, at the close of the book, it gives an account of
his marvellous death and burial. And in the appen-
dix, it tells about his being ground over, and coming

out as young, and as fresh, and as fair as ever. Then, every few pages, is a picture of him to the life.

I have also read Robinson Crusoe, and Reynard the fox, and Moll Flanders; and I have read twelve delightful novels, and Irish Rogues, and Life of Saint Patrick, and Philip Quarle, and Conjuror Crop, and Æsop's Fables, and Laugh and be Fat, and Toby Lumpkin's Elegy on the Birth of a Child, and a Comedy on the Death of his Brother, and an Acrostic, occasioned by a mortal sickness of his dear wife, of which she recovered. This famous author wrote a treatise on the Rise and Progress of Vegetation; and a whole body of Divinity he comprised in four lines.

I have read all the works of Pero Gilpin, whose memory was so extraordinary, that he never forgot the hours of eating and sleeping. This Pero was a rare lad. Why, he could stand on his head, as if it were a real pedestal; his feet he used for drumsticks. He was trumpeter to the foot guards in Queen Betty's time; and if he had not blown his breath away, might have lived to this day.

Then, I have read the history of a man who married for money, and of a woman that would wear her husband's small-clothes in spite of him; and I have read four books of riddles and rebusses; and all that in not half a quarter.

Now what signifies reading so much if one can't tell of it? In thinking over these things, I am sometimes so lost in company, that I don't hear any thing that is said, till some one pops out that witty saying, " A penny for your thoughts." Then I say, to be sure, I was thinking of a book I had been reading. Once, in this mood, I came very near swallowing my cup and saucer; and another time, was upon the very point of taking down a punch-bowl, that held a gallon. Now, if I could fairly have gotten them down, they would not have hurt me a jot; for my mind is capacious enough for a china shop. There is no checking a man of my reading. Why, if my mind can

contain Genii and Giants, sixty feet high, and en-
chanted castles, why not a punch-bowl, and a whole
tea-board?

It was always conjectured that I should be a monstrous great man; and I believe, as much as I do the
Spanish war, that I shall be a perfect Brobdingnag in
time.

Well now, do you see, when I have read a book, I
go right off into the company of the ladies; for they
are the judges whether a man knows any thing or not.
Then I bring on a subject which will show my parts
to the best advantage; and I always mind and say a
smart thing just before I quit.

You must know, moreover, that I have learned a
great deal of wit. I was the first man who invented
all that people say about cold tongues, and warm
tongues, and may-bees. I invented the wit of kissing
the candlestick when a lady holds it; as also the plays
of criminal and cross-question; and above all, I invented the wit of paying toll at bridges. In short,
ladies and gentlemen, take me all in all, I am a
downright curious fellow.

HOWARD AND LESTER.

A DIALOGUE ON LEARNING AND USEFULNESS.

Howard. LIFE is much like a fiddle: every man
plays such a tune as suits him.

Lester. The more like a fiddle, the better I like it.
Any thing that makes a merry noise suits me; and
the man that does not set his hours to music, has a
dull time on't.

How. But, Lester, are there no serious duties in
life? Ought we not to improve our minds, and to
prepare for usefulness?

Lest. Why, in the present day, a man's preparing
himself for usefulness, is like carrying coals to New-
castle. Our country is full of useful men; ten, at

least, to where one is wanted and all of them ten times as ready to serve the public, as the public is to be served. If every man should go to Congress that's fit for it, the federal city would hardly hold them.

How. You mean, if all who think themselves fit for it.

Lest. No; I meant as I said.

How. Then what do you think fits a man for Congress?

Lest. Why he must be flippant and bold.

How. What good will that do him, if he is without knowledge?

Lest. O! he must have knowledge to be sure.

How. Well, must he not be a man in whom the people can trust? Must he not understand politics? and must he not be able and willing to serve his country?

Lest. I agree to all that.

How. Then you suppose that the federal city could hardly hold all our men who unite eloquence with confidence, knowledge with integrity, and policy with patriotism. I fear that a countinghouse would give them full accommodation.

Lest. I don't go so deep into these matters: but this is certain, that when the election comes, more than enough are willing to go.

How. That, my friend, only proves that more than enough are ignorant of themselves: but are there no other ways of serving the public?

Lest. Yes; one may preach, if he will do it for little or nothing. He may practise law, if he can get any body to employ him; or he may be a Doctor or an instructor; but I tell you the country is crowded with learned men begging business.

How. Then you intend to prepare yourself for the ignorant herd; so that you may not be crowded.

Lest. I have serious thoughts of it. You may take your own way, but I'll never wear out a fine pair of eyes in preparing myself for usefulness, till this

G

public will give me a bond to employ me when I am ready to serve them. Till such a bond is signed, sealed, and delivered, I shall set my hours to the tune of "Jack's alive." To-day's the ship I sail in, and that will carry the flag, in spite of the combined powers of yesterdays and to-morrows.

How. Well, Lester, you can take your choice. I shall set my hours to a more serious tune. I ask no bond of the public. If my mind is well furnished with knowledge and that same generous public, which has so uniformly called to her service the discerning, should *refuse* my services, still I shall possess a treasure, which, after a few years of dissipation, you would give the world to purchase, THE RECOLLECTION OF TIME WELL SPENT.

CHRIST's CRUCIFIXION.

——NOW darkness fell
On all the region round; the shrouded sun
From the impen'tent earth withdrew his light:
I thirst, the Saviour cried; and lifting up
His eyes in agony, My God, My God!
Ah! why hast thou forsaken me? exclaim'd.
Yet deem him not forsaken of his God!
Beware that error. 'Twas the mortal part
Of his compounded nature, breathing forth
Its last sad agony, that so complain'd:
Doubt not that veil of sorrow was withdrawn,
And heav'nly comfort to his soul vouchsaf'd,
Ere thus he cry'd, Father! into thy hands
My spirit I commend. Then bow'd his head
And died. Now Gabriel and his heavenly choir
Of minist'ring angels hov'ring o'er the cross
Receiv'd his spirit, at length from mortal pangs
And fleshly pris'n set free, and bore it thence
Upon their wings rejoicing. Then behold

A prodigy, that to the world announc'd
A new religion and dissolv'd the old:
'The temple's sacred veil was rent in twain
From top to bottom, 'midst th' attesting shocks
Of earthquake and the rending up of graves.
Now those mysterious symbols, heretofore
Curtain'd from vulgar eyes, and holiest deem'd
Of holies, were display'd to public view:
The mercy-seat, with its cherubic wings
O'ershadow'd, and the golden ark beneath
Cov'ring the testimony, now through the rent
Of that dissever'd veil first saw the light;
A world redeem'd had now no farther need
Of types and emblems, dimly shadowing forth
An angry Deity withdrawn from sight
And canopied in clouds. Him, face to face,
Now in full light reveal'd, the dying breath
Of his dear Son appeas'd, and purchas'd peace
And reconcilement for offending man.

   Thus the partition wall, by Moses built,
By Christ was levell'd, and the Gentile world
Enter'd the breach, by their great Captain led
Up to the throne of grace, opening █████
Through his own flesh a new and living way.
Then were the oracles of God made known
To all the nations, sprinkled by the blood
Of Jesus, and baptiz'd into his death;
So was the birthright of the elder born,
Heirs of the promise, forfeited; whilst they,
Whom sin had erst in bondage held, made free
From sin, and servants of the living God,
Now gain'd the gift of God, eternal life.

   Soon as those signs and prodigies were seen
Of those who watch'd the cross, conviction smote
Their fear-struck hearts. The sun, at noon-day dark:
The earth convulsive underneath their feet,
And the firm rocks, in shiver'd fragments rent,
Rous'd them at once to tremble and believe.
Then was our Lord by heathen lips confess'd,

When the centurion cry'd, In very truth
This righteous person was the Son of God;
The rest, in heart assenting, stood abash'd,
Watching in silence the tremendous scene.
  The recollection of his gracious acts,
His dying pray'rs and their own impious taunts
Now rose in sad review; too late they wish'd
The deed undone, and sighing smote their breasts.
Straight from God's presence went that angel forth,
Whose trumpet shall call up the sleeping dead
At the last day, and bade the saints arise
And come on earth to hail this promis'd hour,
The day-spring of salvation. Forth they came
From their dark tenements, their shadowy forms
Made visible as in their fleshly state,
And through the holy city here and there
Frequent they gleam'd, by night, by day, with fear
And wonder seen of many: holy seers,
Prophets and martyrs from the grave set free,
And the first fruits of the redeemed dead.
  They, who with Christ transfigur'd on the mount
Were seen of his disciples in a cloud
Of dazzling glory, now, in form distinct,
Mingling amidst the public haunts of men,
Struck terror to all hearts: Ezekiel there,
The captive seer, to whom on Chebar's banks
The heavens were opened and the fatal roll
Held forth, with dire denunciations fill'd,
Of lamentation, mourning and of woe,
Now falling fast on Israel's wretched race:
He too was there, Hilkiah's holy son,
With loins close girt, and glowing lips of fire
By God's own finger touch'd: there might be seen
The youthful prophet, Belteshazzer nam'd
Of the Chaldees, interpreter of dreams,
Knowledge of God bestow'd, in visions skill'd,
And fair, and learn'd and wise: the Baptist here,
Girt in his hairy mantle, frowning stalk'd,
And pointing to his ghastly wound, exclaim'd,

Ye vipers! whom my warning could not move
Timely to flee from the impending wrath
Now fallen on your heads; whom I indeed
With water, Christ hath now with fire baptized:
Barren ye were of fruits, which I prescrib'd
Meet for repentance, and behold! the ax
Is laid to the unprofitable root
Of every sapless tree, hewn down, condemn'd
And cast into the fire. Lo! these are they,
These shadowy forms now floating in your sight,
These are the harbingers of ancient days,
Who witness'd the Messias, and announc'd
His coming upon earth. Mark with what scorn
Silent they pass you by: them had ye heard,
Them had ye noted with a patient mind,
Ye had not crucified the Lord of Life:
He of these stones to Abraham shall raise up
Children, than you more worthy of his stock;
And now his winnowing fan is in his hand,
With which he'll purge his floor, and having stor'd
The precious grain in garners, will consume
With fire unquenchable the refuse chaff.

THE WONDERS OF NATURE.

HOW mighty! how majestic! and how mysterious are Nature's works! When the air is calm,
where sleep the stormy winds? In what chambers are
they reposed, or in what dungeons confined? But
when He, " who holds them in his fist," is pleased
to awaken their rage, and throw open their prison
doors, then with irresistible impetuosity, they rush
forth, scattering dread, and menacing destruction.

The atmosphere is hurled into the most tumultuous
confusion. The aërial torrent bursts its way over mountains, seas, and continents. All things feel the dreadful shock. All things tremble before the furious blast.
The forest, vexed and torn, groans under the scourge.

Her sturdy sons are strained to the very root, and almost sweep the soil they were wont to shade. The stubborn oak, that disdains to bend, is dashed headlong to the ground; and, with shattered arms, with prostrate trunk, blocks up the road. While the flexile reed, that springs up in the marsh, yielding to the gust, (as the meek and pliant temper, to injuries, or the resigned and patient spirit, to misfortunes) eludes the force of the storm, and survives amidst the widespread havoc.

For a moment, the turbulent and outrageous sky seems to be assuaged; but it intermits its wrath, only to increase its strength. Soon the sounding squadrons of the air return to the attack, and renew their ravages with redoubled fury. The stately dome rocks amidst the wheeling clouds. The impregnable tower totters on its basis, and threatens to overwhelm whom it was intended to protect. The ragged rocks are rent in pieces; and even the hills, the perpetual hills, on their deep foundations are scarcely secure. Where now is the place of safety? when the city reels, and houses become heaps! Sleep affrighted flies. Diversion is turned into horror. All is uproar in the elements; all is consternation among mortals; and nothing but one wide scene of rueful devastation through the land.

The ocean swells with tremendous commotions. The ponderous waves are heaved from their capacious bed, and almost lay bare the unfathomable deep. Flung into the most rapid agitation, they sweep over the rocks; they lash the lofty cliffs, and toss themselves into the clouds. Navies are rent from their anchors; and, with all their enormous load, are whirled swift as the arrow, wild as the winds, along the vast abyss. Now they climb the rolling mountain; they plough the frightful ridge; and seem to skim the skies. Anon they plunge into the opening gulf; they lose the sight of day; and are lost themselves to every eye.

How vain is the pilot's art; how impotent the mariner's strength! " They reel to and fro, and stagger like a drunken man." Despair is in every face, and death sits threatening on every surge. But when Omnipotence pleases to command, the storm is hushed to silence; the lightnings lay aside their fiery bolts, and the billows cease to roll.

DIALOGUE ON PHYSIOGNOMY.

Enter FRANK *and* HENRY.

Frank. IT appears strange to me that people can be so imposed upon. There is no difficulty in judging folks by their looks. I profess to know as much of a man, at the first view, as by half a dozen years' acquaintance.

Henry. Pray how is that done? I should wish to learn such an art.

Fr. Did you never read Lavater on Physiognomy?

Hen. No. What do you mean by such a hard word?

Fr. Physiognomy means a knowledge of men's hearts, thoughts, and characters by their looks. For instance, if you see a man, with a forehead jutting over his eyes like a piazza, with a pair of eyebrows, heavy like the cornice of a house; with full eyes, and a Roman nose, depend on it he is a great scholar, and an honest man.

Hen. It seems to me I should rather go below his nose to discover his scholarship.

Fr. By no means: if you look for beauty, you may descend to the mouth and chin; otherwise never go below the region of the brain.

Enter GEORGE.

Geor. Well, I have been to see the man hanged. And he is gone to the other world, with just such a great forehead and Roman nose, as you have always been praising.

Fr. Remember, George, all signs fail in dry weather.

Geor. Now, be honest, Frank, and own that there

is nothing in all this trumpery of yours. The only way to know men is by their actions. If a man commit burglary, think you a Roman nose ought to save him from punishment?

Fr. I don't carry my notions so far as that; but it is certain that all faces in the world are different; and equally true, that each has some marks about it, by which one can discover the temper and character of the person.

Enter PETER.

Peter. [*To Frank.*] Sir I have heard of your fame from Dan to Beersheba; that you can know a man by his face, and can tell his thoughts by his looks. Hearing this, I have visited you without the ceremony of an introduction.

Fr. Why, indeed, I do profess something in that way.

Pet. By that forehead, nose, and those eyes of yours, one might be sure of an acute, penetrating mind.

Fr. I see that *you* are not ignorant of physiognomy.

Pet. I am not; but still I am so far from being an adept in the art, that unless the features are very remarkable, I cannot determine with certainty. But yours is the most striking face I ever saw. There is a certain firmness in the lines, which lead from the outer verge to the centre of the apple of your eye, which denotes great forecast, deep thought, bright invention, and a genius for great purposes.

Fr. You are a perfect master of the art. And to show you that I know something of it, permit me to observe that the form of your face denotes frankness, truth, and honesty. Your heart is a stranger to guile, your lips, to deceit, and your hands, to fraud.

Pet. I must confess that you have hit upon my true character: though a different one, from what I have sustained in the view of the world.

Fr. [*To Henry and George.*] Now see two strong examples of the truth of physiognomy. [*While he is speaking this, Peter takes out his pocket-book, and makes off with himself.*] Now, can you conceive, that without this knowledge, I could fathom the character of a total stranger?

Hen. Pray tell us by what marks you discovered that in his heart and lips was no guile, and in his hands no fraud?

Fr. Ay, leave that to me; we are not to reveal our secrets. But I will show you a face and character, which exactly suits him. [*Feels for his pocket-book in both pockets, looks wildly and concerned.*]

Geor. [*Tauntingly.*] Ay, " in his heart is no guile, in his lips no deceit, and in his hands no fraud! Now we see a strong example of the power of physiognomy!"

Fr. He is a wretch! a traitor against every good sign! I'll pursue him to the ends of the earth. [*Offers to go.*]

Hen. Stop a moment. His fine honest face is far enough before this time. You have not yet discovered the worst injury he has done you.

Fr. What's that? I had no watch or money for him to steal.

Hen. By his deceitful lips, he has robbed you of any just conception of yourself; he has betrayed you into a foolish belief that you are possessed of most extraordinary genius and talents. Whereas, separate from the idle whim about physiognomy, you have had no more pretence to genius or learning than a common school-boy. Learn henceforth to estimate men's hands by their deeds, their lips, by their words, and their hearts, by their lives.

ORATION DELIVERED AT PARIS BY CITIZEN
CARNOT, PRESIDENT OF THE EXECUTIVE DI-
RECTORY, AT THE FESTIVAL OF GRATITUDE
AND VICTORY, CELEBRATED AT THE CHAMP-
DE-MARS, MAY 29, 1796.

IT is at the moment when nature is renovated, when
the earth, adorned with flowers and dressed in
green, promises new harvest; when all beings proclaim
in their own language, the beneficent intelligence which
renovates the universe, that the French people assem-
ble, on this great festival, to render a distinguished
homage to those talents and virtues of the friends of
the country and humanity. What day can better unite
all hearts! What citizen, what man can be a stranger
to the influence of gratitude! We exist only through
an uninterrupted course of beneficence, and our life
is but a continual exchange of services.

As soon as born, our eyes, fixed on the heavens,
appear already to acknowledge a primary Benefactor.
Weak, without support, the love of our parents watches
over our infancy, and provides for wants continually
renewed. They direct our first steps; their patient
solicitude assists in developing our organs; we receive
from them our first ideas of what we are ourselves,
and of surrounding objects. Additional care models
our hearts to affection, our minds to knowledge, and
our bodies to useful labour. It is for our happiness,
that the wise have reflected on the duties of man;
that the learned have dived into the secrets of nature;
that the magistrate watches, and that the legislator
prepares in deliberation protecting laws.

Soon we are enabled to be useful. Good children,
we strew flowers over the age of our parents, and their
trembling voice blesses us in their last moments. Become parents in our turn, we prepare in the education
of our children, the felicity of our declining years

and we thus continue in a new generation the chain of benevolence and gratitude. Sensibility is not restricted within the family circle; the indigent is searched for under the thatch; succors and consolation are lavished; and the donor, at first paid for the good action by the pleasure of having performed it, is doubly rewarded by the gratitude of the object. Benevolence! how happy are thy votaries, and how much to be pitied, the soul that knows thee not!

He who is a good son and a good father is also a good citizen. He loves his country; renders with alacrity the tribute of services; he delights in returning to his brothers the protection he has received from them. Either magistrate or warrior, manufacturer or farmer; in the temple of the arts; in the senate; in the fields of glory, or the workshops of industry, he shows himself ambitious of contributing towards the prosperity of his country, and to deserve one day its gratitude. For there is a national gratitude for individuals. At this moment a people are all assembled to express their gratitude to the virtuous citizens who have deserved it. How agreeable is the task! How we delight in paying you that homage; you to whom the country owes its safety, its glory, and the foundation of its prosperity!

You to whom France owes its political regeneration; courageous philosophers, whose writings have planted the seeds of the revolution, corroded the fetters of slavery, and blunted by degrees the ravings of fanaticism. You, citizens, whose dauntless courage effected this happy revolution, founded the republic, and contended these seven years against crime and ambition, royalism and anarchy. You all, in a word, who labor to render France happy and flourishing; who render it illustrious by your talents, and enrich it by your discoveries; receive the solemn testimony of national gratitude.

Receive that testimony particularly, republican armies; you, whose glory and successes are fresh in the

recollection of all. It is you who have defended us
against ten combined kings; who have driven them
from our territory; have transferred to their dominions
the scourge of war. You have not only conquered
men; you have overcome the obstacles thrown in your
way by nature. You have triumphed over fatigue,
hunger, and winter. What a spectacle for the people!
what a dreadful lesson to the enemies of liberty!

A new-born republic arms its children to defend its
independence; nothing can restrain their impetuosity;
traversing rivers, carrying intrenchments, climbing
rocks. Here, after a series of victories, they pushed
back our limits to those barriers that nature intended
for us, and pursuing over ice the remains of three armies, transformed an oppressed and hostile nation into
a free and allied people. There they fly to extermi-
nate the hordes of traitors and villains, subsidized by
England; punish their thieves, and restore to the republic brothers too long misled. Here surmounting
the Pyrenees, and precipitating themselves from their
summit; overthrowing whatever opposes their progress, and checked only by an honourable peace; there
ascending the Alps and Apennines, they fly across
the Po and Adige.

The ardor of the soldier is seconded by the genius
and boldness of the chiefs. They plan with science,
and execute with energy; now displaying their forces
with calmness; then courting danger at the head of
their brothers in arms. O that I could here display
the immense and glorious picture of their victories!
that I could name our most intrepid defenders! What
a crowd of sublime images and beloved names press
upon my recollection! Immortal warriors, posterity
will not believe the multitude of your triumphs: but
to us history loses all its improbabilities.

But do we not see, even on this spot, a portion of
those brave defenders? Victors over the exterior enemies of the state, they have come to repress our internal enemies; and preserve at home the republic

which they have caused to be respected abroad. Do we not also see those venerable warriors who have grown gray in the service; those whom honourable wounds have obliged to seek premature repose, and whose asylum is in sight? With what pleasure our eyes feed on this interesting reunion. With what agreeable emotions we contemplate those victorious brows!

Heroes who have perished for liberty, why does there remain to us nothing but a recollection of your services? You will, however, live for ever in our hearts; your children will be dear to us; the republic will repay to them the debt they owe to you; and we discharge here the first, by proclaiming your glory and our gratitude. Republican armies, represented here, by warriors from your ranks; invincible phalanxes, whose trophies I observe on all sides, whose fresh successes I foresee, come forward and receive the triumphal crowns which the French people command me to attach to your colours.

ADDRESS OF MR. ADET, FRENCH AMBASSADOR, ON PRESENTING THE COLOURS OF FRANCE TO THE UNITED STATES, 1796.

Mr. President,

I COME to acquit myself of a duty very dear to my heart. I come to deposit in your hands, and in the midst of a people justly renowned for their courage, and their love of liberty, the symbol of the triumph and the enfranchisement of my nation.

When she broke her chain; when she proclaimed the imprescriptible rights of man; when, in a terrible war, she sealed with her blood the covenant made with liberty, her own happiness was not alone the object of her glorious efforts; her views extended also to all free people; she saw their interests blended with

H

her own, and doubly rejoiced in her victories, which, in assuring to her the enjoyments of her rights, became to them new guarantees of their independence.

These sentiments, which animated the French nation, from the dawn of their revolution, have acquired new strength since the foundation of the republic. France, at that time, by the form of its government, assimilated to, or rather identified with free people, saw in them only friends and brothers. Long accustomed to regard the American people as their most faithful allies, she has sought to draw closer the ties already formed in the fields of America, under the auspices of victory over the ruins of tyranny.

The National Convention, the organs of the will of the French Nation, have more than once expressed their sentiments to the American people; but above all these burst forth on that august day, when the minister of the United States presented to the National Representation, the colours of his country, desiring never to lose recollections as dear to Frenchmen as they must be to Americans. The convention ordered that these colours should be placed in the hall of their sittings. They had experienced sensations too agreeable not to cause them to be partaken of by their allies, and decreed that to them the national colours should be presented.

Mr. President, I do not doubt their expectations will be fulfilled; and I am convinced, that every citizen will receive, with a pleasing emotion, this flag, elsewhere the terror of the enemies of liberty; here the certain pledge of faithful friendship; especially when they recollect that it guides to combat, men who have shared their toils, and who were prepared for liberty, by aiding them to acquire their own.

President Washington's Answer.

BORN, Sir, in a land of liberty; having early learned its value; having engaged in a perilous conflict to defend it; having, in a word, devoted the best years of my life to secure it a permanent establishment in my own country; my anxious recollections, my sympathetic feelings, and my best wishes are irresistibly excited, whensoever in any country, I see an oppressed nation unfurl the banners of freedom. But above all the events of the French revolution have produced the deepest solicitude, as well as the highest admiration. To call your nation brave, were to pronounce but common praise. WONDERFUL PEOPLE! ages to come will read with astonishment the history of your brilliant exploits.

I rejoice that the period of your toils and of your immense sacrifices is approaching. I rejoice that the interesting revolutionary movements of so many years have issued in the formation of a constitution designed to give permanency to the great object for which you have contended. I rejoice that liberty, which you have so long embraced with enthusiasm; liberty, of which you have been the invincible defenders, now finds an asylum in the bosom of a regularly organized government; a government, which, being formed to secure the happiness of the French people, corresponds with the ardent wishes of my heart, while it gratifies the pride of every citizen of the United States, by its resemblance of their own. On these glorious events accept, Sir, my sincere congratulations.

In delivering to you these sentiments, I express not my own feelings only, but those of my fellow citizens, in relation to the commencement, the progress, and the issue of the French revolution; and they will cordially join with me in purest wishes to the Supreme Being, that the citizens of our sister republic, our magnanimous allies, may soon enjoy, in peace, that liberty which they have purchased at so great a price, and all the happiness which liberty can bestow.

I receive, Sir, with lively sensibility, the symbol of the triumphs and of the enfranchisement of your nation, the colours of France, which you have now presented to the United States. The transaction will be announced to Congress, and the colours will be deposited with those archives of the United States, which are at once the evidences and the memorials of their freedom and independence. May these be perpetual; and may the friendship of the two republics be commensurate with their existence.

THE OPPRESSIVE LANDLORD.

Enter DON PHILIP and WIFE.

Don Philip. WELL, my dear, I have warned all the families out of my long range of buildings, and ordered them to pay double the rent they have done, for every day they remain. From every new tenant I am determined to have three times the sum. The present rent will never do in these times. Our children will become beggars at this rate; and you and I shall have to betake ourselves to hard labour, like the *common herd*, to earn our daily bread.

Wife. But I fear that some of our tenants are too poor to endure a rent double to what they now pay; and I am certain it will be impossible for them all to remove, on account of the scarcity of houses to be obtained.

Don P. That is not my look out. It is enough for me to attend to my *own* interest, not theirs.

Wife. But you will exercise a little lenity towards them at this distressing time. I am persuaded, my dear, that you will not turn them into the street. Besides, it is thought by some, that they already pay a reasonable rent.

Don P. I have nothing to do with lenity. Wo-

man, would you not have your husband be looking
out against a rainy day? What would become of you
and your children, if I were to spend my time in studying *lenity*, instead of my *interest-table?* I tell you
that now is the harvest time, and I am determined
to thrust in the sickle, and reap my proportion of the
crop, before the season's over. The town is crowded
with foreigners who are exiled from their homes,
and necessity obliges them to pay whatever price is
demanded, for a shelter to cover their heads.

Wife. Would you then profit by the necessities
and misfortunes of your fellow creatures? These ex-
iles are entitled to our compassion, instead of expe-
riencing our oppression.

Don P. You talk like a poor weak woman. Did I
not tell you that I had nothing to do with other people's good or ill fortune? It is more than I can do to
take care of my own dependents. We should make
fine way ahead, if you were at the helm. I believe in
my conscience, that if you possessed the keys of the
strong box, you would squander away to the full
amount of a pistareen a week upon those poor starving runaways. I have not yet forgotten how you lavished a whole gallon of cider upon those three miserable wretches that cleared out our well, the day
before thanksgiving. Does this look like taking a
prudent care of your family? Pray how do you read
your Bible? Has not Nebuchadnezzar said, that,
he who provides not for his own household, has
denied the faith, and is worse than an infidel?"

Wife. If you had studied your Bible as faithfully
as you have your *interest-table*, you would not have
put St. Paul's words into the mouth of the king of
Babylon. Does not the same scripture say, that "He
who oppresseth the poor, and——"

Don P. Hush, I say; one of my tenants approaches.
Banish your womanish feelings; and let not your unruly tongue betray your weakness.

Enter Tenant.

Ten. Sir, I come to inform you, that I have at last been fortunate enough to procure a shelter for my family, though an indifferent one; and have brought you the rent of your tenement, which I quitted with reluctance yesterday.

Don P. It is well you are out; for you would have met with trouble, if you had remained three days longer. I had ordered my attorney to give directions to an officer to tumble all your goods into the street, and you and your children after them.

Ten. Then a good Providence has preserved us.

Don P. Providence has smiled upon me, I confess, in granting me such a riddance.

Ten. I contend not with an adversary who is mantled in gold. Will you please to count your money, and give me a discharge?

Don. P. [*counts the money.*] Why, man, the sum is deficient; I cannot receipt it.

Ten. It is the same, Sir, as I paid the last term.

Don P. That is very true; but did I not double the rent three days ago?

Ten. You did, indeed; but my reply was, that I was utterly unable to pay a higher price; and as the time was so short, I thought you would not stand for trifles.

Don P. Trifles! If you were to receive it, I believe you would not call it a trifle; neither do I. I demand the utmost farthing.

Ten. For the sake of peace, though I think your demand unjust, I will take your receipt for this, and bring the remainder to-morrow.

Don P. Not a cent will I receive without the whole, lest by some quibble of the law I lose the rest.

Ten. Your avaricious disposition leads you to act contrary to your own interest.

Don P. I shall not apply to you for lessons of instruction. I shall conduct my own affairs according to my sovereign will and pleasure. Let me tell you,

Sir, this impudence does not well become a man of your circumstances.

Ten. " Sir, your honoured father never used me thus." Alas! he little thought in what oppressive hands he left his large estate. Could he be permitted to revisit the earth, his ghost would haunt your guilty soul; and, if you have any conscience left, harrow up remorse, and awaken you to repentance.

Don P. I did not admit a tenant into my house to hear a moral lecture from him.

Ten. If you will take your money, I will quit your house with pleasure. But before we part, give me leave to tell you, that, though your great wealth has exalted you above yourself, and in your opinion, placed you beyond the reach of poverty, the time *may* come when you will *feel* what oppression is.

Wife. I entreat you to receive the money, and be content.

Don P. A woman, who can't be silent in her husband's presence, especially when he is negotiating important business, may take a modest hint to leave the room.   [*Exit Wife.*

Ten. If you are resolved not to receive your money, I must carry it home again. And I hope the time is not far distant, when I shall be out of the reach of your oppressive hands.   [*Exit.*

Don P. [*Solus.*] Every man I deal with is trying to cheat me. Mankind are by nature all knaves. I am afraid to trust even my best friends. What an affliction it is to have property! The poor always think that the rich are bound to maintain them, and are never satisfied with what is done for them. My tenants would be glad to live in my houses rent free if they could. This, I am persuaded, they learned of my father; but I'll soon teach them to expect different things. Rather than matters should go on at such loose ends, I'll sell every one of my buildings, and put the money in bank. My mind is constantly on the stretch to contrive ways and means to preserve what little I possess. It is well my father left his property to me. Had he left it to one of only common understanding, these plotting tenants would have run away with the whole of it.

Enter second Tenant.

2d Ten. Sir, I appear before you to crave your compassion. I am the most unfortunate of all your tenants. My misfortune is, to be obliged to remain in your house, after it is your pleasure that I should leave it.

Don P. To-morrow I will cure you of your misfortune; for if you cannot get out yourself, I will help you out.

2d Ten. Why may I not remain? It may be for your interest as well as mine. I have ever made you punctual payment; and stand ready now to give as much as any other man, or as much as your conscience will suffer you to demand.

Don P. My will and pleasure is, that you depart immediately. My reasons for my conduct I give to no man.

2d Ten. But, Sir, I have a claim upon your mercy. You are not insensible of the pains I've taken to accomplish what you wish. Necessity is the only reason why I ask this favour. One special reason why you ought to grant it is, that I am now in your service with the same salary as in years past; when your good father was satisfied with one fourth the sum his craving son demands. I have been, you must allow, a faithful slave to your children. They have long received, and still receive my best instruction, without an augmentation of reward. If you will not hear the plea of mercy, grant me justice. If you increase your price of rent, increase my pay.

Don P. I meddle not with your affairs. Look out for your pay among your employers. I am but one among many, and promise you that I shall not be foremost to enhance the price of instruction, while children are so numerous. My houses are my own. I bought them with my own money; and shall dispose of them at my own pleasure.

2d Ten. You speak as though you were lord of the creation, and had the world at your command.

Don P. I am lord of my own possessions; and shall not ask my tenants how I am to dispose of them.

2d Ten. Did you ever read, that "Riches take to themselves wings, and fly away?"

Don P. I am not apprehensive that any wings are attached to my property.

2d Ten. Your mountain may not stand so strong as you think it does. The cries of the fatherless and the widow, who have groaned under your oppression, have reached the heavens, and you have reason to fear they will be answered with vengeance on your head. Did you but believe in a future day of retribution, as you have impiously professed, you would seriously engage in the work of repentance and reformation; which, let me tell you, it is presumption to neglect.

Re-enter first TENANT, *with a* LAWYER.

1st Ten. I pray you to accept your money, and give me a discharge.

Don P. I told you, not a cent, till the whole amount was paid.

Law. That is sufficient. The law allows no force in paying debts. Every creditor has an undoubted right to refuse his money, when offered by his debtor. This he has done before witness. I now declare it forfeit. Keep it as your own.

Don P. Rogues will always combine against honest men. The whole world are endeavouring to cheat me out of my lawful earnings. My best friends have become my worst enemies.

Law. You have no friends; nor will you ever have, so long as you make an idol of your own dear self.

Don P. My property is my best friend, and one which I trust will never forsake me.

[*Cry of fire without.*]

Enter SERVANT *in haste.*

Ser. Sir, your long row of buildings is all in flames!

Don P. Impossible!—They were all to be insured to-morrow.

Ser. It is seriously true! and the roofs are now tumbling to the ground!

Don P. Then immediately call all hands, and put fire to this, and every other building I possess; that they may all go to destruction together.

2d Ten. That looks something like giving wings to your riches.

Don P. If I had one thimble full of brains, I should have got them insured before. O horrible catastrophe! Not only wicked men and devils, but even the elements themselves have turned against me.

Law. Compose yourself, dear Sir. Your best friend won't be so cruel as to forsake you at this critical moment.

Don P. Is my money safe? If that is burnt, I'll burn myself. Oh that I had permitted my tenants to remain, that they and their property might all have perished in the flames together!

LORD MANSFIELD'S SPEECH, IN SUPPORT OF A BILL FOR PREVENTING DELAYS OF JUSTICE, BY REASON OF PRIVILEGÉ OF PARLIAMENT, 1770.

My Lords,

I HAVE waited with patience to hear what arguments might be urged against the bill; but I have waited in vain; the truth is, there is no argument that can weigh against it. The justice and expediency of the bill are such as render it self-evident. It is a proposition of that nature, that can neither be weakened by argument, nor entangled with sophistry.

We all know, that the very soul and essence of trade are regular payments; and sad experience teaches us, that there are men, who will not make their regular payments without the compulsive power of the laws. The law then ought to be equally open to all. Any exemption to particular men, or particular ranks of men, is, in a free and commercial country, a solecism of the grossest nature.

I will not trouble your lordships with arguments for that which is sufficiently evident without any. I shall only say a few words to some noble lords, who foresee much inconveniency from the persons of their servants being liable to be arrested. One noble lord observes, that the coachman of a peer may be arrested while he is driving his master to the house; and, consequently, he will not be able to attend his duty in Parliament. If this were actually to happen, there are so many ways by which the member might still get to the House, that I can hardly think the noble lord is serious in his objection. Another noble peer said, that by this bill we might lose our most valuable and honest servants. This I hold to be a contradiction in terms: for he can neither be a valuable servant, nor an honest man, who gets into debt which he is neither able nor willing to pay, till compelled by law.

If my servant, by unforeseen accidents, has run into debt, and I still wish to retain him, I certainly would pay the debt. But upon no principle of liberal legislation whatever, can my servant have a title to set his creditors at defiance, while for forty shillings only, the honest tradesman may be torn from his family, and locked up in a jail. It is monstrous injustice! I flatter myself, however, the determination of this day will entirely put an end to all such partial proceedings for the future, by passing into a law the bill now under your lordships' consideration.

I come now to speak, upon what, indeed, I would have gladly avoided, had I not been particularly pointed at for the part I have taken in this bill. It has been said by a noble lord on my left hand, that I likewise am running the race of popularity. If the noble lord means by popularity, that applause bestowed by after-ages on good and virtuous actions, I have long been struggling in that race. But if he mean that mushroom popularity, which is raised without merit & lost without a crime, he much mistakes in his opinion.

I defy the noble lord to point out a single action of my life, where the popularity of the times ever had the smallest influence on my determinations. I have a more permanent and steady rule for my conduct, the dictates of my own breast. Those who have foregone that pleasing adviser, and given up their minds to be the slave of every popular impulse, I sincerely pity. I pity them still more, if their vanity leads them to mistake the shouts of a mob for the trumpet of fame. Experience might inform them, that many who have been saluted with the huzzas of a crowd, one day, have received their execrations the next; and many, who, by the popularity of their times, have been held up as spotless patriots, have, nevertheless, appeared upon the historian's page, when truth has triumphed over delusion, the assassins of liberty.

Why then the noble lord can think I am ambitious of present popularity, that echo of folly, and shadow of renown, I am at a loss to determine. Besides, I do not know that the bill now before your lordships will be popular. It depends much upon the caprice of the day. It may not be popular to compel people to pay their debts; and, in that case, the present must be a very unpopular bill. It may not be popular neither to take away any of the privileges of parliament; for I very well remember, and many of your lordships may remember, that not long ago the popular cry was for the extension of privilege; and so far did they carry it at that time, that it was said that the privilege protected members even in criminal actions. Nay, such was the power of popular prejudices over weak minds, that the very decisions of some of the courts were tinctured with that doctrine.

It was undoubtedly an abominable doctrine. I thought so then, and think so still: but nevertheless, it was a popular doctrine, and came immediately from those who were called the friends of liberty; how deservedly, time will show. True liberty, in my opinion, can only exist when justice is equally administered to all; to the king, and to the beggar. Where is the justice, then, or where is the law, that protects a member of parliament more than any other man, from the punishment due to his crimes? The laws of this country allow of no place, nor any employment, to be a sanctuary for crimes: and where I have the honour to sit as judge, neither royal favour nor popular applause shall ever protect the guilty.

EXTRACT FROM A SERMON ON THE DAY OF JUDGMENT.

LET us endeavour to realize the majesty and terror of the universal alarm on the final Judgment Day. When the dead are sleeping in the silent grave; when the living are thoughtless and unapprehensive of the grand event, or intent on other pursuits: some of them asleep in the dead of night; some of them dissolved in sensual pleasures, eating and drinking, marrying and giving in marriage; some of them planning or executing schemes for riches or honours; some in the very act of sin; the generality stupid and careless about the concerns of eternity, and the dreadful day just at hand; and a few here and there conversing with their God, and looking for the glorious appearance of their Lord and Saviour; when the course of nature runs on uniform and regular as usual, and infidel scoffers are taking umbrage from thence to ask, " Where is the promise of his coming?" In short, when there are no more visible appearances of this approaching day, than of the destruction of Sodom, on that clear morning in which Lot fled away; or of the deluge, when Noah en-

I

tered into the ark: then, in that hour of unapprehensive security, then suddenly shall the heavens open over the astonished world; then shall the alarming clangor break over their heads like a clap of thunder in a clear sky.

Immediately the living turn their gazing eyes upon the amazing phenomenon: some hear the long expected sound with rapture, and lift up their heads with joy, assured that the day of their redemption is come; while the thoughtless world are struck with the wildest horror and consternation. In the same instant the sound reaches all the mansions of the dead; and in a moment, in the twinkling of an eye, they are raised, and the living are changed. This call will be as animating to all the sons of men, as that call to a single person, " Lazarus, come forth." O what a surprise will this be to the thoughtless world! Should this alarm burst over our heads this moment, into what a terror would it strike many in this assembly! Such will be the terror, such the consternation, when it actually comes to pass. Sinners will be the same timorous, self-condemned creatures then as they are now. And then they will not be able to stop their ears, who are deaf to all the gentler calls of the gospel now.

Then the trump of God will constrain them to hear and fear, to whom the ministers of Christ now preach in vain. Then they must all hear; for, " all that are in their graves," all without exception, " shall hear his voice." Now the voice of mercy calls, reason pleads, conscience warns; but multitudes will not hear. But this is a voice which shall, which must, reach every one of the millions of mankind; and not one of them will be able to stop his ears. Infants and giants, kings and subjects, all ranks, all ages of mankind shall hear the call. The living shall start and be changed, and the dead rise at the sound. The dust that was once alive and formed a human body, whether it flies in the air, floats in the ocean, or vegetates on earth, shall hear the new-creating fiat. Wherever the fragments of the human frame are scattered, this all-penetrating call shall reach and speak them into life. We may consider this voice as a summons not only to dead bodies to rise, but to the souls that once animated them, to appear and be reunited to them.

This summons shall spread through every corner of the universe; and Heaven, Earth, and Hell, and all their inhabitants, shall hear and obey. Now methinks I see, I hear the earth heaving, charnel houses rattling, tombs bursting, graves opening. Now the nations under ground begin to stir. There is a noise and a shaking among the dry bones. The dust is all alive, and in motion, and the globe breaks and trembles, as with an earthquake, while this vast army is working its way through, and bursting into life. The ruins of human bodies are scattered far and wide, and have passed through many and surprising transformations. A limb in one country, and another in another; here the head, and there the trunk, and the ocean rolling between.

And now, at the sound of the trumpet, they shall all be collected, wherever they were scattered; all properly sorted and united, however they were confused; atom to its fellow atom, bone to its fellow bone. Now methinks you may see the air darkened with fragments of bodies, flying from country to country, to meet and join their proper parts:

——"Scatter'd limbs and all
The various bones obsequious to the call,
Self-mov'd, advance; the neck perhaps to meet
The distant head, the distant legs, the feet.
Dreadful to view, see through the dusky sky
Fragments of bodies in confusion fly,
To distant regions journeying, there to claim
Deserted members, and complete the frame.
The sever'd head and trunk shall join once more,
Though realms now rise between, and oceans roar.
The trumpet's sound each vagrant mote shall hear,
Or fix'd in earth, or if afloat in air,
Obey the signal, wafted in the wind,
And not one sleeping atom lag behind."

CHRIST TRIUMPHANT OVER THE APOSTATE ANGELS.

SO spake the Son, and into terror chang'd
His count'nance, too severe to be beheld;
And full of wrath bent on his enemies.
At once the Four spread out their starry wings
With dreadful shade contiguous, and the orbs
Of his fierce chariot roll'd, as with the sound
Of torrent floods, or of a numerous host.
He on his impious foes right onward drove,
Gloomy as night; under his burning wheels
The stedfast empyrean shook throughout,
All but the throne itself of God. Full soon
Among them he arriv'd, in his right hand
Grasping ten thousand thunders, which he sent
Before him, such as in their souls infix'd
Plagues; they, astonish'd, all resistance lost,
All courage; down their idle weapons dropt;
O'er shields, and helms, and helmed heads, he rode,
Of thrones and mighty seraphim prostrate,
That wish'd the mountains now might be again
Thrown on them as a shelter from his ire.
  Nor less on either side tempestuous fell
His arrows, from the fourfold-visag'd Four
Distinct with eyes, and from the living wheels
Distinct alike with multitude of eyes;
One spirit in them rul'd, and every eye
Glar'd lightning, and shot forth pernicious fire
Among th' accurs'd, that wither'd all their strength,
And of their wonted vigour left them drain'd,
Exhausted, spiritless, afflicted, fall'n.
Yet half his strength he put not forth, but check'd
His thunder in mid volley; for he meant
Not to destroy, but root them out of Heav'n.
The overthrown he rais'd, and as a herd
Of goats, or tim'rous flock together throng'd,
Drove them before him thunderstruck, pursued

With terrors and with furies to the bounds
And crystal wall of Heav'n, which, opening wide,
Roll'd inward, and a spacious gap disclos'd
Into the wasteful deep; the monstrous sight
Struck them with horror backward, but far worse
Urg'd them behind; headlong themselves they threw
Down from the verge of Heav'n; eternal wrath
Burnt after them to the bottomless pit.

Hell heard th' unsufferable noise; Hell saw
Heav'n ruining from Heav'n, and would have fled
Affrighted! but strict fate had cast too deep
Her dark foundations, and too fast had bound.
Nine days they fell; confounded Chaos roar'd,
And felt tenfold confusion in their fall:
Through his wild anarchy, so huge a rout
Incumber'd him with ruin. Hell at last
Yawning receiv'd them whole, and on them clos'd;
Hell, their fit habitation, fraught with fire
Unquenchable, the house of woe and pain.

Disburden'd Heav'n rejoic'd, and soon repair'd
Her mural breach, returning whence it roll'd.
Sole victor from th' expulsion of his foes,
Messiah his triumphal chariot turn'd:
To meet him all his saints, who silent stood
Eye-witnesses of his almighty acts,
With jubilee advanc'd; and as they went,
Shaded with branching palm, each order bright,
Sung triumph, and him sung victorious King,
Son, Heir, and Lord, to him dominion giv'n
Worthiest to reign. He, celebrated, rode
Triumphant through mid Heav'n, into the courts
And temple of his mighty Father, thron'd
On high; who into glory him receiv'd,
Where now he sits at the right hand of bliss.

I 2

SLAVES IN BARBARY,

A Drama in Two Acts.

Persons of the Drama.

Hamet,	Bashaw of Tunis.
Ozro, *Amandar,* }	Brothers, and Slaves in Tunis
Francisco,	Brother to Ozro and Amandar, sent to redeem them.
Kidnap,	An American Captive.
Oran,	A purchaser of Slaves.
Zanga, *Gorton,* }	Sea Captains.
Teague,	An Irish Captive.
Sharp,	An African, and Kidnap's Slave.

Officer, Auctioneer, Guards, Attendants, Purchasers of Slaves, &c.

ACT I.

Scene I.—*A Garden.*

Amandar *solus, confined with a chain.*

IN vain the flowers spread their gaudy colours, and fill the air with fragrance. The sun has not a cheering beam for me. All nature's smiles are frowns to him, who wears the chain of bondage. Fifteen long months have witnessed my misfortune: what luckless winds delay Francisco's passage?

Enter Oran *with a cane.*

Oran. Moping fugitive! quick to your task. [*Beating him.*] I have not placed you here to mutter to the herbs and flowers: they need the labour of your hands. Let them have it; or heavier blows shall punish your neglect.

Aman. Then do your worst! I ask the fatal blow, to put a period to my miseries.

Oran. Your life is in my hands; but it shall be prolonged; and with your life, I'll lengthen out your miseries.

Aman. Unfeeling tyrant! from you I only ask the murderer's office. Speech was designed for friendly intercourse; it ill becomes the tiger. In brutal silence, you may tear my flesh: add not the sting of words.

Enter OZRO.

Oran. Hah! Ozro. A slave enlarged is no grateful sight to his old master.   [*Aside.*

Ozro. I come, my brother, to end your sufferings.

Aman. Welcome! You know them to be more than man can bear.

Oran. Vile intruder! are you so soon intoxicated with your liberty? Quick, flee this place; or stronger chains, than bound you here before, shall sober you again.

Ozro. Talk not of chains! but rather learn to dread the hand, on which they have been bound. I come to execute the orders of your lord and master; not to be frightened with your threats. Amandar's injuries have reached the ears of the Bashaw; and I am sent ——

Oran. Tale-bearing renegade! Well, I shall learn to husband my own property, and give up no more slaves for Hamet's counsellors. Attend your duty!

[*To Amandar, striking him.*

Ozro. Repeat that blow, and it shall cost you dear.

Oran. Caitiff! begone from hence; or even the Bashaw shall not defend you from my indignation. Quick leave my sight!

Ozro. Not while you have it in your power to exercise your tyranny over my brother. But yesterday, you promised to sell Amandar for this sum: here it is, ready counted to your hand. I demand him of you.

Oran. One half of this sum would have bought him yesterday. It is my present choice to sacrifice my property for my revenge. I will double his task and shorten his allowance, till his pride is reduced, and he becomes more profitable, by additional severity. This is my promise to-day: take it for your solace.

Ozro. Monster! would you forever feast your soul on the miseries of the unfortunate? Your word is passed; recall it at the peril of your life. There is your money. [*Flinging it at his feet.*] Amandar is——

Oran. When foreign ruffians, who ought to wear the chains of bondage, are armed with swords, all right is lost: our property is given to the winds. Were it not for what weak heads, and sickly hearts call justice, I'd feast my dogs upon your flesh.

Ozro. Go vent your railings to the savage beasts, that prey on one another. If you love the laws that sanction cruelty, they are your fit associates. Amandar, you are once more restored to liberty and life. [*Cutting off his bands with his sword.*]

[*Exeunt Amandar and Ozro.*

Oran. [*Taking his money.*] These high-bred fellows make but poor slaves. 'Tis well to shift them off at any rate. I will take care how I lay out my money for the future. [*Exit.*

Scene II.

The Highway.

Ozro *and* Amandar.

Aman. Am I deluded by a dream? or is this real? What angel eye of pity has glanced upon us?

Ozro. I would not interrupt thy bliss, nor stir the dregs, which the fair surface of this draught conceals. But fortune seems to make our happiness her sport.

Aman. Has not the Bashaw purchased our freedom? What are the conditions?

Ozro. That is for time or wild conjecture to determine. We must deliberate what course to take.

Aman. What dost thou say? let me hear the worst.

Ozro. You know the circumstances of my liberation. All had the appearance of affability and pity in the Bashaw. He questioned particularly concerning our situation, and seemed moved with the account I gave. I informed him, our brother was daily expected with the gleanings of an unfortunate father's interest to redeem us from our chains, and restore us to a disconsolate family. He turned aside, as though some sudden emotion had seized his mind; then exclaimed, " They shall be mine!" the money was paid for your ransom, and committed to me. We are considered as his property.

Aman. What then creates suspicion? This favour has some claim upon our gratitude. If we must err, let it be on the side of honour.

Ozro. So thought I, Amandar. These were the impressions of the moment. But avarice often assumes the appearance of generosity: and malice, to make its prey more sure, puts on the guise of pity. If the Bashaw's motive were our happiness, all, but my freedom, I would pledge to pay the debt of gratitude. But I would sooner seek the lion's den, or trust the mercy of a tiger, than commit myself to a mercenary Turk. A father's fortune well may tempt the hypocritic show of kindness to his sons.

Aman. This thought gives weight to your suspicion. Are our misfortunes then the object of base speculation? This well becomes the dignity of rulers; the honour of the prime magistrate of Tunis! to seek us out, like brutes, to buy and sell, and fill his coffers on the ruins of our family. But stay. Is there no room for charity? Tunis, of all the states of Barbary, is famed for its refinement. Every Turk is not an Oran. I think I have heard the Bashaw noted for his humanity.

Ozro. That ruler has but an ill title to humanity, who suffers his subjects to traffic in the dearest rights of man, and shares himself the execrated commerce.

Aman. True, my brother, but let us remember our native Venice. We have seen the Turk sold there in open market, and exposed to all the indignities which we have borne with Oran. Nay more; we may come nearer home, and spread the blush on our own faces. We have both heard the story of the grateful Turk, who, by the intercession of Francisco, was twice released from servitude. He had a noble soul, a feeling heart. Though his virtues were discov-- ered, and finally rewarded by our father, we may blush that they were so long unheeded by our countrymen, and he suffered to languish in ignominious bondage.

Ozro. Your words have weight. For the sake of this noble captive, I will take part of my censure from the Turks, and spare it for my countrymen. Though this was done before my memory, the story paints his virtues to my mind; and had I no other claim, I would call Francisco brother for this deed.

Aman. [*After a pause.*] Can it be? no; 'tis too much to think off.

Ozro. What, Amandar?

Aman. A thought has struck my mind. Help to confirm, or to confute it.

Enter Guards abruptly.

Ozro. [*Drawing.*] Who is here? Stand off!

[*Guards draw.*

1st Guard. But look, my lads! You see you are outmanned. We are more than two to one.

Ozro. Then keep your distance, and let us know your business: else, were you ten to one, I'd make your number less.

1st Guard. As to our business, we are obliged to let you know it; or I believe your swords would not frighten us to it. It is to carry you to the Bashaw.

Ozro. On what conditions must we go?

1st Guard. As to that, we shall not be nice. We have no cavalry, you see; so you must be content to march on foot. You may take the front, or centre, as suits you best. But we shall not trust you in the rear, if you show a disposition to desert us; and, if you are inclined to be hostile, we must secure that sword.

Ozro. I ask the terms on which we are to go; as slaves or freemen?

1st Guard. We don't wish to take the trouble to bind you. If you are not free to go, we must quicken your march with the point of our swords. Our orders are to return immediately.

Ozro. Keep us no longer in suspense. We now are free; and——

1st Guard. As to that, I believe you are a little mistaken. The Bashaw has bought you both, and paid for you; and we shall look better to his interest than to lose you for nothing; d'ye see? Come; march!

Ozro. What is the paltry price, compared with years of misery? Perhaps you know our destiny. If we're for sale again, tell him, we give the terms. This place shall be the fair, and life the price.

1st Guard. I tell you again, we are not easily frighted. But I see you are afraid of getting into Oran's hands again. If you choose to be obstinate, we could easily slice you in pieces, and carry you on the points of our swords. But we don't wish to spoil you in such a manner. Besides, our master keeps no cutthroats. Our orders were to carry you safe to the Bashaw, and neither hurt you ourselves, nor let any body else. You may wonder at this extraordinary honour, and so do we. But he takes a liking to Christians, and is very often doing them a good turn. I fancy something uncommon is going forward to-day by this manœuvre. Perhaps he is inclined to sin a little in your own way, by drinking a few bottles of wine with you.

Ozro. [*To Amandar.*] Their honest frankness quite unarms me. I hope my suspicions have been groundless.

Aman. Let us trust ourselves to their care. I am anxious to know the sequel.

Scene III.

Hamet's House.

Hamet. [*Solus.*] The grateful day returns, that brings to mind my generous benefactors. The birth-day of my happiness, my fortune, and my honour. Let it be sacred to gratitude, and devoted to the sons of sorrow.

Enter OFFICER.

Officer. Noble Sir, the sale of prisoners begins in half an hour. Is it your pleasure to attend the auction?

Hamet. It is. Have them upon the spot; and see that they are treated with humanity. [*Exit Officer.*] Ill-fated men! their lot is miserable indeed. 'Twere almost just to rise above the laws, and give them all their freedom.   [*Exit Hamet.*

Scene IV.

The street in Tunis.

Enter CRIER, *ringing his bell.*

At half an hour from this time! will be sold at public auction! to the highest bidder! prisoners of all colours! sorts and sizes! lately captured! on the Mediterranean! and brought fresh into port! warranted free from sickness and wounds! also, a considerable number! a little damaged! by musket shot! and cannon balls! and careless handling, with long knives and broad swords! and for want of wholesome air! on easy terms for the purchaser.   [*Exit Crier.*

ACT II.

Scene I.

ORAN *walking to the fair.*

Oran. [*Solus.*] Yes, he who frees a slave, arms an assassin. The Bashaw may learn this to his sorrow. Let him look to that. He has given a high price for stock, that I should have been glad to turn upon his hands. The money will purchase two for one. Gorton's and Zanga's freight of prisoners will almost glut the market. The Bashaw may be as ostentatious as he pleases.

of his boyish pity: thank fortune, I am not so tender-
hearted. No: dominion is the right of man. The love
of power is planted in his nature. But all men can't
be kings. If there are lords, there must be slaves.
And what must be is right. Let moralizers murmur
at the doctrine: their arguments are slender threads;
feeble as those who spin them out from lovers' dreams
and children's notions. What is justice without power?
The slave's ideal friend; whom he would wish to
break his chains; on whose credit, he would establish
universal government; then dissolve connexion, and
shut his partner up in prison.   [*Exit Oran.*

SCENE II.

The fair, a large square.

Enter OFFICER, *with a drawn sword;* ZANGA *and*
GORTON, *with swords, followed by prisoners pin-
ioned; Sailors in the rear;* AUCTIONEER, *&c.*
SHARP, *a negro, standing by Gorton.*

OFFICER *bringing forward sick and wounded.*

Auctioneer. Here, gentlemen, is a lot we shall not
differ about. For the sake of despatch we will put up
all the fragments together. Here are a number with
broken legs, arms, &c. and a number more with mortal wounds, that may get well, or may not. That is
your risk; I shall not warrant them. Upwards of a
dozen: count for yourselves. Who bids?

Enter HAMET, *and attendants; silence observed, and
all pay him obeisance.*

Sharp. Dat a man, a planter, masser Gorton.
  [*To Gorton.*

Auct. Examine for yourselves: who bids?

Oran. Four hundred sequins for the whole.

Auct. That is scarce the price of one good able-
bodied slave.

Oran. They will not do me half the service at present. The greater part of them are not able to cook

K

their own food; much less to earn it. Yet they must be fed; or they will die on my hands, you know. And a sick or dead slave is the very worst of dead stock. I'll give no more.

Hamet. These unfortunate men are the objects of compassion, not of unfeeling sarcasm. Raise their price to five hundred and charge them to my account. Servants, see them removed to the hospital. Let a surgeon be employed to heal their wounds, and restore them to health. [*Prisoners bowing respectfully.*]

[*Exeunt servants and prisoners.*]

Sharp. Dat a good planter, masser Gorton. He good to white man; an he be good to poor negur man too.

OFFICER *bringing forward a number.*

Auct. Here are a parcel of lads of the first quality; superfine; the sons of noblemen. Their relations will give their weight in gold to redeem them.

1st Purchaser. And their country, twice their weight, rather than have them return.

Auct. Now is the time to make your fortunes. Who bids?

Zanga. [*To Gorton.*] These, I suppose, are your champions, that took shelter in the hold, with their seafaring brethren, the rats, when you fought them.

Gorton. The same.

Auct. One! two! three! Just going for——nothing.

1st Purchaser. Precisely what they are valued at, at home. You know, captains, these men of the feminine gender, don't pass very current with us. You would do well to exchange them for ballast, or fresh water. I will give you one hundred sequins a piece for them.

Gorton. Strike them off! It is cheaper buying men than raising them at this rate. One, two, three, four, five of them. Clear the hatchway!

[*Exeunt 1st purchaser and prisoners.*]

OFFICER *bringing forward three others.*

Auct. Here are three stout, able-bodied fellows for you; well made for labour. Who bids?

Sharp. Dat a man my masser. [*Pointing to Kidnap.*

2d Purchaser. Mere bladders filled with wine. Our labour and climate will blast them like mushrooms.

3d Purchaser. Let me look at their hands; they are the index of the slave. A good hard hand is worth more than a dozen bloated cheeks and barrel bodies. Let me see how they are put together.

[*Shaking them by the shoulders.*

Kidnap. Stand off! base ruffian. [*Officer strikes him.*

Sharp. Dat larn you strike poor negur. Me wish he killa you.   [*Aside.*

Kidnap. Black imp! be silent.

Officer. This fellow is a rare piece, I'll assure you. Rather mettlesome at present. Discipline him freely with a whip for several weeks, and he will be as patient as a Dutch horse.

Kidnap. Severe reverse! Now, Africans, I learn to pity you.

3d Purchaser. What does he say?

Officer. I fancy he wishes to be excused from reading the new leaf we are turning over for him. His dreams have been very much inclined to tattle, since he has been in prison. If I may judge from them, he has been a wholesale dealer in slaves himself; and is just beginning the hard lesson of repentance.

Gorton. Is this the man, who entertained you so agreeably in his sleep? I should suppose he might afford a deal of amusement when awake.

Officer. He was in a very companionable mood last night. He must have thought himself at home: poor man, I am almost sorry for his delusion. In his social glee, he ordered six dozen of port, gave Liberty and Independence for a toast, sung an ode to freedom; and after fancying he had kicked over the tables, broken all the glasses, and lay helpless on the floor, gave orders, attended by a volley of oaths, to have fifty of his slaves whipped thirty stripes each, for singing a liberty-song in echo to his own; and six more to be hung up by the heels for petitioning him for a draught of milk and water, while he was revelling with his drunken companions. Then waked up, and exclaimed; O happy America! farewell forever! Justice! thou hast overtaken me at last.

Auct. His dreams will be a cash article, who bids?

3d Purchaser. Two hundred sequins apiece, for the three.

Hamet. Officer, forward that man; I wish to speak with him.   [*Officer leads Kidnap to Hamet.*

From whence are you?   [*To Kidnap.*

Kidnap. From North America.

Hamet. The boasted land of liberty?

Kidnap. None more so.

Hamet. Then does she realize those scenes your fancy paints, and which your tongue describes, when off its guard?

Kidnap. Take second-handed dreams for evidence; and judge as you please of me, or of my country.

Hamet. Your arrogance is evidence against you. Stand there in silence. Bring here that African. [*To the Officer.*   [*Officer leads forward Sharp.*
Was that man your master?

Sharp. Yes a masser.   [*Bowing.*

Hamet. Is he a kind master? do you wish to live with him?

Sharp. No, masser planter! he get drunk! he whip me! he knock a me down! he stamp on a me! he will kill a me dead! No! no! let a poor negur live wid a you, masser planter; live wid a masser officer; wid a dat a man; or any udder man, fore I go back America again; fore I live wid a masser Kidnap again.

Hamet. Fear not, honest fellow: nobody shall hurt you.

Sharp. Tank a you, masser! bless a you, good masser planter.   [*Bowing.*

Hamet. [*To Officer.*] Deliver this man to the highest bidder. Let misery teach him, what he could never learn in affluence, the lesson of humanity.

[*3d Purchaser takes off Kidnap and the other two, and returns again.*]

Common sailors brought forward.

Auct. Here are robust fellows for you; reduced to discipline; hardened by toil; proof against heat and cold, wind and weather. Now is your last opportunity. Who bids?

4th Purchaser. Two hundred apiece for the whole.

5th Purchaser. Two hundred and fifty.

Auct. Two hundred and fifty, and going. Their bare bones would be worth half that for skeletons. But they are well strung with nerves, and covered with hardy flesh: none of your mushrooms, grown up in the shade. Look for yourselves: they are almost bullet proof.

Zanga. Quite, you might have said, or we should have made riddling sieves of them.

Oran. Three hundred apiece.

Auct. Three hundred, and going. One! two! three!
[*Strikes.*

Zanga. [*To Oran.*] I am sorry we were obliged to cut so many of them in pieces, before we could persuade them to strike. The whole crew would furnish a fine plantation; and you might live in the style of a West India planter.

Officer. Follow your master. [*Oran going; slaves following. Oran's servants follow the slaves with whips.*

Teague. [*Refusing to follow.*] Ship-mates, you may do as you please. I should be glad of your dear company; but, by my shoul, I will enter no man's ship by sea, or by land, till I know the conditions, and receive a little advance pay.

Oran. Come on, my lad; or my servants shall see to your advance pay. [*Servant strikes him with a whip.*

Teague. [*Bursting his pinions, and seizing Oran's servant.*] If this is your prompt pay, by saint Patrick! you shall have change in your own coin, my honey! D'ye see! I could tear your rigging before and aft like a hurricane. [*Shaking him. Officer attempts to strike him with his sword; other servants with their whips.*

K 2

Hamet. Forbear! his honest indignation is the effusion of humanity. Let him speak for himself. There is something in this ingenuous tar, that moves me to do him a kindness.   [*Aside.*

Teague. I think, an't please your honor, a poor sailor has a hard time enough on't to encounter wind and weather, hunger and thirst, and all the other dangers of the main sea; and when rain and storms have frowned on him for several months, he ought to find a little sunshine in every man's face; and not be bought and sold like dumb beasts in the market. I believe in my shoul, if one were to get rich in a Christian country by such a vile trade, the judgments of Heaven would keep him poor as long as he lived. Ah, and if men were made to be slaves and masters, why was not one man born with a whip in his hand and gold spoon in his mouth; and another, with a chain on his arm, or a fetter to his heel; ay, and without a tongue or a pair of jaws, so long as one must not be allowed to use them? And if I had known I were to live a dog's life in this hard-hearted country, as I am a Christian, I would have fought ye till I died. But look ye! all hands upon deck; this muckle arm of mine is free; and by the blood of my heart, it shall be torn from my body, before I will be bound once more, it shall.

Oran. I must leave that unmanageable creature with you, Zanga; I have had too much to do with such fellows already.

Hamet. Trust him with me. His are the inborn virtues I admire: virtues, that ought to make the tyrant blush before him, and find him friends, wherever there are men.

Teague. On my honest word, I am your honor's good friend and servant, so long as I live, let the winds blow as they will. Yes, I will be any man's good friend and faithful servant, that will secure my liberty in the mean time, I will.

Auct. Here is this honest negro lad, who has been under the benevolent instruction of a task-master, and converted to Christianity by lectures applied to the naked back with a rope's end, or nine-tail whip. He is bred to his business; you will find him an excellent purchase; and he can lose nothing by exchange of masters. Who bids?

5th Purchaser. Three hundred sequins.

3d Purchaser. Four hundred.

Officer. Follow that man; he is your master.

[*To Sharp.*

Sharp. Yes a masser. [*Bowing to his new master.*

5th Purchaser. You give too much. You will raise the price of slaves above their profit.

3d Purchaser. I have my reasons. He is trained to his business: I intend to put his old master under his instruction, that he may occasionally have the advantage of a whip-lecture from his former slave, whom he has treated so kindly.

5th Purchaser. Perfectly right, Sir. Every dog must have his day. [*Exeunt 3d Purchaser and Sharp.*

Zanga. [*Leading forward Francisco.*] This man has cost me dear; he must command a price accordingly.

Auct. Here is the last purchase: who bids?

5th Purchaser. What extraordinary things can this fellow do?

Zanga. He can clip off men's heads and arms with an uncommon slight of hand. Had it not been for his dexterity at this art, and his loud acclamations to his crew, I should not have been repulsed three times from their deck, with the loss of half my men.

5th Purchaser. This is your misfortune; not ours. Men in your way must run the risk of losing an arm and even a head once in a while. Courage is a very good recommendation for a sailor, or soldier; but for a slave, I would give as much for one of your faint-hearted cowards, that you find hid in the hold in time of action, as for half a dozen, who will meet you with a pistol at your head.

Auct. What, does nobody bid?

Zanga. These are the marks of gratitude and honor shown to us, who expose our lives to procure the means of ease and luxury for our countrymen. My men, whose wounds are witnesses against him, would give a generous price to satisfy their vengeance.

Francisco. Detested ruffian! blast not the names of gratitude and honor with your breath. Has not my life already been enough exposed? Then let those men, who wear the marks my courage gave, return me wound for wound. 'Tis not enough that you possess my father's fortune; the effects of an industrious life, designed to purchase from your barbarous land, two darling sons; more than his life to him; and dearer than my own to me. Their misery is not sufficient. Myself, the only stay of his declining years, must be forever exiled from his sight. But I can bear the worst that malice can invent, or tyranny inflict. If you have pity, spare it for my father; for my brothers; they have slain none of your friends; none of your nation. I can endure my own misfortunes: theirs are insupportable.

Hamet. Magnanimous, and dutiful son! your virtues shall be rewarded; and your father's sorrow shall be turned to joy. You say you have two brothers, whom you came to ransom. What are their names? Perhaps they now are free.

Francisco. Ozro and Amandar.

Hamet. Your business is accomplished. They have their liberty. Each minute I expect them here.

Francisco. O kind reverse! Francisco, thou shalt be happy.

Hamet. Francisco! did he say? Good Heavens! Can it be he? [*Aside.*] Art thou Francisco?

Francisco. That is my father's name. I am Francisco the younger.

Hamet. Thou art! O my delivering angel! Dost thou know thy Hamet.

Francisco. It cannot be! Sure I am entranced.

[*Looking earnestly at Hamet.*

Hamet. Come to my arms! I am thy friend, thy Hamet. [*Hamet rises. Francisco meets him pinioned.*

Francisco. Thou art the same! the best of men.

[*Embracing.*

Enter OZRO *and* AMANDAR *at a distance, attended by guards. They advance slowly, looking at each other and at Hamet, in suspense.*

Hamet. [*Unloosing Francisco's pinions.*] Off shameful bands! These ill become thee! Thy hands are worthy of a sceptre. Twice thou hast freed me from the chains of bondage. Thus I, in part, discharge the debt. [*Ozro and Amandar discover Francisco, and run to embrace him.*

Ozro. O Francisco!

Amandar. My brother! [*They embrace each other.*

Francisco. Welcome to my arms again! Bounteous Heaven! thy smiles have pierced the cloud, and changed the night to day. Next to Heaven, Hamet deserves our thanks.

Ozro and Amandar. As first on earth he has them.

Hamet. I am the debtor. Heaven has given me a grateful heart; but it is to you, Francisco I owe my fortune and my honor, and have it in my power to show my gratitude. Had it not been for you, I might till now have been a slave in Venice.

Teague. On my life, I would live and die here all my days, if all the people were like this same good Hamet.   [*Aside.*

Zanga. They sail so pleasantly, I must fall in with them after all. (*Aside.*) [*Takes a chest, containing the money and jewels of Francisco, and carries it to him.*] Good Sir, I have been brought up to the trade of fighting; this, you know, Sir, is not an employment to soften one's heart. I have generally been obliged to resist the current of compassion; but it sets so strong upon me now, I will even follow its motion, as you have been pleased to lead the way. Here is this man's money: I give up my share both in that and him too; and wish him and his good friends a pleasant gale upon whatever course they may steer through life.

Hamet. This deed becomes thee, Zanga, and shall hereafter be rewarded.

Francisco. Zanga, thou hast my thanks. Let me anticipate the joyous hour when our aged father shall hear the transactions of this day; and express in his name the effusions of his grateful heart, when he shall receive his sons from you as the author of their second existence; their delivery from the heavy chains of bondage.   [*To Hamet.*

Hamet. By untoward fortune, my father and myself were slaves in Venice. By your intercession I was emancipated. I cheerfully procured the freedom of a declining parent at the expense of my own. The thought of relieving him from a burden, which his tottering age was unable to support, sweetened my toil, and made that servitude a pleasure, which otherwise had been intolerable. But the generosity of your family exceeded what I dared to hope. You gratuitously restored me to liberty a second time. This was the morning of my prosperity, the birth-day of my happiness. It is by your means, I have it in my power thus to acknowledge and discharge a sacred debt, the debt of gratitude.

Ozro. This day more than compensates for our past misfortunes.

Amandar. Henceforth we will celebrate its anniversary in grateful remembrance of our benefactor.

Hamet. Generous brothers, enjoy your fortune, and let your father participate your happiness. A ship shall be prepared to convey you to your native land, and restore you to your friends. Let it be remembered, there is no luxury so exquisite as the exercise of humanity, and no post so honourable as his, who defends THE RIGHTS OF MAN. [*Exeunt omnes.*

CONCLUSION OF A CELEBRATED SPEECH OF MR.
PITT, IN 1770, IN SUPPORT OF A MOTION MADE
IN PARLIAMENT, TO REQUEST THE KING TO LAY
BEFORE THAT BODY ALL THE PAPERS, RELATIVE
TO CERTAIN DEPREDATIONS OF THE SPANIARDS,
AND LIKEWISE, TO A TREATY WHICH HE WAS
THEN NEGOTIATING WITH SPAIN.

My Lords,

I HAVE taken a wide circuit, and trespassed, I fear,
too long upon your patience. Yet. I cannot conclude without endeavouring to bring home your
thoughts to an object more immediately interesting to
us, than any I have yet considered: I mean the internal condition of this country. We may look abroad
for wealth, or triumphs, or luxury; but England, my
lords, is the main stay, the last resort of the whole
empire. To this point, every scheme of policy, whether foreign or domestic, should ultimately refer.

Have any measures been taken to satisfy, or to
unite the people? Are the grievances they have so
long complained of removed? or do they stand not
only unredressed, but aggravated? Is the right of free
election restored to the elective body? My lords, I
myself am one of the people. I esteem that security
and independence, which is the original birthright of
an Englishman, far beyond the privileges, however
splendid, which are annexed to the peerage. I myself am by birth an English elector, and join with
the freeholders of England as in a common cause.
Believe me, my lords, we mistake our real interest as
much as our duty, when we separate ourselves from
the mass of the people.

Can it be expected that Englishmen will unite heartily in defence of a government, by which they feel themselves insulted and oppressed? Restore them to their

rights; that is the true way to make them unanimous. It is not a ceremonious recommendation from the throne, that can bring back peace and harmony to a discontented people. That insipid annual opiate has been administered so long, that it has lost its effect. Something substantial, something effectual must be done.

The public credit of the nation stands next in degree to the rights of the constitution; it calls loudly for the interposition of Parliament. There is a set of men, my lords, in the city of London, who are known to live in riot and luxury, upon the plunder of the ignorant, the innocent, the helpless; upon that part of the community, which stands most in need of, and best deserves the care and protection of the legislature. To me, my lords, whether they be miserable jobbers of Exchange-Alley, or the lofty Asiatic plunderers of Leadenhall-street, they are all equally detestable. I care but little whether a man walks on foot, or is drawn by eight or six horses. If his luxury be supported by the plunder of his country, I despise and detest him.

My lords, while I had the honor of serving his Majesty, I never ventured to look at the treasury but at a distance; it is a business I am unfit for, and to which I never could have submitted. The little I know of it has not served to raise my opinion of what is vulgarly called the *moneyed interest;* I mean that blood-sucker, that muckworm, which calls itself the friend of government; that pretends to serve this or that administration, and may be purchased, on the same terms, by *any* administration; that advances money to government, and takes special care of its own emoluments.

I hope, my lords, that nothing I have said will be understood to extend to the honest, and industrious tradesman, who holds the middle rank, and has given repeated proofs, that he prefers law and liberty to gold. I love that class of men. Much less would I be thought to reflect upon the fair merchant, whose liberal commerce is the prime source of national wealth. I esteem his occupation, and respect his character.

My lords, if the general representation, which I have had the honor to lay before you, of the situation of public affairs, has in any measure engaged your attention, your lordships, I am sure, will agree with me, that the season calls for more than common prudence and vigor in the direction of our councils. The difficulty of the crisis demands a wise, a firm, and a popular administration. The dishonorable traffic of places has engaged us too long. Upon this subject, my lords, I speak without interest or enmity. I have no personal objection to any of the king's servants. I shall never be minister; certainly, not without full power to cut away all the rotten branches of government. Yet, unconcerned as I truly am for myself, I cannot avoid seeing some capital errors in the distribution of the royal favour.

I know I shall be accused of attempting to revive distinctions. My lords, if it were possible, I would abolish all distinctions. I would not wish the favours of the crown to flow invariably in one channel. But there are some distinctions which are inherent in the nature of things. There is a distinction between right and wrong; between whig and tory.

When I speak of an administration, such as the necessity of the season calls for, my views are large and comprehensive. It must be popular, that it may begin with reputation. It must be strong within itself, that it may proceed with vigor and decision. An administration, formed upon an exclusive system of family connexions, or private friendships, cannot, I am convinced, be long supported in this country.

I shall trouble your lordships with but a few words more. His Majesty tells us in his speech, that he will call upon us for our advice, if it should be necessary in the farther progress of this affair. It is not easy to say whether or not the ministry are serious in this declaration, nor what is meant by the *progress* of an affair,

L

which rests upon one fixed point. Hitherto we have not been called upon. But though we are not consulted, it is our right and duty, as the king's great hereditary council, to *offer* him our advice. The papers, mentioned in the noble duke's motion, will enable us to form a just and accurate opinion of the conduct of his majesty's servants, though not of the actual state of their honorable negotiations.

The ministry, too, seem to want advice upon some points in which their own safety is immediately concerned. They are now balancing between a war, which they ought to have foreseen, but for which they have made no provision, and an ignominous compromise. Let me warn them of their danger. If they are forced into a war, they stand it at the hazard of their heads. If, by an ignominious compromise, they should stain the honor of the crown, or sacrifice the rights of the people, let them look to their consciences, and consider whether they will be able to walk the streets in safety.

SOCRATES' DEFENCE BEFORE HIS ACCUSERS AND JUDGES.

I am accused of corrupting the youth, and of instilling dangerous principles into them, as well in regard to the worship of the gods, as the rulers of government. You know, Athenians, I never made it my *profession* to teach; nor can envy, however violent against me, reproach me with having ever sold my instructions. I have an undeniable evidence for me in this respect, which is my poverty. Always equally ready to communicate my thoughts either to the rich or poor, and to give them entire leisure to question or answer me, I lend myself to every one who is desirous of becoming virtuous; and if amongst those who hear me, there are any who prove either good or bad, neither the virtues of the one, nor the vices of the other, to which I have not contributed, are to be ascribed to me.

My whole employment is to persuade the young and old against too much love for the body, for riches, and all other precarious things of whatsoever nature they be, and against too little regard for the soul, which ought to be the object of their affection. For I incessantly urge to you, that virtue does not proceed from riches, but on the contrary, riches from virtue; and that all the other goods of human life, as well public as private, have their source in the same principle.

If to speak in this manner be to corrupt youth, I confess, Athenians, that I am guilty, and deserve to be punished. If what I say be not true, it is most easy to convict me of my falsehood. I see here a great number of my disciples: they have only to appear. But perhaps the reserve and consideration for a master, who has instructed them, will prevent them from declaring against me: at least their fathers, brothers, and uncles cannot, as good relations and good citizens, dispense with their not standing forth to demand vengeance against the corrupter of their sons, brothers, and nephews. But these are the persons who take upon them my defence, and interest themselves in the success of my cause.

Pass on me what sentence you please, Athenians; but I can neither repent nor change my conduct. I must not abandon or suspend a function, which God himself has imposed on me, since he has charged me with the care of instructing my fellow citizens? If, after having faithfully kept all the posts, wherein I was placed by our generals, the fear of death should at this time make me abandon that in which the Divine Providence has placed me, by commanding me to pass my life in the study of philosophy for the instruction of myself and others; this would be a most criminal desertion indeed, and make me highly worthy of being cited before this tribunal, as an impious man who does not believe the gods.

Should you resolve to acquit me for the future, I should not hesitate to make answer, Athenians, I honor and love you; but I shall choose rather to obey God than you; and to my latest breath shall never renounce my philosophy, nor cease to exhort and reprove you according to my custom. I am reproached with abject fear and meanness of spirit, for being so busy in imparting my advice to every one in private, and for having always avoided to be present in your assemblies, to give my counsels to my country. I think I have sufficiently proved my courage and fortitude, both in the field, where I have borne arms with you, and in the Senate, when I alone, upon more than one occasion, opposed the violent and cruel orders of the thirty tyrants. What is it then that has prevented me from appearing in your assemblies? It is that demon, that voice divine, which you have so often heard me mention, and Melitus has taken so much pains to ridicule.

That spirit has attached itself to me from my infancy; it is a voice, which I never hear, but when it would prevent me from persisting in something I have resolved; for it never exhorts me to undertake any thing. It is the same being that has always opposed me, when I would have intermeddled in the affairs of the republic; and that with the greatest reason; for I should have been amongst the dead long ago, had I been concerned in the measures of the state, without effecting any thing to the advantage of myself, or our country.

Do not take it ill, I beseech you, if I speak my thoughts without disguise, and with truth and freedom. Every man who would generously oppose a whole people, either amongst us or elsewhere, and who inflexibly applies himself to prevent the violation of the laws, and the practice of iniquity in a government, will never do so long with impunity. It is absolutely necessary for him, who would contend for justice, if he has any thoughts of living, to remain in a private station, and never to have any share in public affairs.

For the rest, Athenians, if, in the extreme danger I now am, I do not imitate the behaviour of those, who, upon less emergencies, have implored and supplicated their judges with tears, and have brought forth their children, relations, and friends, it is not through pride or obstinacy; or any contempt for you; but solely for your honour, and for that of the whole city. At my age, and with the reputation, true or false, which I have, would it be consistent for me, after all the lessons I have given upon the contempt of death, to be afraid of it myself, and to belie in my last action all the principles and sentiments of my past life?

But without speaking of my fame, which I should extremely injure by such a conduct, I do not think it allowable to entreat a judge, nor to be absolved by supplications: he ought to be persuaded and convinced. The judge does not sit upon the bench to show favour by violating the laws; but to do justice in conforming to them. He does not swear to discharge with impunity whom he pleases; but to do justice where it is due. We ought not therefore to accustom you to perjury, nor you to suffer yourselves to be accustomed to it; for in so doing, both the one and the other of us equally injure justice and religion, and both are criminals.

Do not therefore expect from me, Athenians, that I should have recourse to means which I believe neither honest nor lawful; especially upon this occasion, wherein I am accused of impiety by Melitus. For, if I should influence you by my prayers, and thereby induce you to violate your oaths, it would be undeniably evident, that I teach you not to believe in the gods; and even in defending and justifying myself, should furnish my adversaries with arms against me, and prove that I believe no divinity. But I am very far from such wicked thoughts. I am more convinced of the existence of God than my accusers; and so convinced that I abandon myself to God and you, that you may judge of me as you shall think it best.

DIALOGUE ON COWARDICE AND KNAVERY.

CHARACTERS.

HECTOR, *An Officer cashiered for Cowardice.*
HAMBURGH, *A fraudulent Bankrupt.*
SIMON, *A Pawn-Broker.*
TRUSTY, *In disguise, acquainted with all.*

(Sitting together; some with segars.)

SCENE, *A Tavern.*

Enter LANDLORD.

Landlord. GENTLEMEN, you all come different ways; and I s'pose are strangers; but may be, you'd like to cut and come again upon a roast turkey with good trimmings.

Trusty. With all my heart. I'd play knife and fork even with a cut-throat over such a supper: and I dare say, you will find none of us cowards or bankrupts in that business.

Up start HECTOR, HAMBURGH, *and* SIMON.

All three. [*To Trusty.*] Do you call me names, Sir?

Trusty. Gentlemen, I meant no personalities.

Hector. [*Puts his hand to his sword.*] But you called me a coward, you rascal.

Hamb. [*Takes off his coat.*] You called me a bankrupt, you knave.

Simon. [*Doubles his fist.*] You called me a cut-throat, you villain.

Trusty. I told you all, I meant no personalities; but [*To Hector*] pray what are you?

Hector. A soldier, to your sorrow. Fear and tremble.

Trusty. [*To Hamburgh.*] Pray what are you?

Hamb. A merchant.

Trusty. [*To Simon.*] And what are you?

Simon. A banker.

Trusty. Then if you are such as soldiers, merchants, and bankers *ought to be*, I could not mean you; otherwise you may take the words, cut-throat, bankrupt, and coward, and divide 'em among you. And as to knave, rascal, and villain, I return them to the right owners.

Hector. Gentlemen, stand by. I'll fight for you all. [*Draws and turns to Trusty.*] I challenge you to fight me.

Land. Poh! challenge him to eat with you; the supper's waiting.

Hector. [*To Landlord.*] Don't interfere, Sir: here's serious work: blood will be spilt.

Trusty. Well, spill your own then: I have no notion of having my veins pricked.

Hector. Choose your mode of fighting instantly, or fall beneath this sword, which has drunk the blood of thousands.

Trusty. Well, if I must fight, my mode will be to use that sword five minutes upon your body: then you shall use it upon me as long, and so we will take turns.

Hector. You inflame my choler.

Trusty. Then unpin your collar.

Hector. I shall burst with rage.

Trusty. Then we shall have one less at table.

Hector. [*Brandishes his sword.*] Are you prepared for your exit?

Trusty. I am.   [*Exit.*]

Hector. Now he is gone to arm himself with panoply to meet this valorous sword. Guard me, ye powers! who, in the day of battle, 'mid clashing swords and all the thunder of my father Mars, have been my shield and buckler. Now I am ready for him: why does he not return?

Land. He's gone to supper. This is an eating house, not a fighting house. Sheathe your sword.

Hector. [*Sheathes.*] There, sword, smother thy rage till some dauntless adversary shall call thee out: then seek his heart and make report of victory.

                              [*Exeunt omnes.*

Interval five minutes.

Enter TRUSTY *and* LANDLORD.

Land. I take that officer-looking man to be Colonel Home, one of the bravest men in the army.

Trusty Colonel Home and he are very different characters. That wretch was but an ensign, and was cashiered for cowardice.

Land. Is that possible? Why, he told me himself that he had alone surprised a whole regiment and cut them in pieces; and that all the army stood in awe of him.

Trusty. Well, you may depend on what I tell you: and the one that sits next to him is a bankrupt, who has been guilty of every shameful practice to defraud his creditors; and the other is a base pawnbroker, who has got all the property of this bankrupt in his hand for concealment.

Land. You surprise me! Why, that bankrupt, as you call him, was just now telling the other, how he was afraid the late storms at sea might affect his shipping; and the other was offering to insure them.

Enter HECTOR, HAMBURGH, *and* SIMON.

Hector. [*To Trusty.*] Since my wrath is a little abated, I am persuaded you meant no offence; but look ye, Sir, if any man was seriously to dispute my courage, you see my sword!

Trusty. I see it.

Hector. And don't you fear it?

Trusty. No; nor its owner. [*Hector offers to draw.*] Forbear, or " I will tell a tale will make it blush."

[*Hector sneaks off.*

Hamb. [*To Trusty.*] I am not disposed, Sir, to believe that you meant me by any expression you made: as to coward and cut-throat, they certainly don't belong to me. And as to bankrupt, the four winds can give the lie to such a charge.

Trusty. They could give but *windy* testimony in your favour.

Hamb. Then I appeal to this worthy gentleman, [*Speaking of Simon,*] and an honester man lives not on earth, if I have not thousands in his hands.

Simon. [*Aside to Hamb.*] You had better leave it to the four winds.

Hamb. [*Loud and hastily.*] Have I not moneys of a great amount in your hands?

Simon. Did you not take an oath, a few days since, that you had not directly nor indirectly, five pounds on earth?

Hamb. Yes. I had not *on earth;* but it was then in your coffers, and you know it.

Simon. If your oath that you had no property can't be relied on, why should your word be taken, that you have?

Hamb. But I ask you, have you not my property in your hands?

Simon. Not a farthing. You are a bankrupt for thousands, and the four winds may tell of that.

Hamb. O knavery!

Simon. O perjury!

Trusty. You are perfectly welcome to use the words I just now tossed out to you; and it appears to me, they are a very proper currency between you.

Hamb. O that I had the money out of that wretch's hands, to give to my honest creditors!

Simon. O that I had the character, which I have lost by my connexion with you!

Trusty. I am sorry for the depravity of you both. It has led you to deceive honest men, and to betray each other. You have now learned the value of reputation and peace of mind, by the loss of them. Let your future days be days of atonement. Let them be devoted to honesty and fair dealing; and ever remember that integrity is the only road to desirable wealth, and that the path of virtue is alone the path of peace.

MR. SHERIDAN'S SPEECH AGAINST MR. TAYLOR.

WE have this day been honored with the counsels of a complete gradation of lawyers. We have received the opinion of a Judge, of an Attorney General, of an Ex-Attorney-General, and of a practising Barrister. I agree with the learned gentleman in his admiration of the abilities of my honorable friend, Mr. Fox. What he has said of his quickness and of his profoundness, of his boldness and his candor, is literally just and true, which the mental accomplishment of my honorable friend is, on every occasion, calculated to extort even from his adversaries.

The learned gentleman has, however, in this insidious eulogium, connected such qualities of mind with those he has praised and venerated, as to convert his encomiums into reproach, and his tributes of praise into censure and invective. The boldness he has described is only craft, and his candor, hypocrisy. Upon what grounds does the learned gentleman connect those assemblages of great qualities and of cardinal defects? Upon what principles, either of justice or of equity, does he exalt with one hand, whilst he insidiously reprobates and destroys with the other?

If the wolf is to be feared, the learned gentleman may rest assured, it will be the wolf in sheep's clothing, the masked pretender to patriotism. It is not from the fang of the lion, but from the tooth of the serpent, that reptile which insidiously steals upon the vitals of the constitution, and gnaws it to the heart, ere the mischief is suspected, that destruction is to be feared.

With regard to the acquisition of a learned gentleman, Mr. Taylor, who has declared that he means to vote with us this day, I am sorry to acknowledge, that from the declaration he has made at the beginning of his speech, I see no great reason to boast of such an auxiliary. The learned gentleman, who has with peculiar modesty styled himself a *chicken lawyer*, has declared, that, thinking us in the right with respect to the subject of this day's discussion, he shall vote with us; but he has at the same time thought it necessary to assert, that he has never before voted differently from the minister and his friends, and perhaps he never shall again vote with those whom he means to support this day.

It is rather singular to vote with us, professedly because he finds us to be in the right, and, in the very moment that he assigns so good a reason for changing his side, to declare, that in all probability he never shall vote with us again. I am sorry to find the chicken is a bird of ill omen, and that its augury is so unpropitious to our future interests. Perhaps it would have been as well, under these circumstances, that the chicken had not left the barn-door of the treasury; but continued side by side with the old cock, to pick those crumbs of comfort which would doubtless be dealt out in time, with a liberality proportioned to the fidelity of the feathered tribe.

PART OF CICERO'S ORATION AGAINST CATILINE.

IT is now a long time, conscript fathers, that we have trod amidst the dangers and machinations of this conspiracy: but I know not how it comes to pass, the full maturity of all those crimes, and of this long-ripening rage and insolence, has now broken out during the period of my consulship. Should Catiline alone be removed from this powerful band of traitors, it may abate, perhaps, our fears and anxieties for a while; but the danger will still remain, and continue lurking in the veins and vitals of the republic.

For, as men, oppressed with a severe fit of illness, and labouring under the raging heat of a fever, are often at first seemingly relieved by a draught of cold water; but afterwards find the disease return upon them with redoubled fury; in like manner, this distemper, which has seized the commonwealth, eased a little by the punishment of this traitor, will, from his surviving associates, soon assume new force. Wherefore, conscript fathers, let the wicked retire; let them separate themselves from the honest; let them rendezvous in one place. In fine, as I have often said, let a wall be between them and us; let them cease to lay snares for the consul in his own house; to beset the tribunal of the city prætor; to invest the senatehouse with armed ruffians, and to prepare fireballs and torches for burning the city: in short, let every man's sentiments with regard to the public be inscribed on his forehead.

This I engage for, and promise, conscript fathers, that by the diligence of the consuls, the weight of your authority, the courage and firmness of the Roman knights, and the unanimity of all the honest, Catiline being driven from the city, you shall behold all his treasons detected, exposed, crushed, and punished.

With these omens, Catiline, all of prosperity to the republic, but of destruction to thyself, and all those who have joined themselves with thee in all kinds of parricide, go thy way then to this impious and abominable war: whilst thou, Jupiter, whose religion was established with the foundation of this city, whom we truly call Stator, the stay and prop of this empire, wilt drive this man and his accomplices from thy altars and temples, from the houses and walls of the city, from the lives and fortunes of us all; and wilt destroy with eternal punishments, both living and dead, all the haters of good men, the enemies of their country, the plunderers of Italy, now confederated in this detestable league and partnership of villany.

DESCRIPTION OF THE FIRST AMERICAN CONGRESS;
FROM THE VISION OF COLUMBUS.

COLUMBUS look'd; and still around them spread,
  From south to north, th' immeasurable shade;
At last, the central shadows burst away,
And rising regions open'd on the day.
He saw, once more, bright Del'ware's silver stream,
And Penn's throng'd city cast a cheerful gleam;
The dome of state, that met his eager eye,
Now heav'd its arches in a loftier sky.
The bursting gates unfold: and lo, within,
A solemn train, in conscious glory, shine.
The well-known forms his eye had trac'd before,
In diff'rent realms along th' extended shore;
Here, grac'd with nobler fame, and rob'd in state,
They look'd and mov'd magnificently great.
  High on the foremost seat, in living light,
Majestic Randolph caught the hero's sight:
Fair on his head, the civic crown was plac'd,
And the first dignity his sceptre grac'd.
He opes the cause, and points in prospect far,
Through all the toils that wait th' impending war,
But, hapless sage, thy reign must soon be o'er,
To lend thy lustre, and to shine no more.
So the bright morning star, from shades of ev'n,
Leads up the dawn, and lights the front of heav'n,
Points to the waking world the sun's broad way,
Then veils his own, and shines above the day.
And see great Washington behind thee rise,
Thy following sun, to gild our morning skies;
O'er shadowy climes to pour the enlivening flame,
The charms of freedom and the fire of fame.
Th' ascending chief adorn'd his splendid seat,
Like Randolph, ensign'd with a crown of state,
Where the green patriot bay beheld, with pride,
The hero's laurel springing by its side;
His sword hung useless, on his graceful thigh,

M

On Britain still he cast a filial eye;
But sovereign fortitude his visage bore,
To meet their legions on th' invaded shore.
　Sage Franklin next arose, in awful mien,
And smil'd, unruffl'd, o'er th' approaching scene.
High, on his locks of age, a wreath was placed,
Palm of all arts, that e'er a mortal grac'd;
Beneath him lies the sceptre kings have borne,
And crowns and laurels from their temples torn.
Nash, Rutledge, Jefferson, in council great,
And Jay and Laurens op'd the rolls of fate.
The Livingstons, fair freedom's generous band,
The Lees, the Houstons, fathers of the land,
O'er climes and kingdoms turn'd their ardent eyes,
Bade all th' oppress'd to speedy vengeance rise;
All pow'rs of state, in their extended plan,
Rise from consent, to shield the rights of man.
Bold Wolcott urg'd the all important cause;
With steady hand the solemn scene he draws;
Undaunted firmness with his wisdom join'd,
Nor kings nor worlds could warp his stedfast mind.
　Now, graceful rising from his purple throne,
In radiant robes, immortal Hosmer shone;
Myrtles and bays his learned temples bound,
The statesman's wreath, the poet's garland crown'd:
Morals and laws expand his liberal soul,
Beam from his eyes, and in his accents roll.
But lo! an unseen hand the curtain drew,
And snatch'd the patriot from the hero's view;
Wrapp'd in the shroud of death, he sees descend
The guide of nations and the muse's friend.
Columbus dropp'd a tear. The angel's eye
Trac'd the freed spirit mounting through the sky.
　Adams, enrag'd, a broken charter bore,
And lawless acts of ministerial power;
Some injur'd right in each loose leaf appears,
A king in terrors, and a land in tears;
From all the guileful plots the veil he drew,
With eye retortive look'd creation through:

Op'd the wide range of nature's boundless plan,
Trac'd all the steps of liberty and man;
Crowds rose to vengeance while his accents rung,
And independence thunder'd from his tongue.

SPEECH OF BONAPARTE, COMMANDER IN CHIEF OF
THE FRENCH ARMY IN ITALY, TO HIS BRETHREN
IN ARMS.

Soldiers,

YOU are precipitated like a torrent from the
height of the Apennines; you have overthrown
and dispersed all that dared to oppose your march.
Piedmont, rescued from Austrian tyranny, is left to
its natural sentiments of regard and friendship to the
French. Milan is yours; and the republican standard
is displayed throughout all Lombardy. The dukes of
Parma and Modena are indebted for their political
existence only to your generosity.

The army, which so proudly menaced you, has had
no other barrier than its dissolution, to oppose your
invincible courage. The Po, the Tessen, the Adda,
could not retard you a single day. The vaunted bulwarks of Italy were insufficient. You swept them with
the same rapidity that you did the Apennines. Those
successes have carried joy into the bosom of your
country. Your representatives decreed a festival dedicated to your victories, and to be celebrated throughout all the communes of the republic. Now your fathers, your mothers, your wives, and your sisters,
will rejoice in your success, and take pride in their
relation to you.

Yes, soldiers, you have done much; but more still
remains for you to do. Shall it be said of us, that we
know how to conquer, but not to profit by our victories? Shall posterity reproach us with having found a
Capua in Lombardy? But already I see you fly to
arms. You are fatigued with an inactive repose. You
lament the days that are lost to your glory! Well,

then, let us proceed; we have other forced marches to make; other enemies to subdue; more laurels to acquire, and more injuries to avenge.

Let those who have unsheathed the daggers of civil war in France; who have basely assassinated our ministers; who have burnt our ships at Toulon; let them tremble! the knell of vengeance has already tolled!

But to quiet the apprehensions of the people, we declare ourselves the friends of all, and particularly of those who are the descendents of Brutus, of Scipio, and those other great men whom we have taken for our models.

To reestablish the capitol; to replace the statues of those heroes who have rendered it immortal; to rouse the Roman people entranced in so many ages of slavery; this shall be the fruit of your victories. It will be an epoch for the admiration of posterity; you will enjoy the immortal glory of changing the aspect of affairs in the finest part of Europe. The free people of France, not regardless of moderation, shall accord to Europe a glorious peace; but it will indemnify itself for the sacrifices of every kind which it has been making for six years past. You will again be restored to your firesides and homes; and your fellowcitizens, pointing you out, shall say, " There goes one who belonged to the army of Italy!"

REFLECTIONS OVER THE GRAVE OF A YOUNG MAN.

HERE lies the grief of a fond mother, and the blasted expectation of an indulgent father. The youth grew up, like a well watered plant; he shot deep, rose high, and bade fair for manhood. But just as the cedar began to tower, and promised ere long, to be the pride of the wood, and prince among the neighbouring trees, behold! the ax is laid unto the root, the fatal blow struck; and all its branching honors tumbled to the dust. And did he fall alone? No: the hopes of his father that begat him, and the pleasing prospects of her that bare him, fell, and were crushed together with him.

Doubtless it would have pierced one's heart, to have beheld the tender parents following the breathless youth to his long home. Perhaps, drowned in tears, and all overwhelmed with sorrows, they stood, like weeping statues, on this very spot. Methinks I see the deeply distressed mourners attending the sad solemnity. How they wring their hands, and pour forth floods from their eyes! Is it fancy? or do I really hear the passionate mother, in an agony of affliction, taking her final leave of the darling of her soul? Dumb she remained, while the awful obsequies were performing; dumb with grief, and leaning upon the partner of her woes. But now the inward anguish struggles for vent; it grows too big to be repressed. She advances to the brink of the grave. All her soul is in her eyes. She fastens one more look upon the dear doleful object, before the pit shuts its mouth upon him. And as she looks, she cries; in broken accents, interrupted by many a rising sob, she cries, Farewell, my son! my son! my only beloved! would to God I had died for thee! Farewell, my child! and farewell all earthly happiness! I shall never more see good in the land of the living. Attempt not to comfort me. I will go mourning all my days, till my gray hairs come down with sorrow to the grave.

SCENE FROM THE DRAMA OF " MOSES IN THE BULRUSHES."

JOCHEBED, MIRIAM.

Jochebed. WHY was my prayer accepted? why did Heaven
In anger hear me, when I ask'd a son?

M 2

Ye dames of Egypt! happy! happy mothers!
No tyrant robs you of your fondest hopes;
You are not doom'd to see the babes you bore,
The babes you nurture, bleed before your eyes!
You taste the transports of maternal love,
And never know its anguish! Happy mothers!
How diff'rent is the lot of thy sad daughters,
O wretched Israel! Was it then for this—
Was it for this the righteous arm of God
Rescu'd his chosen people from the jaws
Of cruel want, by pious Joseph's care?
Joseph th' elected instrument of Heav'n,
Decreed to save illustrious Abram's race,
What time the famine rag'd in Canaan's land.
Israel, who then was spar'd, must perish now!
O thou mysterious Pow'r! who hast involv'd
Thy wise decrees in darkness, to perplex
The pride of human wisdom, to confound
The daring scrutiny, and prove the faith
Of thy presuming creatures! clear this doubt;
Teach me to trace this maze of providence;
Why save the fathers, if the sons must perish?

 Miriam. Ah me, my mother! whence these floods
  of grief?

 Joch. My son! my son! I cannot speak the rest.
Ye who have sons can only know my fondness!
Ye who have lost them, or who fear to lose,
Can only know my pangs! None else can guess them.
A mother's sorrows cannot be conceived,
But by a mother. Wherefore am I one?

 Mir. With many prayers thou didst request this son,
And Heav'n has granted him.

 Joch.   O sad estate
Of human wretchedness! so weak is man,
So ignorant and blind, that did not God
Sometimes withhold in mercy what we ask,
We should be ruin'd at our own request.
Too well thou know'st, my child, the stern decree
Of Egypt's cruel king, hard-hearted Pharaoh;

" 'That every male, of Hebrew mother born,
" Must die." O! do I live to tell it thee?
Must die a bloody death! My child! my son,
My youngest born, my darling must be slain!

   Mir. The helpless innocent! and must he die?

   Joch. No: if a mother's tears, a mother's prayers,
A mother's fond precautions can prevail,
He shall not die. I have a thought, my Miriam!
And sure the God of mercies, who inspir'd,
Will bless the secret purpose of my soul,
To save his precious life.

   Mir.   Hop'st thou that Pharaoh——

   Joch. I have no hope in Pharaoh; much in God;
Much in the Rock of Ages.

   Mir.   Think, O think,
What perils thou already hast incurr'd;
And shun the greater which may yet remain.
Three months, three dang'rous months thou hast pre-
      serv'd
Thy infant's life, and in thy house concealed him!
Should Pharaoh know!

   Joch. O! let the tyrant know,
And feel what he inflicts! Yes, hear me, Heav'n!
Send the right aiming thunderbolts——But hush,
My impious murmurs! Is it not thy will,
Thou infinite in mercy? Thou permitt'st
This seeming evil for some latent good.
Yes, I will laud thy grace, and bless thy goodness
For what I have, and not arraign thy wisdom
For what I fear to lose. O, I will bless thee,
That Aaron will be spar'd! that my first born
Lives safe and undisturb'd! that he was giv'n me
Before this impious persecution rag'd!

   Mir. And yet who knows, but the fell tyrant's rage
May reach *his* precious life?

   Joch.   I fear for him,
For thee, for all. A doting parent lives
In many lives; through many a nerve she feels;
From child to child the quick affections spread,
Forever wand'ring, yet forever fix'd.

Nor does division weaken, nor the force
Of constant operation e'er exhaust
Parental love. All other passions change,
With changing circumstances: rise or fall,
Livendent on their object; claim returns;
Depeon reciprocation, and expire
Unfed by hope. A mother's fondness reigns
Without a rival, and without an end.

 Mir. But say what Heaven inspires, to save thy son?
 Joch. Since the dear fatal morn which gave him
   birth,
I have revolv'd in my distracted mind
Each mean to save his life: and many a thought,
Which fondness prompted, prudence has oppos'd
As perilous and rash. With these poor hands
I've fram'd a little ark of slender reeds!
With pitch and slime I have secured the sides.
In this frail cradle I intend to lay
My little helpless infant, and expose him
Upon the banks of Nile.
 Mir.   'Tis full of danger.
 Joch. 'Tis danger to expose, and death to keep him.
 Mir. Yet, O reflect! should the fierce crocodile,
The native and the tyrant of the Nile,
Seize the defenceless infant!
 Joch.   O, forbear!
Spare my fond heart. Yet not the crocodile,
Nor all the deadly monsters of the deep,
To me are half so terrible as Pharaoh,
That heathen king, that royal murderer!
 Mir. Should he escape, which yet I dare not hope,
Each sea-born monster; yet the winds and waves
He cannot 'scape.
 Joch.   Know, God is every where;
Not to one narrow, partial spot confin'd;
No, not to chosen Israel. He extends
Through all the vast infinitude of space.
At his command the furious tempests rise,
The blasting of the breath of his displeasure:
He tells the world of waters when to roar;

And at his bidding, winds and seas are calm.
In Him, not in an arm of flesh I trust;
In him, whose promise never yet has fail'd,
I place my confidence.

Mir.   What must I do?
Command thy daughter, for thy words have wak'd
An holy boldness in my youthful breast.

Joch. Go then, my Miriam; go, and take the infant,
Buried in harmless slumbers, there he lies;
Let me not see him. Spare my heart that pang.
Yet sure, one little look may be indulg'd;
One kiss; perhaps the last. No more, my soul!
That fondness would be fatal. I should keep him.
I could not doom to death the babe I clasp'd:
Did ever mother kill her sleeping boy?
I dare not hazard it. The task be thine.
O! do not wake my child; remove him softly;
And gently lay him on the river's brink.

Mir. Did those magicians, whom the sons of Egypt
Consult and think all-potent, join their skill,
And was it great as Egypt's sons believe;
Yet all their secret wizard arts combined,
To save this little ark of bulrushes,
Thus fearfully exposed, could not effect it.
Their spells, their incantations, and dire charms
Could not preserve it.

Joch.   Know, this ark is charm'd
With spells, which impious Egypt never knew.
With invocations to the living God,
I twisted every slender reed together,
And with a prayer did ev'ry osier weave.

Mir. I go.

Joch. Yet ere thou go'st, observe me well.
When thou hast laid him in his wat'ry bed,
O leave him not; but at a distance wait,
And mark what Heav'n's high will determines for
        him.
Lay him among the flags on yonder beach,
Just where the royal gardens meet the Nile.
I dare not follow him. Suspicion's eye

Would note my wild demeanor; Miriam, yes,
The mother's fondness would betray the child.
Farewell! God of my fathers, Oh, protect him!

SPEECH OF CAIUS CASSIUS TO HIS COLLECTED FORCES, AFTER THE DEATH OF CESAR.

Soldiers and fellow citizens,

THE unjust reproaches of our enemies we could easily disprove, if we were not, by our numbers, and by the swords which we hold in our hands, in condition to despise them. While Cesar led the armies of the republic against the enemies of Rome, we took part in the same service with him; we obeyed him; we were happy to serve under his command. But when he declared war against the commonwealth, we became his enemies; and when he became an usurper and a tyrant, we resented, as an injury, even the favours which he presumed to bestow upon ourselves.

Had he been to fall a sacrifice to private resentment, we should not have been the proper actors in the execution of the sentence against him. He was willing to have indulged us with preferments and honors; but, we were not willing to accept, as the gift of a master, what we were intitled to claim as free citizens. We conceived, that, in presuming to confer the honors of the Roman republic, he encroached on the prerogatives of the Roman people, and insulted the authority of the Roman senate. Cesar cancelled the laws, and overturned the constitution of his country; he usurped all the powers of the commonwealth, set up a monarchy, and himself affected to be a king. This our ancestors, at the expulsion of Tarquin, bound themselves and their posterity, by the most solemn oaths, and by the most direful imprecations, never to endure. The same obligation has been entailed upon as a debt by our fathers; and we have faithfully paid and discharged it, have performed the oath, and averted the consequences of failure from ourselves, and from our posterity.

In the station of soldiers, we might have committed ourselves, without reflection, to the command of an officer, whose abilities and whose valor we admired; but, in the character of Roman citizens, we have a far different part to sustain. I must suppose, that I now speak to the Roman people, and to citizens of a free republic; to men who have never learned to depend upon others for gratifications and favours; who are not accustomed to own a superior, but who are themselves the masters, the dispensers of fortune and of honor, and the givers of all those dignities and powers by which Cesar himself was exalted, and of which he assumed the entire disposal.

Recollect from whom the Scipios, the Pompeys, and even Cesar himself derived his honors; from your ancestors, whom you now represent, and from yourselves, to whom, according to the laws of the republic, we, who are now your leaders in the field, address ourselves as your fellow-citizens in the commonwealth, and as persons depending on your pleasure for the just reward and retribution of our services. Happy in being able to restore to you what Cesar had the presumption to appropriate to himself, the power and the dignity of your fathers, with the supreme disposal of all the offices of trust that were established for your safety, and for the preservation of your freedom; happy in being able to restore to the tribunes of the Roman people the power of protecting you, and of procuring to every Roman citizen that justice, which, under the late usurpation of Cesar, was withheld, even from the sacred persons of those magistrates themselves.

An usurper is the common enemy of all good citizens; but the task of removing him could be the business only of a few. The senate and the Roman people, as soon as it was proper for them to declare their judgment, pronounced their approbation of those who were concerned in the death of Cesar, by the rewards and the honors which they bestowed upon them; and they are now become a prey to assassins and murderers; they bleed in the streets, in the temples, in the most secret retreat, and in the arms of their families; or they are dispersed, and fly wherever they hope to escape the fury of their enemies.

Many are now present before you, happy in your protection, happy in witnessing the zeal which you entertained for the commonwealth, for the rights of your fellow citizens, and for your own. These respectable citizens, we trust, will soon, by your means, be restored to a condition in which they can enjoy, together with you, all the honors of a free people; concur with you, in bestowing, and partake with you in receiving, the rewards which are due to such eminent services as you are now engaged to perform.

PART OF MR. ERSKINE's SPEECH AGAINST MR. PITT, 1784.

Mr. Speaker,

IT becomes us to learn, not from the ministry, but from the throne itself, whether this country is to be governed by men, in whom the House of Commons can confide, or whether we, the people of England's Representatives, are to be the sport and football of any junto that may hope to rule over us, by an unseen and unexplorable principle of government, utterly unknown to the Constitution. This is the great question, to which every public-spirited citizen of this country should direct his view. A question which goes very wide of the policy to be adopted concerning India, about which very wise and very honest men, not only might, but have, and did materially differ.

The total removal of all the executive servants of the crown, while they are in the full enjoyment of the confidence of that House, and, indeed, without any other visible or avowed cause of removal, than because they do enjoy that confidence; and the appointment of others in their room, without any other apparent ground of selection than because they enjoy it not, is, in my mind, a most alarming and portentous attack on the public freedom; because, though no outward form of the government is relaxed or violated by it, so as instantly to supply the constitutional remedy of opposition, the whole spirit and energy of the government is annihilated by it.

If the Right Honorable Gentleman retain his own opinions, and if the House likewise retain its own, is it not evident that he came into office without the most distant prospect of serving the public? Is it not evident that he has brought on a struggle between executive and legislative authority, at a time when they are pointing with equal vigor, unity, and effect, to the common interests of the nation?

The Right Honorable Gentleman may imagine that I take pleasure in making these observations. If so, I can assure him, upon my honor, that it is far from being the case. So very far the contrary, that the inconveniences which the country suffers at this moment, from the want of a settled government, are greatly heightened to my feelings, from the reflection that they are increased by his unguided ambition.

Our fathers were friends; and I was taught, from my infancy, to reverence the name of Pitt; an original partiality, which, instead of being diminished, was strongly confirmed by an acquaintance with the Right Honorable Gentleman himself, which I was cultivating with pleasure, when he was taken from his profession, into a different scene. Let him not think that I am the less his friend, or the mean envier of his talents, because they have been too much the topic of panegyric here already; and both I and the public are now reaping the bitter fruits of these intemperate praises.

N

"It is good," said Jeremiah, "for a man to bear the yoke in his youth;" and if the Right Honorable Gentleman had attended to this maxim, he would not, at so early a period, have declared against a subordinate situation; but would have lent the aid of his faculties to carry on the affairs of his country, which wanted nothing but stability to render them glorious, instead of setting up at once for himself to be the first.

How very different has been the progress of my honorable friend, who sits near me; who was not hatched at once into a minister, by the heat of his own ambition; but who, as it was good for him to do, in the words of the prophet, " bore the yoke in his youth;" passed through the subordinate offices, and matured his talents, in long and laborious oppositions; arriving, by the natural progress of his powerful mind, to a superiority of political wisdom and comprehension, which this House had long, with delight and satisfaction, acknowledged.

To pluck such a man from the councils of his country in the hour of her distresses, while he enjoyed the full confidence of the House, to give effect to vigorous plans for her interest; and to throw every thing into confusion, by the introduction of other men, introduced, as it should seem, for no other purpose than to beget that confusion, is an evil, which, if we cannot rectify, we may at least have leave to lament.

These evils are, however, imputed, by the Right Honorable Gentleman and his colleagues, to another source; to the bill for the regulation of the East Indies; from the mischiefs of which they had stepped forth to save the country; a language most indecent in this House of Commons, which thought it their duty to the public to pass it by a majority of above one hundred; but which was, however, to be taken to be destructive and dangerous, notwithstanding that authority: because it had been disapproved by a majority of eighteen votes in the House of Lords. Some of whose opinions I reverence as conscientious and independent; but the majority of that small majority voted upon principles which the forms of the House will not permit me to allude to, farther than to say, that individual *Noblemen* are not always *Gentlemen*.

———

EXTRACT FROM PRESIDENT WASHINGTON's ADDRESS TO THE PEOPLE OF THE UNITED STATES, SEPT. 17, 1796.

Friends and Fellow Citizens,

THE period for a new election of a citizen to administer the executive government of the United States, being not far distant; and the time actually arrived, when your thoughts must be employed in designating the person, who is to be clothed with that important trust, it appears to me proper, especially as it may conduce to a more distinct expression of the public voice, that I should now apprise you of the resolution I have formed, to decline being considered among the number of those, out of whom a choice is to be made.

I beg you, at the same time, to do me the justice to be assured, that this resolution has not been taken, without a strict regard to all the considerations appertaining to the relation, which binds a dutiful citizen to his country; and that, in withdrawing the tender of service which silence in my situation might imply, I am influenced by no diminution of zeal for your future interest; no deficiency of grateful respect for your past kindness; but am supported by a full conviction that the step is compatible with both.

The acceptance of, and continuance hitherto in the office to which your suffrages have twice called me, have been a uniform sacrifice of inclination to the opinion of duty, and to a deference for what appeared to be your desire. I constantly hoped, that it would have been much earlier in my power, consistently with motives, which I was not at liberty to disregard, to return to that retirement from which I had been reluctantly drawn. The strength of my inclination to do this, previous to the last election, had even led to the preparation of an address to declare it to you; but mature reflection on the then perplexed and critical posture of our affairs with foreign nations, and the unanimous advice of persons intitled to my confidence, impelled me to abandon the idea.

I rejoice, that the state of your concerns, external as well as internal, no longer renders the pursuit of inclination incompatible with the sentiment of duty, or propriety; and am persuaded, whatever partiality may be retained for my services, that in the present circumstances of our country, you will not disapprove my determination to retire.

The impressions, with which I first undertook the arduous trust, were explained on the proper occasion. In the discharge of this trust, I will only say, that I have with good intentions contributed towards the organization and administration of the government, the best exertions of which a very fallible judgment was capable. Not unconscious, in the outset, of the inferiority of my qualifications, experience in my own eyes, perhaps still more in the eyes of others, has strengthened the motives to diffidence of myself: and every day the increasing weight of years admonishes me more and more, that the shade of retirement is as necessary to me as it will be welcome. Satisfied that if any circumstances have given peculiar value to my services, they were temporary, I have the consolation to believe, that while choice and prudence invite me to quit the political scene, patriotism does not forbid it.

In looking forward to the moment which is intended to terminate the career of my public life, my feelings do not permit me to suspend the deep acknowledgment of that debt of gratitude which I owe to my beloved country, for the many honors it has conferred upon me; still more for the stedfast confidence with which it has supported me; and for the opportunities I have thence enjoyed of manifesting my inviolable attachment, by services faithful and persevering, though in usefulness unequal to my zeal. If benefits have resulted to our country from these services, let it always be remembered to your praise, as an instructive example in our annals, that under circumstances in which the passions, agitated in every direction, were liable to mislead; amidst appearances sometimes dubious; vicissitudes of fortune often discouraging; in situations in which, not unfrequently, want of success has countenanced the spirit of criticism; the constancy of your support was the essential prop of the efforts, and a guarantee of the plans by which they were effected.

Profoundly penetrated with this idea, I shall carry it with me to my grave, as a strong incitement to unceasing vows that Heaven may continue to you the choicest tokens of its beneficence; that your union and brotherly affection may be perpetual; that the free constitution, which is the work of your hands, may be sacredly maintained; that its administration in every department may be stamped with wisdom and virtue; that, in fine, the happiness of the people of these States, under the auspices of liberty, may be made complete, by so careful a preservation and so prudent a use of this blessing, as will acquire to them the glory of recommending it to the applause, the affection, and adoption of every nation, which is yet a stranger to it.

Though in reviewing the incidents of my administration, I am unconscious of intentional error; I am nevertheless too sensible of my defects not to think it probable that I may have committed many errors. Whatever they may be, I fervently beseech the Almighty to avert or mitigate the evils to which they tend. I shall also carry with me the hope that my country will never cease to view them with indulgence; and after forty-five years of my life dedicated to its service, with an upright zeal, the faults of incompetent abilities will be consigned to oblivion, as myself must soon be to the mansions of rest.

Relying on its kindness in this as in other things; and actuated by that fervent love towards it, which is so natural to a man who views in it the native soil of himself and his progenitors for several generations, I anticipate with pleasing expectation that retreat, in which I promise myself to realize, without alloy, the sweet enjoyment of partaking, in the midst of my fellow citizens, the benign influence of good laws under a free government; the ever favorite object of my heart, and the happy reward, as I trust, of our mutual cares labors, and dangers.

DIALOGUE ON THE CHOICE OF BUSINESS FOR LIFE.

Enter EDWARD, CHARLEY, *and* THOMAS.

Edward. IT appears to me high time for us to choose our business for life. Our academical studies will soon be completed; and I wish to look a little forward. What say you? am I right?

Charley. It may be well for *you:* poor men's sons must look out for themselves. My father is able to support me at my ease; and my mamma says she would rather see me laid in a coffin than shut up in a study, spoiling my eyes and racking my brains, plodding over your nonsensical minister, doctor, and lawyer books; and I am sure she would never have me confined behind a counter, or a merchant's desk. She intends I shall be brought up a gentleman. My mother is of noble blood, and she don't intend that I shall disgrace it.

Edw. Pray, master Charley, who was the father of your noble-blooded mother?

Char. A gentleman, I'd have you to know.

Edw. Yes, a gentleman cobler, to my knowledge.

Char. Ay, he followed that business, to be sure, sometimes, to stop the clamor of the vulgar. Then poor people could not bear to see a rich man living at his ease, or give a nobleman his title. But times are altering for the better, my mamma says: the rich begin to govern now. We shall soon live in style, and wear titles here as well as in England. She intends to send over and get my coat of arms, and she hopes to add a title to them.

Edw. High style! titles! and coats of arms! fine things in America, to be sure! Well, after all, I can't really disapprove of your mamma's plan. A lapstone, an awl, and shoe-hammer will make a fine picture, and may appear as well in your mother's parlour, as in her father's shop: and the title of cobler, or shoe-maker, would well become her darling Charley.

Char. I will not be insulted on account of my grand-father's employment, I'll have you to know! I have heard my mother say, her father was grandson of an aunt of 'squire Thorn, who once had a horse that run a race with the famous horse of a cousin of the Duke of Bedford, of ——.

Edw. Quite enough! I am fully convinced of the justice of your claim to the title of Duke, or whatever you please. About as much merit in it, I perceive, as in your father's title to his estate. Ten thousand dollars drawn in a lottery! already two thirds spent. A title to nobility derived from the grandson of an aunt of 'squire Thorn, from 'squire Thorn's horse, or perhaps from some monkey, that has been a favorite playmate with the prince of Wales. These are to be the support of your ease and honor through life. Well, I believe there is no need of your troubling yourself about your future employment: that is already determined. Depend upon it, you will repent of your folly, or scratch a poor man's head as long as you live. I advise you to set about the former, in order to avoid the latter.

Char. I did not come to you for advice. I'll not bear your insults, or disgrace myself with your company any longer. My parents shall teach you better manners.

[*Exit Charley.*

Thomas. I pity the vanity and weakness of this poor lad. But reflection and experience will teach him the fallacy of his hopes.

Edw. Poor child! he does not know that his lottery money is almost gone; that his father's house is mortgaged for more than it is worth; and that the only care of his parents is to keep up the appearance of present grandeur, at the expense of future shame. Happy for us, that we are not deluded with such deceitful hopes.

Tho. My parents were poor; not proud. They experienced the want of learning; but were resolved their children should share the benefit of a good education. I am the fourth son, who owe the debt of filial gratitude. All but myself are well settled in business, and doing honor to themselves and their parents. If I fall short of their example, I shall be most ungrateful.

Edw. I have neither father nor mother to excite my gratitude, or stimulate my exertions. But I wish to behave in such a manner, that if my parents could look down and observe my actions, they might approve my conduct. Of my family neither root nor branch remains: all have paid the debt of nature. They left a name for honesty; and I esteem that higher than a pretended title to greatness. They have left me a small farm, which, though not enough for my support, will, with my own industry, be sufficient. For employment, to pass away the winter season, I have determined upon keeping a school for my neighbours' children.

Tho. I heartily approve of your determination. Our mother Earth rewards, with peace and plenty, those who cultivate her face; but loads with anxious cares, those who dig her bowels for treasure. The life you contemplate is favorable to the enjoyment of social happiness, improvement of the mind, and security of virtue; and the task of training the tender mind is an employment, that ought to meet the encouragement, the gratitude of every parent, and the respect of every child.

Edw. I am pleased that you approve my choice. Will you frankly tell me your own?

Tho. I will: my intention is to follow the inclination of my kind parents. It is their desire that I should be a preacher. Their other sons have taken to other callings; and they wish to see one of their children in the desk. If their prayers are answered, I shall be fitted for the important task. To my youth, it appears formidable; but others, with less advantages, have succeeded, and been blessings to society, and an honor to their profession.

Edw. You have chosen the better part. Whatever the licentious may say to the contrary, the happiness of society must rest on the principles of virtue and religion; and the pulpit must be the nursery, where they are cultivated.

Tho. " ———— The pulpit;
And I name it, fill'd with solemn awe,
Must stand acknowledg'd, while the world shall stand,
The most important and effectual guard,
Support and ornament of virtue's cause.
There stands the messenger of truth. There stands,
The legate of the skies: his theme divine,
His office sacred, his credentials clear.
By him the violated law speaks out
Its thunders, and by him, in strains as sweet
As angels use, the gospel whispers peace."

My heart glows with the subject; and if my abilities could equal my zeal, I could at least hope to realize the sublime character so beautifully drawn by Cowper.

Edw. It is a laudable ambition to aim at eminence in religion, and excellence in virtue.

SPEECH OF BONAPARTE, COMMANDER IN CHIEF OF
THE FRENCH ARMY IN ITALY, BEFORE HIS AT-
TACK ON MILAN, APRIL 26, 1796.

Soldiers,

YOU have in a fortnight gained six victories; taken
twenty-one stands of colors; seventy-one pieces
of cannon; several strong places; conquered the richest
part of Piedmont; you have made fifteen thousand
prisoners, and killed or wounded more than ten thousand men. You have hitherto fought only for sterile
rocks, rendered illustrious by your courage, but useless to the country; you have equalled by your services
the victorious army of Holland and the Rhine. Deprived of every thing, you have supplied every thing.
You have won battles without cannon; made forced
marches without shoes; watched without brandy, and
often without bread. The republican phalanxes, the
soldiers of liberty, were alone capable of suffering what
you have suffered.

Thanks be to you, soldiers. The grateful country
will, in part, be indebted to you for her prosperity;
and if, when victorious at Toulon, you predicted the
immortal campaign of 1794, your present victories will
be the presages of more brilliant victories. The two
armies which attacked you with audacity, fly disheart-
ened before you. Men, who smiled at your misery,
and rejoiced in thought at the idea of the triumphs
of your enemies, are confounded and appalled. But it
must not, soldiers, be concealed from you, that you
have done *nothing*, since *something* remains yet to be
done. Neither Turin nor Milan are in your power.
The ashes of the conquerors of the Tarquins are still
disgraced by the assassins of Basseville. At the commencement of the campaign you were destitute of
every thing; now you are amply provided; the maga-

zines taken from your enemies are numerous; the artillery for the field and for besieging is arrived.

Soldiers, the country has a right to expect great things from you; justify her expectations. The greatest obstacles are undoubtedly overcome; but you have still battles to fight, cities to take, rivers to pass. Is there one among you whose courage is diminished? Is there one who would prefer returning to the summits of the Alps and the Apennines? No: all burn with the desire of extending the glory of the French; to humble the proud kings who dare to meditate putting us again in chains; to dictate a peace that shall be glorious, and that shall indemnify the country for the immense sacrifices which she has made. All of you burn with a desire to say on your return to your home, I belonged to the victorious army of Italy.

Friends, I promise this conquest to you; but there is one condition which you must swear to fulfil; it is to respect the people whom you deliver; to repress the horrible pillage which some wretches, instigated by our enemies, have practised. Unless you do this, you will no longer be the friends, but the scourges of the human race; you will no longer form the honor of the French people. They will disavow you. Your victories, your successes, the blood of your brethren who died in battle; all, even honor and glory, will be lost. With respect to myself, to the generals, who possess your confidence, we shall blush to command an army without discipline, and who admit no other law than that of force.

People of Italy, the French army comes to break your chains; the French people are the Friends of all people; come with confidence to them; your property, religion, and customs, shall be respected. We make war as generous enemies; and wish only to make war against the tyrants who oppress you.

MR. PITT'S SPEECH, NOV. 18, 1777, IN OPPOSI-
TION TO LORD SUFFOLK, WHO PROPOSED TO PAR-
LIAMENT TO EMPLOY THE INDIANS AGAINST THE
AMERICANS; AND WHO SAID, IN THE COURSE OF
THE DEBATE, THAT "THEY HAD A RIGHT TO
USE ALL THE MEANS, THAT GOD AND NATURE
HAD PUT INTO THEIR HANDS, TO CONQUER AME-
RICA."

My Lords,

I AM astonished to hear such principles confessed!
I am shocked to hear them avowed in this House,
or in this country! Principles, equally unconstitutional,
inhuman, and unchristian!

My lords, I did not intend to have encroached
again on your attention; but I cannot repress my indignation, I feel myself impelled by every duty. My
lords we are called upon as members of this House,
as men, as christian men, to protest against such notions standing near the throne, polluting the ear of
Majesty. " That God and nature put into our hands!"
I know not what ideas that lord may entertain of God
and nature; but I know that such abominable principles are equally abhorrent to religion and humanity.

What! to attribute the sacred sanction of God and
nature to the massacres of the Indian scalping knife!
to the cannibal savage, torturing, murdering, roasting,
and eating; literally, my lords, *eating* the mangled
victims of his barbarous battles! Such horrible notions
shock every precept of religion, divine or natural, and
every generous feeling of humanity. And, my lords,
they shock every sentiment of honor; they shock me
as a lover of honorable war, and a detester of mur-
derous barbarity.

These abominable principles, and this more abominable avowal of them, demand the most decisive indignation. I call upon that Right Reverend bench, those

holy ministers of the gospel, and pious pastors of our Church: I conjure them to join in the holy work, and vindicate the religion of their God. I appeal to the wisdom and the law of this *learned bench*, to defend and support the justice of their country. I call upon the bishops to interpose the unsullied sanctity of their *lawn;* upon the learned judges, to interpose the purity of their *ermine*, to save us from this pollution. I call upon the honor of your lordships, to reverence the dignity of your ancestors, and to maintain your own. I call upon the spirit and humanity of my country, to vindicate the national character. I invoke the genius of the constitution.

From the tapestry that adorns these walls, the immortal ancestor of this noble lord frowns with indignation at the disgrace of his country. In vain he led your victorious fleets against the boasted armada of Spain; in vain he defended and established the honor, the liberties, the religion, the protestant religion of this country, against the arbitrary cruelties of popery and the inquisition, if these more than popish cruelties and inquisitorial practices are let loose among us; to turn forth into our settlements, among our ancient connexions, friends, and relations, the merciless cannibal, thirsting for the blood of man, woman and child! to send forth the infidel savage—against whom? against your protestant brethren; to lay waste their country; to desolate their dwellings, and extirpate their race and name, with these horrible hell-hounds of savage war!

Spain armed herself with blood-hounds, to extirpate the wretched natives of America; and we improve on the inhuman example even of Spanish cruelty. We turn loose these savage hell-hounds against our brethren and countrymen in America, of the same language, laws, liberties, and religion; endeared to us by every tie that should sanctify humanity.

My lords, this awful subject, so important to our honor, our constitution, and our religion, demands the most solemn and effectual inquiry. And I again call

O

upon your lordships, and the united powers of the state, to examine it thoroughly, and decisively, and to stamp upon it an indelible stigma of the public abhorrence. And I again implore those holy prelates of our religion, to do away these iniquities from among us. Let them perform a lustration; let them purify this House, and this country from this sin.

My lords, I am old and weak, and at present unable to say more; but my feelings and indignation were too strong to have said less. I could not have slept this night in my bed, nor reposed my head on my pillow, without giving this vent to my eternal abhorrence of such preposterous and enormous principles.

DIALOGUE BETWEEN A SCHOOLMASTER, AND SCHOOL-COMMITTEE.

[N B. The Author is happy in believing, that the following Dialogue is applicable to but *few* towns, and *few* teachers in this country; but, so long as there are any remaining to whom it may apply, he thinks a sufficient apology exists for its publication]

SCENE, *a Public House in the Town of*——

Enter SCHOOLMASTER, *with a pack on his back.*

Schoolmaster. HOW fare you, landlord? what have you got that's good to drink?

Landlord. I have gin, West-India, genuine New-England, whiskey, and cider brandy.

Schoolm. Make us a stiff mug of sling. Put in a gill and a half of your New-England; and sweeten it well with lasses.

Land. It shall be done, Sir, to your liking.

Schoolm. Do you know of any vacancy in a school in your part of the country, landlord?

Land. There is a vacancy in our district; and I expect the parson, with our three school-committee men, will be at my house directly, to consult upon matters relative to the school.

Schoolm. Well, here's the lad that will serve them as *cheap* as any man in America; and I believe I may venture to say as *well* too; for I profess no small share of skill in that business. I have kept school eleven winters, and have often had matter of fifty scholars at a time. I have teach'd a child its letters in a day, and to read in the Psalter in a fortnight: and I always feel very much ashamed, if I use more than one quire of paper in larnin a boy to write as well as his master. As for government, I'll turn my back to no man. I never flog my scholars; for that monstrous doctrine of whippin children, which has been so long preached and practised by our rigid and superstitious forefathers, I have long since exploded. I have a rare knack of *flattering* them into their duty. And this, according to a celebrated Doctor at Philadelphia, whose works I have heard of, though I never read them, is the grand criterion of school government. It is, landlord, it is the very philosopher's stone. I am told, likewise, that this same great Doctor does not believe that Solomon and others really meant *lickan*, in the proper sense of the word, when they talked so much about using the rod, &c. He supposes they meant confining them in dungeons; starving them for three or four days at a time; and then giving them a portion of tatromattucks, and such kinds of mild punishment. And, zounds, landlord, I believe he's about half right.

Land. [*Giving the cup to the master.*] Master—— What may I call your name, Sir, if I may be so bold?

Schoolm. Ignoramus, at your service, Sir.

Land. Master Ignoramus, I am glad to see you. You are the very man we wish for. Our committee won't hesitate a moment to employ you, when they become acquainted with your talents. Your sentiments on government I know will suit our people to a nicety. Our last master was a tyrant of a fellow, and very extravagant in his price. He grew so important the latter part of his time, that he had the frontery to demand *ten dollars* a month and his board. And he might truly be said to rule with a rod of iron; for he kept an *ironwood* cudgel in his school, four feet long; and it was enough to chill one's blood to hear the shrieks of the little innocents, which were caused by his barbarity. I have heard my wife say, that Sue Gossip told her, that she had seen the marks of his lashes on the back of her neighbour Rymple's son Darling for twelve hours after the drubbing. At least, the boy told her with his own mouth, that they *might* be seen, if they would only take the trouble to strip his shirt off. And, besides, Master Ignoramus, he was the most niggardly of all the human race. I don't suppose that my bar room was one dollar the richer for him, in the course of the whole time which he tarried with us. While the young people of the town were recreating themselves, and taking a sociable glass, of an evening, at my house, the stupid blockhead was etarnally in his chamber, poring over his musty books. But finally he did the job for himself, and I am rejoiced. The wretch had the dacity to box little Sammy Puney's ears at such an intolerable rate, that his parents fear the poor child will be an idiot all the days of his life. And all this, for nothing more, than, partly by design, and partly through mere accident, he happened to spit in his master's face. The child being nephew to the 'squire, you may well suppose, that the whole neighbourhood was soon in an uproar. The indignation of the mother, father, aunts, uncles, cousins, and indeed the whole circle of acquaintance, was roused; and the poor fellow was hooted out of town in less than twenty-four hours.

Schoolm. [*Drinking off his liquor.*] This is a rare dose. Believe me, landlord, I have not tasted a drop before, since six o'clock this morning. [*Enter Parson and Committee Men.*] Your humble sarvant, gentlemen. I understand you are in want of a schoolmaster.

Parson. Yes, Sir; that is the occasion of our present meeting. We have been so unfortunate as to lose one good man; and we should be very glad to find another.

1st Committee Man. Pray don't say *unfortunate*, Parson. I think we may consider ourselves as very *fortunate*, in having rid the town of an extravagant coxcomb, who was draining us of all the money we could earn, to fill his purse, and rig himself out with fine clothes.

2d Com. Ten dollars a month, and board, for a man whose task is so easy, is no small sum.

3d Com. I am bold to affirm, that we can procure a better man for half the money.

Schoolm. That I believe, friend; for, though I esteem myself as good as the best; that is to say, in the common way; yet I never ax'd but five dollars a month in all my life.

Par. For my own part, whatever these gentlemen's opinion may be, I must tell you, that I am much less concerned about the wages we are to give, than I am about the character and abilities of the man with whom we intrust the education of our children. I had much rather you had said you had received forty dollars a month, than five.

1st Com. Dear Sir, you are beside yourself. You will encourage the man to *rise* in his price; whereas I was in hopes he would have *fallen*, at least one dollar.

Par. Before we talk any further about the price, it is necessary that we examine the gentleman according to law, in order to satisfy ourselves of his capability to serve us. Friend, will you be so obliging as to inform us where you received your education, and what your pretensions are, with respect to your profession?

Schoolm. Law, Sir! I never went to college in my life.

Par. I did not ask you whether you had been to college or not. We wish to know what education you have had; and whether your abilities are such, as that you can do yourself honor in taking the charge of a common English School.

Schoolm. Gentlemen, I will give you a short history of my life. From seven to fifteen years of age, I went to school perhaps as much as one year. In which time, I went through Dilworth's Spelling-Book, the Psalter, the New-Testament; and could read the newspaper without spelling more than half the words. By this time feeling a little above the common level, I enlisted a soldier in the army, where I continued six years; and made such a proficiency in the military art, that I was frequently talked of for a corporal. I had likewise larn'd to write considerably, and to cypher as fur as Division. The multiplication table I had at my tongue's end, and have not forgot it to this day. At length having received a severe flogging for nothing at all, I am not ashamed to own that I deserted, and went into one of the back settlements, and offered myself as a teacher. I was immediately employed in that service; and, though I am obliged to say it myself, I do assure you I soon became very famous. Since that time, which is eleven years, I have followed the business constantly; at least, every winter; for in the summer, it is not customary in the towns in general, to continue a man's school. One thing I would not forget to mention; and that is, I have travelled about the country so much, and been in the army so long (which is allowed to be the best school in the world) that I consider myself as being thoroughly acquainted with mankind. You will not be insensible, gentlemen, of what great importance this last acquisition is, to one who has the care of youth.

3d Com. I admire his conversation. I imagine, by this time, you have cyphered *clear through;* have you not, Sir?

Schoolm. Why, as to that I have gone so fur, that I thought I could *see through.* I can tell how many minutes old my great grandfather was when his first son was born; how many barley corns it would take to measure round the world; and how old the world will be at the end of six thousand years from the creation.

1st Com. It is very strange! You must have studied hard, to learn all these things, and that without a master too.

Schoolm. Indeed I have, Sir; and, if I had time, I could tell you things stranger still.

Par. Can you tell in what part of the world you were born; whether in the torrid, frigid, or temperate zone?

Schoolm. I was not born in the *zoon*, Sir; nor in any other of the West-India Islands; but I was born in New-England, in the state of New-Jersey, and Commonwealth of the United States of America.

Par. Do you know how many parts of speech there are in the English language?

Schoolm. How many speeches! Why as many as there are "stars in the sky, leaves on the trees, or sands on the sea shore."

1st Com. Please to let *me* ask him a question, Parson. How many commandments are there?

Schoolm. Ten, Sir; and I knew them all before I went into the army.

2d Com. Can you tell when the moon changes by the almanac?

Schoolm. No! but I'll warrant you, I could soon tell by cyphering.

3d Com. How many varses are there in the 119th Psalm?

Schoolm. Ah! excuse me there, if you please, Sir; I never meddle with psalmody or metaphysics.

Par. Will you tell me, my friend, what is the difference between the circumference and the diameter of the globe?

Schoolm. There you are too hard for me again. I never larn'd the rule of circumstance nor geometry. I'll tell you what, gentlemen, I make no pretensions to minister larnin, lawyer larnin, or docter larnin; but put me upon your clear schoolmaster larnin, and there I am even with you.

1st Com. I am satisfied with the gentleman. He has missed but one question, and that was such a metatisical one, that it would have puzzled a Jesuit himself to have answered it. Gentlemen, shall the master withdraw a few minutes, for our further consultation?

[*Exit Master.*

2d Com. I am much pleased with the stranger. He appears to be a man of wonderful parts; and I shall cheerfully agree to employ him.

3d Com. For my part, I don't think we shall find a *cheaper* master; and I move for engaging him at once.

Par. Gentlemen, how long will you be blind to your own interest? I can say with you, that I am perfectly satisfied—that the m n is, in his profession, emphatically what he calls himself by name, an *ignoramus;* and totally incapable of instructing our children. You know not who he is, or what he is; whether he be a thief, a liar, or a drunkard. The very terms, on which he offers himself, ought to operate as a sufficient objection against him. I am sensible that my vote will now be of no avail, since you are all agreed. I have been for years striving to procure a man of abilities and morals, suitable for the employment; and such a one I had obtained; but, alas! we were unworthy of him. We aspersed his character; invented a multitude of falsehoods; magnified every trifling error in his conduct; and even converted his virtues into vices. We refused to give him that pecuniary reward which his services demanded; and he, knowing his own worth, and our unworthiness, has left us forever.

1st Com. Come, come, Parson, it is easy for salary men to talk of *liberality*, and to vote away money which they never earned; but it won't do. The new master, I dare engage, will do as well, or better than the old one. Landlord, call him in for his answer.

Par. I protest against your proceeding; and withdraw myself forever from the committee. But I must tell you, your children will reap the bitter consequences of such injudicious measures. It has always been surprising to me that people in general are more willing to pay their money for any thing else, than for "the one thing needful," that is, for the education of their children. Their taylor must be a workman, their carpenter, a workman, their hairdresser, a workman; their hostler, a workman; but the instructer of their children must——work *cheap!*   [*Exit Parson.*

Re-enter SCHOOLMASTER.

1st Com. We have agreed to employ you, Sir; and have only to recommend to you, not to follow the steps of your predecessor. This is an "age of reason;" and we do not imagine our children so stupid, as to need the rod to quicken their ideas, or so vitious, as to require a moral lesson from the ferule. Be gentle and accommodating, and you have nothing to fear.

Land. I'll answer for him. He's as generous and merry a lad as I've had in my house this many a day.

EXTRACT FROM MR. PITT'S SPEECH, IN ANSWER TO LORD MANSFIELD, ON THE AFFAIR OF MR. WILKES, 1770.

My Lords,

THERE is one plain maxim to which I have invariably adhered through life; that in every question in which my liberty or my property was concerned, I should consult and be determined by the dictates of common sense. I confess, my lords, that I am apt to distrust the refinements of learning, because I have seen the ablest and most learned men equally liable to deceive themselves, and to mislead others.

The condition of human nature would be lamentable indeed, if nothing less than the greatest learning and talents which fall to the share of so small a number of men, were sufficient to direct our judgment and our conduct. But Providence has taken better care of our happiness, and given us, in the simplicity of common sense, a rule for our direction, by which we shall never be misled.

I confess, my lords, I had no other guide in drawing up the amendment, which I submitted to your consideration. And before I heard the opinion of the noble lord who spoke last, I did not conceive, that it was even within the limits of possibility for the greatest human genius, the most subtle understanding, or the acutest wit, so strangely to misrepresent my meaning; and to give it an interpretation so entirely foreign from what I intended to express, and from that sense, which the very terms of the amendment plainly and distinctly carry with them.

If there be the smallest foundation for the censure thrown upon me by that noble lord; if, either expressly or by the most distant implication, I have said or insinuated any part of what the noble lord has charged me with, discard my opinions forever; discard the motion with contempt.

My lords, I must beg the indulgence of the House. Neither will my health permit me, nor do I intend to be qualified, to follow that learned lord minutely through the whole of his argument. No man is better acquainted with his abilities and learning, nor has a greater respect for them, than I have. I have had the pleasure of sitting with him in the other House, and always listened to him with attention. I have not now lost a word of what he said, nor did I ever. Upon the present question, I meet him without fear.

- The evidence, which truth carries with it, is superior to all arguments; it neither wants the support, nor dreads the opposition of the greatest abilities. If there be a single word in the amendment to justify the interpretation, which the noble lord has been pleased to give it, I am ready to renounce the whole. Let it be read, my lords; let it speak for itself. In what instance does it interfere with the privileges of the

House of Commons? In what respect does it question their jurisdiction, or suppose an authority in this House to arraign the justice of their sentence?

I am sure that every lord who hears me, will bear me witness that I said not one word touching the merits of the Middlesex election. Far from conveying any opinion upon that matter in the amendment, I did not even in discourse, deliver my own sentiments upon it. I did not say that the House of Commons had done either right or wrong; but when his Majesty was pleased to recommend it to us to cultivate unanimity amongst ourselves, I thought it the duty of this House, as the great hereditary council of the crown, to state to his majesty the distracted condition of his dominions, together with the events which had destroyed unanimity among his subjects.

But, my lords, I stated those events merely as facts, without the smallest addition either of censure or of opinion. They are facts, my lords, which I am not only convinced are true, but which I know are indisputably true.

Do they not tell us, in so many words, that Mr. Wilkes, having been expelled, was thereby rendered incapable of serving in that Parliament? and is it not their resolution alone, which refuses to the subject his common right? The amendment says farther, that the electors of Middlesex are deprived of their free choice of a representative. Is this a fact, my lords? or have I given an unfair representation of it? Will any man presume to affirm that Colonel Luttrell is the free choice of the electors of Middlesex? We all know the contrary.

We all know that Mr. Wilkes (whom I mention without either praise or censure) was the favourite of the county, and chosen, by a very great and acknowledged majority, to represent them in Parliament. If the noble lord dislikes the manner in which these facts are stated, I shall think myself happy in being advised by him how to alter it. I am very little anxious about terms, provided the substance be preserved; and these are facts, my lords, which I am sure will always retain their weight and importance, in whatever form of language they are described.

The constitution of this country has been openly invaded in fact; and I have heard, with horror and astonishment, that very invasion defended upon principle. What is this mysterious power, undefined by law, unknown to the subject; which we must not approach without awe, nor speak of without reverence; which no man may question, and to which all men must submit? My lords, I thought the slavish doctrine of passive obedience had long since been exploded: and, when our kings were obliged to confess that their title to the crown, and the rule of their government, had no other foundation than the known laws of the land, I never expected to hear a divine right, or a divine infallibility, attributed to any other branch of the legislature.

My lords, I beg to be understood. No man respects the House of Commons more than I do, or would contend more strenuously than I would, to preserve to them their just and legal authority. Within the bounds prescribed by the constitution, that authority is necessary to the well-being of the people: beyond that line, every exertion of power is arbitrary, is illegal; it threatens tyranny to the people, and destruction to the State. Power without right is the most odious and detestable object that can be offered to the human imagination: it is not only pernicious to those who are subject to it, but tends to its own destruction.

ON THE GENERAL JUDGMENT-DAY; FROM DWIGHT'S
CONQUEST OF CANAAN.

MID these dire scenes, more awful scenes shall rise;
Sad nations quake, and trembling seize the skies.
From the dark tombs shall fearful lights ascend,
And sullen sounds the sleeping mansion rend;
Pale ghosts with terror break the dreamer's charm,
And death-like cries the listening world alarm.
Then midnight pangs shall toss the cleaving plains;
Fell famine wanton o'er unburied trains;
From crumbling mountains baleful flames aspire;
Realms sink in floods, and towns dissolve in fire;
In every blast the spotted plague be driven,
And angry meteors blaze athwart the Heaven.
Clouds of dark blood shall blot the sun's broad light,
Spread round th' immense, and shroud the world in
    night;
With pale and dreadful ray, the cold moon gleam;
The dim, lone stars diffuse an anguish'd beam;
Storms rock the skies; afflicted oceans roar,
And sanguine billows dye the shuddering shore;
And round earth thunder, from th' Almighty throne,
The voice irrevocable, IT IS DONE.
    Rous'd on the fearful morn, shall nature hear
The trump's deep terrors rend the troubled air;
From realm to realm the sound tremendous roll;
Cleave the broad main, and shake th' astonish'd pole;
The slumbering bones th' archangel's call inspire;
Rocks sink in dust, and earth be wrapt in fire;
From realms far distant, orbs unnumber'd come,
Sail through immensity, and learn their doom:
And all yon changeless stars, that, thron'd on high,
Reign in immortal lustre round the sky,
In solemn silence shroud their living light,
And leave the world to undistinguish'd night.
    Hark, what dread sounds descending from the pole,
Wave following wave, in swelling thunders roll!
P

How the tombs cleave! What awful forms arise!
What crowding nations pain the failing eyes!
From land to land behold the mountains rend;
From shore to shore the final flames ascend;
Round the dark poles with boundless terror reign,
With bend immeasurable sweep the main;
From morn's far kingdoms stretch to realms of even,
And climb and climb with solemn roar to heaven.
What smoky ruins wrap the lessening ground!
What fiery sheets sail through the vaulted round!
Pour'd in one mass, the lands and seas decay;
Involv'd, the heavens, dissolving, fleet away;
The moon departs; the sun's last beams expire,
And nature's buried in the boundless fire.
  Lo, from the radiance of the bless'd abode
Messiah comes, in all the pomp of God!
Borne on swift winds, a storm before him flies;
Stars crown his head, and rainbows round him rise;
Beneath his feet a sun's broad terrors burn,
And cleaving darkness opes a dreadful morn:
Through boundless space careering flames are driven;
Truth's sacred hosts descend, and all the thrones of
      heaven.
See crowding millions, call'd from earth's far ends,
See hell's dark world, with fearful gloom, ascends,
In throngs incomprehensible! Around,
Worlds after worlds, from nature's farthest bound,
Call'd by th' archangel's voice from either pole,
Self-moved, with all created nations, roll.
From this great train, his eyes the just divide,
Price of his life, and being's fairest pride;
Rob'd by his mighty hand, the starry throngs
From harps of transport call ecstatic songs.
Hail, heirs of endless peace! ordain'd to rove
Round the pure climes of everlasting love.
For you the sun first led the lucid morn;
The world was fashion'd and Messiah born;
For you high heaven with fond impatience waits,
Pours her fair streams, and opes her golden gates;

Each hour, with purer glory, gaily shines,
Her courts enlarges, and her air refines.

But O unhappy race! to woes consign'd,
Lur'd by fond pleasure, and to wisdom blind,
What new Messiah shall the spirit save,
Stay the pent flames, and shut the eternal grave?
Where sleeps the music of his voice divine?
Where hides the face, that could so sweetly shine?
Now hear that slighed voice to thunder turn!
See that mild face with flames of vengeance burn!
High o'er your heads the storm of ruin roars,
And,'round th' immense, no friend your fate deplores.

Lo, there to endless woe in throngs are driven,
What once were angels, and bright stars of heaven!
The world's gay pride! the king with splendor crown'd!
The chief resistless, and the sage renown'd!
Down, down the millions sink; where yon broad main
Heaves her dark waves, and spreads the seats of pain;
Where long, black clouds, emblazed with awful fire,
Pour sullen round their heads, and in dread gloom
    retire.

----●♦----

ON THE WORKS OF CREATION AND PROVIDENCE.

WHEN I contemplate those ample and magnificent structures, erected over all the etherial plains: when I look upon them as so many repositories of light, or fruitful abodes of life: when I remember that there may be other orbs, vastly more remote than those which appear to our unaided sight; orbs, whose effulgence, though travelling ever since the creation, is not yet arrived upon our coasts: when I stretch my thoughts to the innumerable orders of being, which inhabit all those spacious systems; from the loftiest seraph, to the lowest reptile; from the armies of angels which surround the Almighty's throne, to the *puny* nations, which tinge with purple the surface of the plum, or mantle the standing pool with green; how various appear the links of this immeasurable chain! how vast the gradations in this universal scale of existence! Yet all these, though ever so vast and various, are the work of the Creator's hand, and are full of his presence.

He rounded in his palm those stupendous globes, which are pendulous in the vault of heaven. He kindled those astonishing bright fires, which fill the firmament with a flood of glory. By Him they are suspended in fluid ether, and cannot be shaken; by Him they dispense a perpetual tide of beams, and are never exhausted. He formed with inexpressible nicety, that delicately fine collection of tubes; that unknown multiplicity of subtile springs, which organize and actuate the frame of the minutest insect.

He bids the crimson current roll; the vital movements play; and associates a world of wonders, even in an animated point. In all these is a signal exhibition of creating power; to all these are extended the special regards of preserving goodness. From hence let me learn to rely on the providence, and to revere the presence, of Supreme Majesty. Amidst that inconceivable number and variety of beings, which swarm through the regions of creation, not one is overlooked, not one is neglected, by the great Omnipotent Cause of all.

_____

Speech of Mr. Fox, in the British Parliament, on American Affairs, 1778.

YOU have now two wars before you, of which you must choose one, for both you cannot support. The war against America has hitherto been carried on against her alone, unassisted by any ally whatever. Notwithstanding she stood alone, you have been obliged uniformly to increase your exertions, and to push your efforts to the extent of your power, without being able to bring it to an issue. You have exerted all your force hitherto without effect, and you cannot now divide a force, found already inadequate to its object.

My opinion is for withdrawing your forces from America entirely; for a defensive war you can never think of there. A defensive war would ruin this nation at any time; and in any circumstances, offensive war is pointed out as proper for this country; our situation points it out; and the spirit of the nation impels us to attack rather than defend. Attack France, then, for she is your object. The nature of the wars is quite different: the war against America is against your own countrymen; you have stopped me from saying against your fellow subjects; that against France is against your inveterate enemy and rival. Every blow you strike in America is against yourselves; it is against all idea of reconciliation, and against your own interest, though you should be able, as you never will be, to force them to submit. Every stroke against France is of advantage to you: America must be conquered in France; France never can be conquered in America.

The war of the Americans is a war of passion; it is of such a nature as to be supported by the most powerful virtues, love of liberty and of their country; and, at the same time, by those passions in the human heart which give courage, strength, and perseverance to man; the spirit of revenge for the injuries you have done them; of retaliation for the hardships you have inflicted on them; and of opposition to the unjust powers you have exercised over them. Every thing combines to animate them to this war, and such a war is without end; for whatever obstinacy enthusiasm ever inspired man with, you will now find in America. No matter what gives birth to that enthusiasm; whether the name of religion or of liberty, the effects are the same; it inspires a spirit which is unconquerable, and solicitous to undergo difficulty, danger, and hardship: and as long as there is a man in America, a being formed such as we are, you will have him present himself against you in the field.

The war of France is a war of another sort; the war of France is a war of interest: it was her interest which first induced her to engage in it, and it is by that inter-

est that she will measure its continuance. Turn your
face at once against her; attack her wherever she is
exposed; crush her commerce wherever you can; make
her feel heavy and immediate distress throughout the
nation: the people will soon cry out to their government. Whilst the advantages she promises herself are
remote and uncertain, inflict present evils and distresses upon her subjects: the people will become discontented and clamorous; she will find it a bad bargain,
having entered into this business; and you will force
her to desert any ally that brings so much trouble and
distress upon her.

What is become of the ancient spirit of this nation?
Where is the national spirit that ever did honor to
this country? Have the present ministry spent that too,
with almost the last shilling of your money? Are they
not ashamed of the temporizing conduct they have
used towards France? Her correspondence with America has been clandestine. Compare that with their
conduct towards Holland, some time ago; but it is
the characteristic of little minds to be exact in little
things, whilst they shrink from their rights in great
ones.

The conduct of France is called clandestine: look
back but a year ago to a letter from one of your Se-
cretaries of State to Holland; "it is with surprise and
indignation" your conduct is seen, in something done
by a petty governor of an island, while they affect to
call the measures of France clandestine. This is the
way that ministers support the character of the nation,
and the national honor and glory. But look again how
that same Holland is spoken of to-day. Even in your
correspondence with her, your littleness appears.

From this you may judge of your situation: from
this you may know what a state you are reduced to.
How will the French party in Holland exult over you,
and grow strong! She will never continue your ally,
when you meanly crouch to France, and do not dare
to stir in your defence! But it is nothing extraordinary
that she should not, while you keep the ministers you

have. No power in Europe is blind; there is none blind enough to ally itself with weakness, and become partner in bankruptcy; there is no one blind enough to ally itself to obstinacy, absurdity, and imbecility.

The Conjurer, a Dialogue.

Richard and Jack.

Jack. WHAT a strange man this is, Richard! did you ever see a conjurer before?

Richard. There was one travelled this way before your remembrance; but he missed his figure very much. I was to have been an officer before this time, according to his predictions; and you, Jack, were to have had a fine rich young lady for your sister-in-law. But he was only an apprentice in the art; no more than A, B, C, to this man.

Jack. Ay, he is master of his trade, I warrant you. I dare say, when father comes home, he can tell him which way the thief is gone with our old Trot. Uncle Bluster is coming over here this evening to find out who has got his watch. The conjurer is just gone out to look at the stars. I suppose, after he has viewed them a while, he will cast a figure in his great black-art book in the other room, and tell in a trice what things are stolen, and where they are, to a hair's breadth.

Rich. He must have a hawk's eye to see the stars this evening. Why don't you know, Jack, it is cloudy out o' doors?

Jack. That's nothing with him. He could look through the clouds with his glass, if it was as dark as Egypt, as easy as you can look into the other room; or, if he had a mind he could brush away the clouds in a trice, with that long wand he carries in his hand.

Rich. No doubt he is a great almanac maker. I'll be bound he could foretel the weather to a tittle for a thousand years to come. I wish I knew the tenth part as much about the planets as he does.

Jack. So do I. Don't you think our neighbours could hire him to keep our school, instead of Master Thinkwell? I believe he has fifty times as much learning. Aunt Betty told me this afternoon, that he knew every star in the sky as well as I do the cattle in our stable; and that he was as well acquainted with every crook and turn in the milky-way, as I am with the road to mill. They say he rode round to all the planets one night, in a chaise made of moonlight, drawn by flying horses.

Conjurer. [*Without in a grum hollow voice.*] Hoc noxe conventio planetorum tenetur est in domus Jovum.

Rich. Hark! he is going by the window: don't you hear him talking to himself?

Jack. What a strange language he uses! He is talking to the man in the moon, I dare say. He will go into the back room and cast a figure now: I will look through the key-hole and see him. [*Exit Jack.*

Rich. [*Solus.*] What a prodigious learned man this conjurer must be! I should suppose he had read all the books in the world, and conversed with spirits a hundred years, to know as much as he does.

Enter THINKWELL.

I am glad to see you, Master Thinkwell. Have you heard the rare news of the conjurer that is come to town?

Thinkwell. Yes; and I am informed he has taken up lodgings at your house to-night. You are greatly honored to be sure.

Rich. He is a very extraordinary man, I'll assure you.

Think. So far I agree with you, Richard. I believe he is an extraordinary man, and an extraordinary impostor too.

Rich. You are always on the side of contraries, Master Thinkwell; but every body is not of so stubborn faith as you. Why, there is as great a stir in town as there was when Prince Edward went through it. All the ladies are as much in the fidgets to see the conjurer, as they were to see him.

Think. It is much easier to account for these things than to justify them. We shall always act beneath ourselves, while we look up to such worthless wretches as our superiors. Prince Edward was certainly no more than a man. This conjurer in my opinion, is much less: I consider him beneath contempt. I am as great a friend to mirth as yourself; but it is really mortifying that my friends should be so anxious to make themselves the objects of ridicule.

Rich. This is your old strain, Master Thinkwell. I know you are apt to get round me in your arguments; but I believe the conjurer knows much more than both of us. I might go to you to learn grammar, arithmetic, and the common branches that are taught at school; but I shall go to him to have my fortune told.

Think. Have patience; and time, the only true fortune-teller, will disclose the future, without any pay, fast enough for your happiness or profit. Let me advise you to lay out your money for more valuable commodities than such gross imposition. Believe me, Richard, this man was never admitted into the cabinet of futurity any more than you or I, and knows no more of the events of to-morrow, next day, or next year, than the orang outang.

Rich. All our neighbours think very differently. He has told Mrs. Primble where she may find her silver spoon; and Sam Hodkins, the very day he is to be married; and the very first moment he cast his eyes on Bill Blunder's face, he saw the scar on his foot, and told him he had been wounded with an ax.

Think. Depend on it, Richard, it is all gross imposition. What careless lad is there, who uses an axe, that has not a scar on his feet?

Rich. If a man of common learning can foretel what is past, I don't see, for my part, why a conjurer may not foretel what is to come. [*Knocking at the door.*] Ah! Aunt Betty Wrinkle, I know by her rap.

Enter BETTY WRINKLE.

Betty. How do you do, Richard? a word with you, if you please cousin. [*To Richard. They go to the other side of the room.*] Is the fortune teller at your house, Richard?

Rich. He is casting a figure in the back room.

Betty. Can I see him? I wish to ask him a few questions in private.

Enter Mrs. CREDULOUS *and* JACK, *in haste.*

Mrs. Credulous. Law, sister Betty! I am glad to see you! I am half frighted out of my senses!

Betty. What is the matter, sister?

Mrs. Cred. I have been looking through the keyhole to see the conjurer. I believe there is a spell of enchantment on him! The room will be full of spirits in five minutes!

Betty. O, don't be frighted, sister; if he can conjure them up, he can conjure them down again. He won't let them hurt you. I shouldn't be afraid to go right into the room among them, not I.

Rich. If they were to come in the shape of widowers or old bachelors, perhaps you would not.

Betty. Law, how you joke, cousin. [*Cuffing his ears.*

Mrs. Cred. This is no jesting matter, I assure you. I could see plainly the candle burnt blue; there was a circle of fire round his head, and it began to smoke out of his mouth and nose.

Betty, Poh! nothing more than his breath, I dare say.

Jack. And I thought I saw the shadow of a spirit. The cat saw it too; for she looked as wild as though she would fly out of the window.

Betty. Well you won't frighten me. I am determined to see him, if he breathes nothing but fire and smoke.

Conj. [*Speaking loud in the other room.*] Horum quorum spiritorum, veniunto!

Mrs. Cred. Law, me! the very ghosts are come now! he is talking to them.

Think. They will never understand him, unless he uses better Latin.

Mrs. Cred. O, good master Thinkwell! you can talk Latin; do go and pray them, for mercy's sake! beseech them to leave the house. Do, quick!

Think. Do compose yourself, Mrs. Credulous: there are no worse spirits here than ignorance and folly; and they, of all others, are the most incorrigible. If you please, I will go and turn this scape-gallows out of your house, and put an end to your fears. [*Going.*

Mrs. Cred. O, stop! don't think of such a thing for the world. If we should affront him, he would raise a tempest and carry the house away in a minute. Mercy on me! he knows what you have said now! How dark it grows! O, the wind begins to rise! I will leave the house! we shall all be flying in the air in an instant!

Rich. Don't be terrified, ma'am. I dont hear any wind.

Jack. I do; and see it too, [*Looking out at the window.*] Dear me! how black it is!

Betty. You are very much frighted, sister. For my part, I am not afraid of the conjurer or any other man.

Rich. You were never quite so shy of them as they are of you.

Betty. Shy of me!

Mrs. Cred. Well, you must all take care of yourselves. I will run over to Mr. Rector's the minister. He may save the house; he is a good man. What would I give if I had never seen this wicked conjurer! [*Going out of the door.*] Mercy! the ground rises up under my feet; I can almost hear it thunder! Dear me, I shall meet a spirit! Master Thinkwell, you are not apt to be frighted; do go with me to the minister's.

Think. At your request I will. For your credit's sake, compose yourselves, and let not this shameful affair be related abroad.   [*Exit Thinkwell.*

Betty. I'm sure I don't see any cause for all this flutteration.

Jack. I believe I was more scared than hurt. The cat, I see, has got over her fright: she is playing in the entry as sprightly as you, aunt Betty.

Betty. Well said, Jack. [*Patting his cheeks.*] Do you think I could speak with the conjurer now, Richard?

Rich. I see nothing of any spirits yet. We will venture to go and see what he is about.

[*They go out of the room.*

SCENE *changes and discovers the Conjurer sitting at a table and making characters in a large book. He rises, takes his wand, and moves it slowly round a large circle, drawn on the floor, and filled with characters.*

Betty. [*Advancing slowly.*] Law me, my heart is in my mouth! I dare not speak to him. [*She stands and looks at him, and on Richard and Jack at the other side of the room, alternately.*

Conj. Horum charactarius in hoc circulum omnes planetorum atque eorum inhabitantibusque recto representur; et atque genii spiritorumque.

Betty. Bless me! what a world of learning he has! I can't understand a word he says.

Jack. [*To Richard.*] That circle is full of spirits, I suppose he has made them put on their coats of air that we might not see them.

Conj. I perceive, lady, by the mystic characters of this circle, you approach this way to inquire into the occult mysteries of fate, and to know of me your future destiny.

Betty. He knows my very thoughts. [*Aside.*] Learned Sir, be so good as to take this, and answer me a few questions I shall ask you.

[*Offering him a piece of money.*

Conj. You must first answer *me* a few questions. Your name, madam?

Betty. Elizabeth Wrinkle, at your service, Sir.

Conj. [*Writing her name in his book*.] Do you recollect whether the day that Burgoyne was captured was clear or cloudy?

Betty. That was quite before my remembrance, Sir, [*Looking in a glass.*] I am sure no body could take me for more than twenty-five.

Conj. I am not to be deceived, madam.

[*Looking out at the window through his glass*.

Jack. [*To Richard*.] Hark! we shall know her age now. He looks clear through time, with that glass, as easy as you can look through a key-hole.

Betty. Good Sir, don't expose me! pray speak low.

Conj. Young men, withdraw, and shut that door.

[*Richard and Jack leave the room*.

I told you I was not to be deceived. You were born, Anno Domini, one thousand, seven hundred and —

Betty. Law me! how should he know I was born in fifty-five? The treacherous stars must have betrayed me; not my looks, I am sure.   [*Aside*.

Conj. I tell you furthermore, the very man, whom the fates had singled out for your husband, by the fatal destiny of the stars, was slain at the taking of Burgoyne.

Betty. Dear me! O cruel stars, and more cruel Britons! how many husbands and wives have ye separated! Were it not for you, I should have been married twenty years ago. But since the fates have been so very cruel, don't you think they will be so kind as to provide me——you know what I mean, Mr. Conjurer.

Conj. Another husband. I will inquire.

[*Moving his wand round the circle*.

Enter *Mr*. CREDULOUS *and* BLUSTER.

Betty. Law, Brother, you have come in the very nick of time. I was just going to ask the Conjurer about your horse.

Conj. By the mysterious numbers of this circle,

Q

and the hidden virtue of this wand, I perceive you have lost a horse.

Cred. You have cast your figure right. My poor Trot has been gone ever since the twentieth day of June.

Conj. [*Moving his wand over the circle, and touching particular characters.*] Aries, Taurus, Gemini, Cancer; that is it precisely. You are under a little mistake, Sir; it was on the twentieth *night* of June.

Bluster. You are right, you are right, Mister Conjurer. The same night I had my watch stolen.

Conj. Aries, March; Taurus, April; Gemini, May; Cancer, June. On the night of June twentieth, precisely at twenty-three minutes past twelve, the horse was stolen from your pasture by a thief.

Blust. There, brother Credulous, you have it as exact as the multiplication table.

Cred. Strange what learning will do! [*Giving a piece of money to the Conjurer.*] Now, Sir, be so good as to tell me where the horse is, and how I shall find the very thief. Rascal! I shall have you now.

[*To himself.*

Conj. [*Making characters in his book.*] The stars are inauspicious at present. Mercury, the patron of thieves, bears rule to-night. I shall be able to detect him to-morrow. Hah! that is a lucky figure. Quod erat demonstrandum. I have got a clue to the watch in spite of Mercury.

Blust. Put me in a way of finding it, and you shall be well paid. We must secure our houses, brother Credulous, or this rogue of a Mercury will have our very beds from under us, before morning.

Conj. It shall be forthcoming immediately. [*Figuring in his book.*] One hundred and twenty-seven rods northeasterly from this table, in Chinese measure, lies a hollow tree; in that tree lies your watch.

Enter LONGSTAFF, *an* OFFICER, *two* WITNESSES, *and* THINKWELL.

Betty. Bless me! half the town will be here: it is time for me to go. [*Exit.*

Blust. Mr. Longstaff, be so good as not to interrupt the Conjurer. He has just told me where my watch is, and will detect the thief with a few figures more.

Longstaff. My duty obliges me to interrupt him. We have your watch, and are come to secure the thief. [*To the Conjurer.*] You have run at large, and defrauded the honest and ignorant long enough. By virtue of this warrant, you are the state's prisoner.

Conj. What trick shall I try now! I am detected at last. [*Aside.*]

Cred. You must be misinformed, Mr. Longstaff. This man is so far from being a thief, that he is a greater torment to them than their own consciences.

Long. Hear the evidence of these gentlemen, and you may alter your mind.

1st Witness. I suppose this watch to be yours, Mr. Bluster.

Blust. It is the very same; the chain only changed.

1st Wit. I happened to overhear him talking with one of his gang last evening. This watch, with a number of other articles, was to be hidden in a hollow tree. This impostor, to maintain the credit of a Conjurer was to inform the owners, on inquiry, where they were, upon their paying him for the imposition. I have been so fortunate as to secure one of the partners in this trade. And as I heard this gentleman, for whom you have so much regard, had taken up lodgings at your house, I did not choose to interrupt you till there was full proof of his guilt. The stolen goods which he described, and we have found, are sufficient evidence against him.

Cred. Villain! a halter is too good for your neck. May I be taught common sense by a monkey, if ever I am duped again in such a manner.

2d Wit. My evidence tends rather to impeach the character of my townsmen, than this worthless fellow's. All I can say, is that several months ago, he travelled this road in character of a tinker; and now all our young girls, old maids, and ignorant fellows, are running after this wise Conjurer to buy the history of their lives, which a little while since, they were weak enough to give him for nothing.

Think. I hope the impostor will be brought to justice, and we to our senses; and that after paying this infatuated devotion to vice and ignorance, virtue and true knowledge may have our more serious veneration.

Long. Gentlemen, assist me to conduct him to prison. [*Exeunt omnes.*

EXTRACT FROM MR. PITT'S SPEECH IN THE BRITISH PARLIAMENT, JAN. 20, 1775.

WHEN your lordships look at the papers transmitted to us from America; when you consider their decency, firmness and wisdom, you cannot but respect their cause and wish to make it your own. For myself, I must declare and avow, that in all my reading and observation, (and it has been my favourite study: I have read Thucydides, and have studied and admired the master-states of the world:) I say I must declare, that, for solidity and reasoning, force of sagacity, and wisdom of conclusion, under such a complication of difficult circumstances, no nation, or body of men can stand in preference to the General Congress at Philadelphia. I trust it is obvious to your lordships, that all attempts to impose servitude upon such men, to establish despotism over such a mighty continental nation, must be vain, must be fatal.

We shall be forced, ultimately, to retract; let us retract while we *can*, not when we *must*. I say we must necessarily undo these violent oppressive acts. They must be repealed. You WILL repeal them. I pledge myself for it, that you will in the end repeal them. I stake my reputation on it. I will consent to be taken for an idiot, if they are not finally repealed.

Avoid, then, this humiliating, disgraceful necessity. With a dignity becoming your exalted situation, make the first advances to concord, peace and happiness: for it is your true dignity, to act with prudence and justice. That *you* should first concede, is obvious from sound and rational policy. Concession comes with better grace, and more salutary effects from superior power; it reconciles superiority of power with the feelings of men; and establishes solid confidence on the foundations of affection and gratitude.

Every motive, therefore, of justice and of policy, of dignity and of prudence, urges you to allay the ferment in America, by a removal of your troops from Boston; by a repeal of your acts of Parliament; and by demonstration of amicable dispositions towards your colonies. On the other hand, every danger and every hazard impend, to deter you from perseverance in your present ruinous measures. Foreign war hanging over your heads by a slight and brittle thread: France and Spain watching your conduct, and waiting for the maturity of your errors; with a vigilant eye to America, and the temper of your colonies, more than their own concerns, be they what they may.

To conclude, my lords; if the ministers thus persevere in misadvising and misleading the King, I will not say, that they can alienate the affections of his subjects from his crown; but I will affirm, that they will make the crown not worth his wearing: I will not say that the King is betrayed; but I will pronounce, that the kingdom is undone.

———◆———

SPEECH OF GALGACHUS TO THE CALEDONIAN ARMY.

Countrymen, and Fellow-Soldiers,

WHEN I consider the cause, for which we have drawn our swords, and the necessity of striking an effectual blow before we sheathe them again, I feel joyful hopes arising in my mind, that this day an opening will be made for the restoration of British

liberty, and for shaking off the infamous yoke of Roman slavery. Caledonia is yet free. The all-grasping
power of Rome has not yet been able to seize our
liberty. But it is to be preserved only by valor.

You are not to expect to escape the ravage of the
general plunderers of mankind, by any sentiment of
justice in them. When the countries which are more
accessible have been subdued, they will then force
their way into those which are harder to be overcome.
And if they should conquer the dry land, over the
whole world, they will then think of carrying their
arms beyond the ocean, to see whether there be not
certain unknown regions, which they may attack, and
reduce under subjection to the Roman empire.

For we see that if a country is thought to be powerful in arms, the Romans attack it because the conquest will be glorious; if inconsiderable in the military art, because the victory will be easy; if rich, they
are drawn thither by the hope of plunder; if poor, by
the desire of fame.

The east, and the west, the south, and the north,
the face of the whole earth is the scene of their military achievments. The world is too little for their
ambition, and their avarice. Their supreme joy seems
to be ravaging, fighting, and shedding of blood; and
when they have unpeopled a region, so that there are
none left alive to bear arms, they say they have giv-
en peace to that country.

Our distance from the seat of government, and our
natural defence by the surrounding ocean, render us
obnoxious to their suspicions: for they know that
Britons are born with an instinctive love of liberty:
and they conclude that we must naturally be led to
think of taking the advantage of our detached situation, to disengage ourselves, one time or other, from
their oppression.

Thus, my countrymen and fellow-soldiers, suspected and hated as we ever must be by the Romans,
there is no prospect of our enjoying even a tolerable

state of bondage under them. Let us then in the name of all that is sacred, and in defence of all that is dear to us, resolve to exert ourselves, if not for glory, at least for safety; if not in vindication of British honor, at least in defence of our lives.

But, after all, who are these mighty Romans? Are they Gods; or mortal men, like ourselves? Do we not see that they fall into the same errors and weaknesses, as others? Does not peace effeminate them? Does not abundance debauch them? Does not wantonness enervate them? Do they not even go to excess in the most unmanly vices? And can you imagine that they who are remarkable for their vices are likewise remarkable for their valor? What then do we dread? Shall I tell you the truth, my fellow-soldiers? It is by means of our intestine divisions, that the Romans have gained such great advantage over us. They turn the misconduct of their enemies to their own praise. They boast of what they have done, and say nothing of what we might have done, had we been so wise, as to unite against them.

What is this formidable Roman army? Is it not composed of a mixture of people from different countries; some more, some less capable of bearing fatigue and hardship? They keep together while they are successful. Attack them with vigor: distress them: you will see them more disunited than we are now. Can any one imagine, that Gauls, Germans, and with shame I must add, Britons, who basely lend their limbs and lives, to build up a foreign tyranny; can one imagine that these will be longer enemies than slaves? or that such an army is held together by sentiments of fidelity or affection? No: the only bond of union among them is fear. And whenever terror ceases to work upon the minds of that mixed multitude, they who now fear, will then hate their tyrannical masters.

On our side there is every possible incitement to valour. The Roman courage is not, as ours, inflamed by the thoughts of wives and children in danger of falling into the hands of the enemy. The Romans have not parents, as we have, to reproach them if they should desert their infirm old age. They have no country here to fight for. They are a motley collection of foreigners, in a land wholly unknown to them; cut off from their native country, hemmed in by the surrounding ocean; and given, I hope, a prey into our hands, without any possibility of escape. Let not the sound of the Roman name affright your ears, nor let the glare of gold or silver, upon their armour, dazzle your eyes. It is not by gold or silver, that men are either wounded or defended; though they are rendered a richer prey to the conquerors. Let us boldly attack this disunited rabble. We shall find among themselves a reinforcement to our army.

And what will there be then to fear? A few half garrisoned forts; a few municipal towns, inhabited by worn-out old men; discord universally prevailing, occasioned by tyranny in those who command, and obstinacy in those who should obey. On our side, an army united in the cause of their country, their wives, their children, their aged parents, their lives. At the head of this army, I hope I do not offend against modesty in saying, there is a General ready to exert all his abilities such as they are, and to hazard his life, in leading you to victory, and to freedom.

I conclude, my countrymen and fellow-soldiers, with putting you in mind, that on your behaviour this day depends your future enjoyment of peace and liberty, or your subjection to a tyrannical enemy, with all its grievous consequences. When, therefore, you come to engage, think of your ancestors and think of your posterity.

Modern Education.

Dialogue between a Preceptor of an Academy and Parent of an offered Pupil.

Preceptor. I AM heartily sick of this modern mode
[*Solus.*] of education. Nothing but trash will
suit the taste of people at this day. I am perplexed
beyond all endurance with these frequent solicitations
of parents, to give their children graceful airs, polite
accomplishments, and a smattering of what they call
the fine arts; while nothing is said about teaching them
the substantial branches of literature. If they can but
dance a little, fiddle a little, flute a little, and make a
handsome bow and courtesy, that is sufficient to make
them famous in this *enlightened* age. Three-fourths
of the teachers of those arts, which once were esteemed most valuable, will soon be out of employment at
this rate. For my part, I am convinced, that, if I
had been a dancing master, music master, stage
player, or mountebank, I should have been much
more respected, and much better supported, than I
am at present.

Enter Parent.

Parent. Your humble servant, Sir, are you the
principal of this Academy?

Precep. I am, at your service, Sir.

Par. I have heard much of the fame of your institution, and am desirous of putting a son, of about
twelve years of age, under your tuition. I suppose
you have masters who teach the various branches of
the polite arts.

Precep. We are not inattentive to those arts, Sir;
but the fame of our Academy does not rest upon
them. *Useful* learning is our grand object. What studies do you wish to put your son upon?

Par. I wish him to be perfected in music, dancing,
drawing, &c. and as he possesses a promising genius
for poetry, I would by all means have that cultivated.

Precep. These are not all the branches, I trust, in which he is to be instructed. You mention nothing of reading, writing, arithmetic, language, &c. Are these to be wholly neglected?

Par. Why, as to these *every-day* branches, I cannot say I feel very anxious about them. The boy reads well now; writes a decent hand; is acquainted with the ground rules of arithmetic, and pronounces the English language genteelly. He has been a long time under the care of Mr. Honestus, our town school-master, who has taught him all these things sufficiently. So that I think any more time devoted to them would be wasted.

Precep. If he is such an adept that there is no room for his progressing in those arts; yet I think at least there is need of practice, lest, at his age, he should forget what he has learned.

Par. That I shall leave to your discretion. But there is one branch, of great importance, which I have not yet mentioned, and to which I would have particular attention paid; I mean the art of speaking. You will find him not deficient in that respect; though perhaps it requires as much practice to make one perfect in that, as in any art whatever. He has already learned by heart a great number of pieces, and has acted a part in several comedies and tragedies with much applause. It has been the custom of our master to have an exhibition at least once a quarter; and my son has always been considered as one of his best performers. He lately took the part of Jemmy Jumps, in the farce called The Farmer; and acted it to universal acceptation.

Precep. I must confess, Sir, that your account of your son does not appear to me to be very flattering.

Par. Why so, pray? have you not an ear for eloquence?

Precep. Indeed I have, Sir. No man is more charmed than I am with its enrapturing sounds. No music rests sweeter on my ear than the melodious notes, proceeding from the mouth of a judicious, well-instructed and powerful orator. But I must tell you plainly, that I am by no means pleased to see parents take so much pains to transform their children into monkeys instead of men. What signs of oratory do you imagine you can discern in a boy, rigged out in a fantastical dress, skipping about the stage like a baboon, in the character of Jemmy Jumps, Betty Jumps, or any other jumper?

Par. Do you not approve of exhibitions then?

Precep. Not much I confess, in the way they are generally conducted. A master who has four in a year, must necessarily rob his pupils of one quarter of that time, which in my opinion, might be much better employed in attending to what would be useful for them in life.

Par. What can be more useful for a child, under such a government as ours than to be able to speak before an audience with a graceful ease, and a manful dignity? My son, for ought I know, may be a member of Congress before he dies.

Precep. For that very reason I would educate him differently. I would lay the foundation of his future fame on the firm basis of the *solid sciences;* that he might be able in time to do something more than a mere parrot, or an ape, who are capable only of speaking the words, and mimicking the actions of others. He should first be taught to *read.* He should likewise be taught to compose for himself; and I would not be wanting in my endeavours to make him a speaker.

Par. Surely, Mr. Preceptor, you must be very wrong in your notions. I have ever pursued a different plan with my children; and there are none in the country, though I say it myself, who are more universally caressed. I have a daughter that has seen but fourteen years, who is capable of gracing the politest circles. It is allowed that she can enter, and leave a room, with as much ease and dignity as any lady of quality whatever. And this is evidently owing altogether to her polite education. I boarded her a year in the capital, where she enjoyed every possible advantage. She attended the most accomplished masters in the ornamental branches of science; visited the genteelest families, and frequented all the scenes of amusement. It is true, her letters are not always written quite so accurately as could be wished; yet she dances well, plays well on the piano-forte, and sings like a nightingale.

Precep. Does she know the art of making a good pudding? Can she darn a stocking well? or is she capable of patching the elbows of her husband's coat, should she ever be so lucky as to get one? If she is to remain ignorant of all such domestic employments, as much as I value her other accomplishments, and as much as I might be in want of a wife, I would not marry her with twice her weight in gold.

Par. Her accomplishments will command her a husband as soon as she wishes. But so long as a single cent of my property remains, her delicate hands shall never be so unworthily employed.

Precep. But suppose a reverse of fortune should overtake you, what is to become of the child; as you say she understands nothing of domestic affairs? Will it be more honourable, do you imagine for her to be maintained by the charity of the people, than by her own industry?

Par. There are many ways for her to be supported. I would not have you think she is wholly ignorant of the use of the needle, though she never employed it in so disgraceful a manner as that of darning stockings! or botching tattered garments! But we will waive that subject, and attend to the other. Will you receive the boy for the purposes before mentioned?

Precep. Why, indeed, Sir, I cannot. Though I am far from condemning altogether your favourite branches, yet I consider them all as subordinate, and some of them at least, totally useless. We devote but a small portion of our time to the attainment of such superficial accomplishments. I would therefore recommend it to you, to commit him to the care of those persons, who have been so successful in the instruction of his sister.

Par. I confess I am so far convinced of the propriety of your method, that, if you will admit him into your Academy, I will renounce all right of dictating to you his lessons of instruction, except in one single instance; and in that I am persuaded we shall not disagree; I mean the art of speaking.

Precep. I shall agree to that only under certain limitations. That is an art which undoubtedly demands our solicitous attention; but it ought never to be pursued to the injury of other studies. I am sensible that it is no less useful to a pupil than entertaining to an audience, to exercise him occasionally on the stage in declaiming judicious and well written compositions, and pronouncing such selected dialogues, as will tend to give gracefulness to his attitude, and familiarity to his tones and gestures. But, admitting that time could be spared from more important pursuits, I see but little *good* resulting from the exhibition of whole comedies and tragedies in our academies and schools: while much *evil* is to be feared, both from the immorality of the plays, and the dissipation it introduces into society. Besides, all boys are not calculated for orators; and though Demosthenes surmounted almost insuperable difficulties in the acquirement of his art, it is folly to suppose that his example is capable of universal imitation. I cannot believe it a very pleasing entertainment to a discerning audience, to see a boy without talents, mounted upon the rostrum, *spouting* forth sentences which he does not understand, and which, perhaps, are chosen with as little judgment as they are delivered with propriety. But what can be more disgusting than to see innocent, and timid females, whose excellence, in part, consists in their modesty and silence before superiors, encouraged to reverse the order of nature by playing the orator on a public stage! And what often enhances our disgust, and sickens all our

R

feelings, is, that their lips are taught to pronounce sentiments, extracted from the very dregs of the European drama.

Par. Then it seems you do not approve of females speaking at all.

Precep. Not on a public stage, unless I wished to see them divested of half their charms. Such masculine employments as ill become them, as the labours of the field, or the habits of the stronger sex. I would have them taught to read and pronounce well at school; but nature never designed them for public orators; much less, that they should be degraded to the vile purpose of entertaining the votaries of theatrical amusements.

Par. Why, you differ widely from many, whose pride it is to be considered as the standards of modern taste. It does not now offend against the rules of delicacy, for the different sexes to make exchange of garments now and then, provided the grand object of amusement be promoted by it. I was in Boston last week, and there I saw a beautiful young lady, rigged out from top to toe in men's apparel, astride a gay horse, parading through the streets, for the entertainment of the ladies and gentlemen of that polite metropolis. And none appeared to be offended, except a few who had not attained a relish for refined pleasures.

Precep. Yes, and I am told, that, at their theatres, it is no uncommon thing for a woman to make her appearance in that apparel, with a sword by her side, strutting across the stage, and swearing oaths big enough to choke an Algerine pirate; and yet it is so agreeable to the modern *ton*, that even ladies of distinguished refinement are *ashamed* to *blush* at her!

Par. You have made me so far a convert to your sentiments on this subject, and given me such proofs of your superior judgment in the education of youth, that I am determined to commit my son, without any reserve, to your care and instruction. Till you hear from me again, I am, Sir, your obedient servant.

THE EXISTENCE OF GOD, DEMONSTRATED FROM THE WORKS OF CREATION; BEING A SERMON PREACHED AT PROVIDENCE, BY JONATHAN MAXCY, A. M. PRESIDENT OF RHODE ISLAND COLLEGE, 1795; FROM ROMANS i. 20.

[N. B. When found expedient, the following Sermon may conveniently be divided into three or four parts, suitable for declamations. The author of this work did not intend at first to insert the whole; but, in attempting to make a selection, he could find no part which he was willing to *leave*.]

NOTHING will more effectually guard us against vice, than a firm belief in the existence of God. For surely if we realize that there is such a Being, we shall naturally infer from his perfections, from the nature of his moral government, and from our situation as rational creatures, that we are amenable at his awful tribunal. Superior power, wisdom, and goodness, always lay us under restraint, and command our veneration. These, even in a mortal, overawe us. They restrain not only the actions, but the words and thoughts of the most vitious and adandoned. Our happiness depends on our virtue. Our virtue depends on the conformity of our hearts and conduct to the laws prescribed us by our beneficent Creator.

Of what vast importance then is it to our present as well as future felicity, to possess in our hearts a feeling sense and in our understanding a clear conviction, of the existence of that Being whose power and goodness are unbounded, whose presence fills immensity, and whose wisdom, like a torrent of lightning, emanates through all the dark recesses of eternal duration! How great must be the effect of a sense of the presence of the great Creator and Governor of all things, to whom belong the attributes, eternity, independency, perfect holiness, inflexible justice, and inviolable veracity; complete happiness and glorious majesty; supreme right and unbounded dominion!

A sense of accountability to God will retard the eager pursuit of vice; it will humble the heart of the proud, it will bridle the tongue of the profane, and snatch the knife from the hand of the assassin. A belief of the existence of God is the true original source of all virtue, and the only foundation of all religion, natural or revealed. Set aside this great luminous truth, erase the conviction of it from the heart, you then place virtue and vice on the same level; you drive afflicted innocence into despair; you add new effrontery to the marred visage of guilt; you plant thorns in the path, and shed an impenetrable gloom over the prospects of the righteous.

Sin has alienated the affections, and diverted the attention of men from the great Jehovah. " Darkness has covered the earth, and gross darkness the people." Men have worshipped the works of their own hands, and neglected the true God, though his existence and perfections were stamped in glaring characters on all creation. From the regularity, order, beauty, and conservation of this great system of things, of which man makes a part; from the uniform tendency of all its divisions to their proper ends, the existence of God shines as clearly as the sun in the heavens. "From the things that are made," says the text, " are seen his eternal power and Godhead."

1. Man himself is a proof of God's existence. Let us place him before us in his full stature. We are at once impressed with the beautiful organization of his body, with the orderly and harmonious arrangement of his members. Such is the disposition of these, that their motion is the most easy, graceful, and useful, that can be conceived. We are astonished to see the same simple matter diversified into so many different substances, of different qualities, size, and figure. If we pursue our researches through the internal economy, we shall find, that all the different opposite parts correspond to each other with the utmost exactness and order; that they all answer the most beneficent purposes.

This wonderful machine, the human body, is animated, cherished, and preserved, by a spirit within, which pervades every particle, feels in every organ, warns us of injury, and administers to our pleasures. Erect in stature, man differs from all other animals. Though his foot is confined to the earth, yet his eye measures the whole circuit of heaven, and in an instant takes in thousands of worlds. His countenance is turned upward, to teach us that he is not like other animals, limited to the earth, but looks forward to brighter scenes of existence in the skies.

Whence came this erect, orderly, beautiful constitution of the human body? Did it spring up from the earth, self-formed? Surely not. Earth itself is inactive matter. That which has no motion can never produce any. Man surely could not, as has been vainly and idly supposed, have been formed by the fortuitous concurrence of atoms. We behold the most exact order in the constitution of the human body. Order always involves design. Design always involves intelligence. That intelligence, which directed the orderly formation of the human body, must have resided in a Being whose power was adequate to the production of such an effect.

Creation surely is the prerogative of a self existent uncaused Being. Finite creatures may arrange and dispose, but they cannot create; they cannot give life.

It is a universal law through all nature, that like produces like. The same laws most probably obtain through the whole system in which we are connected. We have therefore no reason to suppose that angels created man. Neither can we, without the greatest absurdity, admit that he was formed by himself, or by mere accident. If in the latter way, why do we never see men formed so in the present day? Why do we never see the clods of earth brightening into human flesh, and the dust under our feet crawling into animated forms, and starting up into life and intelligence?

R 2

If we even admit that either of the aforementioned causes might have produced man, yet neither of them could have preserved him in existence one moment. There must therfore be a God uncaused, independent, and complete. The nobler part of man clearly evinces this great truth. When we consider the boundless desires and the inconceivable activity of the soul of man, we can refer his origin to nothing but God! How astonishing are the reasoning faculties of man! How surprising the power of comparing, arranging, and connecting his ideas! How wonderful is the power of imagination! On its wings, in a moment, we can transport ourselves to the most distant part of the universe. We can fly back, and live the lives of all antiquity, or surmount the limits of time, and sail along the vast range of eternity. Whence these astonishing powers, if not from a God of infinite wisdom, goodness, and power?

2. " The invisible things of him from the creation of the world," says the text, " are clearly seen." Let us for a moment behold our earth. With what a delightful scene are we here presented! the diversification of its surface into land and water, islands and lakes, springs and rivers, hills and valleys, mountains and plains, renders it to man doubly enchanting. We are entertained with an agreeable variety, without being disgusted by a tedious uniformity. Every thing appears admirably formed for our profit and delight. There the valleys are clothed in smiling green, and the plains are bending with corn. Here is the genle hill to delight the eye, and beyond, slow rising from the earth, swells the huge mountain, and, with all its load of waters, rocks, and woods heaves itself up into the skies. Why this pleasing, vast deformity of nature? Undoubtedly for the benefit of man. From the mountains descend streams to fertilize the plains below, and cover them with wealth and beauty.

The earth not only produces every thing necessary to support our bodies, but to remedy our diseases, and gratify our senses. Who covered the earth with such a pleasing variety of fruits and flowers? Who gave them their delightful fragrance, and painted them with such excellent colours? Who causes the same water to whiten in the lily, that blushes in the rose? Do not these things indicate a Cause infinitely superior to any finite being? Do they not directly lead us to believe the existence of God, to admire his goodness, to revere his power, to adore his wisdom, in so happily accommodating our external circumstances to our situation and internal constitution?

3. But how are we astonished to behold the vast ocean, rolling its immense burden of waters! Who gave it such a configuration of particles as to render it movable by the least pressure, and at the same time so strong as to support the heaviest weights? Who spread out this vast highway of all the nations under heaven? Who gave it its regular motion? Who confined it within its bounds? A little more motion would disorder the whole world! A small incitement on the tide would drown whole kingdoms. Who restrains the proud waves, when the tempest lifts them to the clouds? Who measured the great waters, and subjected them to invariable laws? That great Being, " who placed the sand for the bound thereof, by a perpetual decree that it cannot pass; and though the waves thereof toss themselves, yet they cannot prevail; though they roar, yet can they not pass over." With reason may we believe, that from the things that are made are clearly seen eternal power and wisdom.

4. Passing by the numerous productions and appendages of the earth, let us rise from it and consider the body of air with which we are surrounded. What a convincing proof do we here find of the existence of God! Such is the subtility and transparency of the air, that it receives the rays of the sun and stars, conveying them with inconceivable velocity to objects on the earth, rendering them visible, and decorating the

whole surface of the globe with an agreeable inter-
mixture of light, shade, and colours. But still this air
has a sufficient consistency and strength to support
clouds, and all the winged inhabitants. Had it been
less subtile it would have intercepted the light. Had
it been more rarified, it would not have supported its
inhabitants, nor have afforded sufficient moisture for
the purposes of respiration. What then but infinite
wisdom could have tempered the air so nicely, as to
give it sufficient strength to support clouds for rain,
to afford wind for health, and at the same time to
possess the power of conveying sound and light? How
wonderful is this element! How clearly does it discover infinite wisdom, power, and goodness!

5. But when we cast our eyes up to the firmament
of heaven, we clearly see that it declares God's handy
work. Here the immense theatre of God's works opens
upon us, and discloses ten thousand magnificent
splendid objects. We dwindle to nothing in comparison with this august scene of beauty, majesty, and glory. Who reared this vast arch over our heads? Who
adorned it with so many shining objects, placed at
such immense distances from each other, regular in
their motions, invariably observing the laws to which
they were originally subjected? Who placed the sun
at such a convenient distance as not to annoy, but re-
fresh us? Who, for so many ages, has caused him to
rise and set at fixed times? Whose hand directs, and
whose power restrains him in his course, causing him
to produce the agreeable changes of day and night, as
well as the variety of seasons?

The order, harmony, and regularity in the revolu-
tions of the heavenly bodies, are such incontestable
proofs of the existence of God, that an eminent poet well
said, " An undevout astronomer is mad." In the time
of Cicero, when the knowledge of astronomy was very
imperfect, he did not hesitate to declare, that in his opinion the man who asserted the heavenly bodies were not
framed and moved by a divine understanding, was him-

self void of all understanding. Well indeed is it said, that the heavens declare the glory of God.

This great Being is every where present. He exists all around us. He is not, as we are apt to imagine, at a great distance. Wherever we turn, his image meets our view. We see him in the earth, in the ocean, in the air, in the sun, moon, and stars. We feel him in ourselves. He is always working round us; he performs the greatest operations, produces the noblest effects, discovers himself in a thousand different ways, and yet the real GOD remains unseen. All parts of creation are equally under his inspection. Though he warms the breast of the highest angel in heaven, yet he breathes life into the meanest insect on earth. He lives through all his works, supporting all by the word of his power. He shines in the verdure that clothes the plains, in the lily that delights in the vale, and in the forest that waves on the mountain. He supports the slender reed that trembles in the breeze, and the sturdy oak that defies the tempest. His presence cheers the inanimate creation.

Far in the wilderness, where human eye never saw, where the savage foot never trod, there he bids the blooming forest smile, and the blushing rose opens its leaves to the morning sun. There he causes the feathered inhabitants to whistle their wild notes to the listening trees and echoing mountains. There nature lives in all her wanton wildness. There the ravished eye, hurrying from scene to scene, is lost in one vast blush of beauty. From the dark stream that rolls through the forest, the silver scaled fish leap up, and dumbly mean the praise of God. Though man remain silent, yet God will have praise. He regards, observes, upholds, connects, and equals all.

The belief of his existence is not a point of mere speculation and amusement. It is of inconceivable importance to our present, as well as future felicity. But while we believe there is a God, we should be extremely careful to ascertain, with as much accuracy as possible, what is his real nature. The most prominent features of this are exhibited in that incomprehensible display of wisdom, power, and goodness, made in the works of creation. A virtuous man stands in a relation to God which is peculiary delightful. The divine perfections are all engaged in his defence. He feels powerful in God's power, wise in his wisdom, good in his goodness.

The vitious man, on the contrary, stands in a relation to God, which is of all things the most dreadful. He is unwilling to know that God has sufficient wisdom to search out all his wickedness, sufficient goodness to the universe to determine to punish that wickedness, and sufficient power to execute that determination. A firm belief in the existence of God will heighten all the enjoyments of life, and, by conforming our hearts to his will, will secure the approbation of a good conscience, and inspire us with the hopes of a blessed immortality.

Never be tempted to disbelieve the existence of God, when every thing around you proclaims it in a language too plain not to be understood. Never cast your eyes on creation without having your souls expanded with this sentiment, "There is a God." When you survey this globe of earth, with all its appendages; when you behold it inhabited by numberless ranks of creatures, all moving in their proper spheres, all verging to their proper ends, all animated by the same great source of life, all supported at the same great bounteous table: when you behold not only the earth, but the ocean and the air, swarming with living creatures, all happy in their situation; when you behold yonder sun darting an effulgent blaze of glory over the heavens, garnishing mighty worlds, and waking ten thousand songs of praise; when you behold unnumbered systems diffused through vast immensity, clothed in splendour, and rolling in majesty; when you behold these things, your affections will rise above all the vanities of time; your full souls will struggle with ecstasy;

and your reason, passions, and feelings, all united, will rush up to the skies, with a devout acknowledgment of the existence, power, wisdom, and goodness of God.

Let us behold him, let us wonder, let us praise and adore. These things will make us happy. They will wean us from vice, and attach us to virtue. As a belief of the existence of God is a fundamental point of salvation, he who denies it runs the greatest conceivable hazard. He resigns the satisfaction of a good conscience, quits the hopes of a happy immortality, and exposes himself to destruction. All this for what? for the shortlived pleasures of a riotous, dissolute life. How wretched, when he finds his atheistical confidence totally disappointed! Instead of his beloved sleep and insensibility, with which he so fondly flattered himself he will find himself still existing after death, removed to a strange place; he will then find that there is a God, who will not suffer his rational creatures to fall into annihilation as a refuge from the just punishment of their crimes; he will find himself doomed to drag on a wretched train of existence in unavailing woe and lamentation. Alas! how astonished will he be to find himself plunged in the abyss of ruin and desperation! God forbid that any of us should act so unwisely as to disbelieve, when every thing around us proclaims his existence!

The Dignity of Human Nature.

Extract of an Oration delivered at Rhode-Island College, 1796.

GUIDED by reason, man has travelled through the abstruse regions of the philosophic world. He has originated rules by which he can direct the ship through the pathless ocean, and measure the comet's flight over the fields of unlimited space. He has established society and government. He can aggregate the profusions of every climate, and every season. He can meliorate the severity, and remedy the imperfections, of nature herself. All these things he can perform by the assistance of reason.

By imagination, man seems to verge towards creative power. Aided by this, he can perform all the wonders of sculpture and painting. He can almost make the marble speak. He can almost make the brook murmur down the painted landscape. Often, on the pinions of imagination, he soars aloft where the eye has never travelled; where other stars glitter on the mantle of night, and a more effulgent sun lights up the blushes of morning. Flying from world to world, he gazes on all the glories of creation; or, lighting on the distant margin of the universe, darts the eye of fancy over the mighty void, where power creative never yet has energized; where existence still sleeps in the wide abyss of possibility.

By imagination he can travel back to the source of time; converse with the successive generations of men, and kindle into emulation while he surveys the monumental trophies of ancient art and glory. He can sail down the stream of time until he loses " sight of stars and sun, by wandering into those retired parts of eternity, when the heavens and the earth shall be no more."

To these unequivocal characteristics of greatness in man, let us adduce the testimony of nature herself. Surrounding creation subserves the wants and proclaims the dignity of man. For him day and night visit the world. For him the seasons walk their splendid round. For him the earth teems with riches, and the heavens smile with beneficence.

All creation is accurately adjusted to his capacity for bliss. He tastes the dainties of festivity, breathes the perfumes of morning, revels on the charms of melody, and regales his eye with all the painted beauties of vision. Whatever can please, whatever can charm, whatever can expand the soul with ecstasy of bliss, allures and solicits his attention. All things beautiful, all things grand, all things sublime, appear in native loveliness, and proffer men the richest pleasures of fruition.

INFERNAL CONFERENCE.

Satan. FRIENDS, and confederates, welcome!
　　　　　　　for this proof
Of your affiance, thanks. On every call,
Whether we need your counsel or your arms,
Joyful I see your ready zeal displays
Virtues, which hell itself cannot corrupt.
I mean not to declaim: the occasion told
Speaks its own import, and the time's despatch
All waste of words forbids. God's Son on earth,
Christ, the reveal'd Messias, how t' oppose
Is now the question; by what force, or power;
(Temptations have been tried, I name not them;)
Or dark conspiracy, we may pull down
This Sun of Righteousness from his bright sphere,
Declare, who can. I pause for a reply.

　　Baal. Why thus on me, as I were worthy; me,
Lost being like yourselves; as I alone
Could compass this high argument; on me,
Least in your sapient conclave; why you point
These scrutinizing looks, I muse; and, aw'd
By this your expectation, fain would shrink
From the great task to silence, had you not
O'er these poor faculties such full control,
As to put by all pleas, and call them forth
In heaven or earth, or hell's profound abyss,
Yours in all uses, present at all hours.
Our kingly chief hath told us we are met
To combat Christ on earth. Be't so! We yet
May try our fortune in another field;
Worse fortune than in heaven befel our arms
Worse downfal than to hell, we cannot prove.
But with the scene our action too must change;
How? to what warfare? Circumvention, fraud,
Seduction; these are earthly weapons; these
As man to man opposes, so must we
To Christ incarnate. There be some, who cry,

S

Hence with such dastard arts! War, open war!
I honor such bold counsellors, and yield
All that I can, my praise: till one be found,
One that may rival God's own Son in power,
And miracle to miracle oppose,
More than my praise I cannot; my assent
I will not give; 'twere madness. And how war
With God? what arms may we employ 'gainst him,
Whose very prophets can call down heaven's fires
Upon our priests and altars? For myself,
What powers I had I shall not soon forget;
What I have left I know, and for your use
Shall husband as I may, not vainly risk
Where they must surely fail. The Jews pretend
That Christ colludes with Beelzebub; the Jews
As far mistake my nature as my name.
The fallacy, O peers, confutes itself,
Forg'd to disparage Christ, not honor me.
Oh! that I had his wonder-working powers;
I'm not that fool to turn them on myself:
No, my brave friends, I've yet too much to lose.
Therefore no more of Beelzebub and Christ;
No league, no compact can we hold together.
What then ensues? Despair! Perish the thought!
The brave renounce it, and the wise prevent;
You are both wise and brave. Our leader says
Temptations have been tried, and tried in vain,
Himself the tempter. Who will tread that ground
Where he was foil'd? For Adam a mere toy,
An apple serv'd; Christ is not brib'd by worlds:
So much the second Man exceeds the first
In strength and glory. But though Christ himself
Will not be tempted, those who hear him may:
Jews may be urg'd to envy, to revenge,
To murder: a rebellious race of old!
Wist ye not what a train this preacher hath,
What followers, what disciples? These are men,
Mere men, frail sons of Adam, born in sin.
Here is our hope. I leave it to your thoughts.

Moloch. My thoughts it seems are known before I
    speak;
War, open war is all my note. I rise
To thank the prophet, who thus reads my heart,
Where honesty should wear it, in my face;
That face from danger I did never hide;
How then from him? Nor am I by his praise
More honor'd than by his dissenting voice:
For whilst he counsels circumvention, fraud,
Seduction, (if my memory wrong his words
I yield it to correction) we stand off,
Wide as the poles apart. Much I had hop'd,
When the great tempter fail'd, and in your ears
Sung his own honor's dirge, we had heard the last
Of plots and mean temptations; mean I call them,
For great names cannot sanctify mean deeds.
Satan himself knows I oppos'd th' attempt,
Appeal'd, protested; my thrice honor'd chief
Knows it full well, and blushes for th' event.
And are we now caballing how t' outwit
A few poor harmless fishermen; for such
Are Christ's disciples; how to gull and cheat
Their simple hearts of honesty? Oh peers,
For shame, if not for pity, leave them that,
That beggars virtue. And is this the theme,
The mighty theme, which now employs the thoughts
Of your immortal synod? Shame, Oh shame!
Princes, dominions, arch-angelic thrones,
Imperial lords! These were your titles once;
By these names ye were known above the stars:
Shame not your ancient dignities, nor sink
Beneath the vilest of the sons of men,
Whisperers, informers, spies. If Christ be God;
Fight, as becometh you to fight, with God:
If man, and sure his birth bespeaks no more,
Why all this preparation, this consult,
These mighty machinations and cabals?
Off with your foe at once; dismiss him hence
Where all his brother prophets have been sent;

Where his precursor John is gone before;
Whose voice still echoes through this wilderness,
" Repent ye, for God's kingdom is at hand!
Prepare ye the Lord's way!" It is prepar'd;
It leads to death; it marshals him the road
To that oblivious bourne, whence none return.
Herod yet lives; another royal feast,
Another wanton dance, and he, for whom
So many innocents were slain, shall fall.
Once vanquish'd, are we therefore to despair?
In heav'n, unequal battle we provok'd;
Though vast our host, the million was with God.
On earth, inquire of all the nations round
Whom they will serve; with one voice they reply,
We are their gods; they feed us with their blood,
Their sons and daughters they make pass through fire
To do us grace; if their own flesh they give,
Shall they withhold to sacrifice a foe?
Twelve tribes were all Jehovah had on earth,
And ten are lost; of this small remnant, few
And wretched are the friends that league with heav'n.
And where is now Christ's promis'd reign on earth?
When God's own servants rise against his Son,
And those, to whom the promises were giv'n,
Revolt from their Messias, can we wish
Greater revenge? What need have we to tempt
Those who have hearts rebellious as our own,
As prompt to malice, no less prone to vex
God's righteous Spirit? And let come what may,
It comes not to our loss, rather our gain.
Let God arise to vengeance; let him pour
Destruction on his temple, whose proud height
Our chief can witness, measur'd by his fall:
Let him not leave one stone upon another,
As his rash Son hath menac'd; let his wrath
Through all the inhospitable earth disperse
His scatter'd tribes; such ever be the fate
Of all his worshippers! May scorn, contempt,
Derision be their lot, and may their God

Never recal his curse! Are we, O peers,
To mourn for his Jerusalem? Our joy
Springs from confusion: enmity 'twixt God
And man is our best triumph. For myself,
War is my harvest; then my altars blaze
Brightest, when human victims feed the flame.

   Belial. After so many peaceful ages past
Since first emerging from hell's dark abyss,
Rous'd by our arch-angelic chief, we sprung
Up to this middle region, and here seiz'd
On this terrestrial globe, created first
For man, our vassal now, where, at full ease,
Lords of the elements and gods ador'd,
We reign and revel undisturb'd of Heav'n.
If God, whose jealousy be sure ill brooks
That this fair world should be so long possess'd
By us his exil'd angels, and his name,
Pent up in Palestine, should now arouse
His slumbering wrath, and his best strength put forth
To wrestle for lost empire, and our earth,
As we in evil hour his heaven, assail;
Who of this mighty synod but must own
The provocation warrants the retort?
If then the Maker of mankind hath cause
To meditate their rescue, we no less
Have cause t' oppose th' attempt, and hold them fast
To their allegiance in despite of Heav'n.
Much then we owe to our great leader's care,
Who, ever watchful o'er the public weal,
Calls us to this full council, here to meet
In grave consult how best we may repair
Past disappointments, and repel the spite
Of this new Champion, levell'd at our shrines.
Great is the trouble of my thoughts, O peers,
And much perplex'd am I with doubts, what name,
Nature, and office to ascribe to Christ;
In form the lowliest of the sons of men,
In miracles omnipotent as God;
Whose voice controls the stoutest of our host.

Bids the graves open and their dead come forth;
Whose very touch is health; who with a glance
Pervades each heart, absolves it or condemns;
Whose virgin birth credulity scarce owns,
And nature disavows. Prais'd to all time,
Immortal as himself be the renown
Of that wise spirit, who shall devise the means
By force or fraud to overthrow the power
Of this mysterious foe: what shall I say?
Priest, Prophet, King, Messias, Son of God?
Yet how God's unity, which well we know
Endures no second, should adopt a Son,
And essence indivisible divide,
Baffles my weak conjecture. Let that pass.
To such hard doctrines I subscribe no faith:
I'll call him man inspir'd, and wait till death
Gives sentence of mortality upon him.
Meanwhile let circumspection on our part
Fill all the anxious interim; alarm
Rome's jealousy: stir up the captious spleen
Of the proud Pharisee; beset him round
With snares to catch him; urge the envious priests,
For envy still beneath the altar lurks;
And note the man he trusts. Mammon could tell,
Though Mammon boasts not of his own success,
How few of human mould have yet withstood
His glittering, golden lures. The sword can kill
Man's body; gold destroys his very soul.
Yet mark me well, I counsel not to tempt
The Master; poverty can do no more
Than his own mortifying penance does,
Hunger and thirst and obstinately starve,
When his mere wish could make the rock a spring,
And its hard fragments, bread. Yet sure I am
All are not Christ's in heart, who with their lips
Confess him; these are men, and therefore frail,
Frail and corruptible. And let none say,
Fear prompts this counsel; I disclaim all fear
But for the general cause. In every heart

Nature had built my altar; every sect,
Nation and language with one voice confess
Pleasure the sovereign good. The Stoic churl,
The dogged cynic snarling in his tub,
And all the ragged moralizing crew,
Are hypocrites; philosophy itself
Is but my votary beneath a cloak.
It harms not me, though every idol god
Were tumbled from his base; alike I scorn
Sampson's strong nerve and Daniel's flaming zeal:
And let Christ preach his mortifying rules;
Let him go forth through all the Gentile world,
And on the ruin of our fanes erect
His church triumphant o'er the gates of hell,
Still, still man's heart will draw the secret sigh
For pleasures unenjoyed; the gloomy cell
And melancholy fast, the midnight prayer,
And pale contrition weeping o'er her lamp,
Are penances from which the sense revolts,
Fines, that compounding superstition pays
For pleasures past, or bribes, for more to come.
   Satan. Enough of this vain boast,
More than enough of these voluptuous strains,
Which, though they lull the ear, disarm the soul
Of its best attribute. Not gaudy flowers
Are cull'd for med'cine, but the humble weed.
True wisdom, ever frugal of her speech,
Gives sage advice in plain and homely words.
The sum of all our reasoning ends in this,
That nothing but the death of Christ can solve
The myst'ry of his nature: till he falls,
Scarce can I say we stand. All voices then,
Though varying in the means, conspire his death;
Some cautiously as Baal; some with zeal
Precipitate as Moloch, whose swift thought
Vaults over all impediments to seize
The goal of his ambition. But, O peers,
Ours is no trivial care; direct your sight
Along the ranks of that redeemed host,

On us hangs all their safety. Night and day
My anxious thoughts are lab'ring in their cause;
And whilst Christ walks the earth, I take no rest;
A watchful spy forever at his side,
Noting each word and deed; sometimes I mix
With the selected Twelve that page his steps;
Of these, though some have waver'd, none is false
Save one alone, Iscariot he by name;
The taint of avarice hath touch'd his heart;
I've mark'd him for my own. Hear, princes, hear!
This night the priests and elders will convene
Their secret conclave: I am in their hearts.
Burning with envy, malice, and revenge,
Their only thought is how to tangle Christ,
In whom of force I own no guile is found,
But gentleness instead, and perfect truth;
A lamb in nature without spot and pure;
Fit victim therefore for their Paschal rites,
Which now are near at hand: apt is the hour,
Apt are the instruments. What now remains
But to send forth a tempter to persuade
Iscariot to betray his Master's life,
And damn himself for gold? Speak, is there one,
One in this patriot circle, whom all eyes
Point out this emprise? Most sure there is;
Belial hath well predicted of our choice:
Mammon, stand forth! on thee the election lights.

    Mammon. Prince of this world! to whom these
        armies owe,
(Lost but for thee in everlasting night)
The glorious prospect of yon rising sun,
'Tis not t'evade the labor, but prevent
The failure of your hopes, that I beseech
Your wisdom to correct its choice, and lodge
This arduous embassy in abler hands:
Nathless, if such your will, and my compeers
Adjudge me to this service, I submit.
In me is no repugnance, no delay;
For ever what these toiling hands could do,

Or patient thoughts devise, that I have done;
Whether in heav'n ordain'd to undermine
God's adamantine throne, or doom'd to dig
The solid sulphur of hell's burning soil,
Fearless I wrought, and were there no tongues else
To vouch my services, these scars would speak.
How many daintier spirits do I see
Fair as in heav'n and in fresh bloom of youth,
Whilst I, with shrivell'd sinews, cramp'd and scorch'd,
'Midst pestilential damps and fiery blasts,
Drag as you see, a miserable load,
Age-struck without the last resource of death:
This for myself: no more. You're not to learn
The snares which I employ are golden snares;
These are my arts; and like the crafty slave,
Who in Rome's circus hurls the fatal net
Over his fierce pursuer, so oft times
Have I entangled the proud hearts of men,
And made their courage stoop to shameful bribes,
Paid for dishonest deeds, perjuries and plots,
That draw them off from God, who else had fill'd
His courts ere now with guests, and peopled heav'n.
These weapons and these hands you still command;
So dear I hold the general cause at heart,
So disciplin'd am I in duty's school,
That reckless of all hazard I present
Myself your servant, or, if so fate wills,
Your sacrifice: for though from mortal man
Discomfiture I dread not; yet if Christ,
Whom the great tempter foil'd not, shall stand forth
The champion of his followers, witness for me,
You, my brave peers, and this angelic host,
I sought not this bold height, whence, if I fall,
I do but fall where Satan could not stand.
    Satan. Go then;
Go, brave adventurer, go where glory calls:
Auspicious thoughts engender in my breast,
And now prophetic visions burst upon me:
I see the traitor Judas with a band

Of midnight ruffians seize his peaceful Lord:
They drag him to the bar, accuse, condemn;
He bleeds, he dies! Darkness involves the rest.
Ascend the air, brave spirit, and midst the shout
Of grateful myriads wing thy course to fame.

EXTRACT FROM MR. PITT'S SPEECH IN THE BRIT-
ISH PARLIAMENT, MAY 13, 1777.

My Lords,

THIS is a flying moment; perhaps but six weeks
left to arrest the dangers that surround us. It is
difficult for government, after all that has passed, to
shake hands with defiers of the king, defiers of the parliament, defiers of the people. I am a defier of nobody;
but if an end is not put to this war, there is an end to
this kingdom. I do not trust my judgment in my present state of health; this is the judgment of my better
days; the result of forty years' attention to America.
They are rebels! but what are they rebels for? Surely
not for defending their unquestionable rights! What
have these rebels done heretofore! I remember when
they raised four regiments on their own bottom, and
took Louisbourg from the veteran troops of France.

But their excesses have been great! I do not mean
their panegyric; but must observe, in extenuation, the
erroneous and infatuated counsels, which have pre-
vailed. The door to mercy and justice has been shut
against them. But they may still be taken up upon
the grounds of their former submission. I state to you
the importance of America; it is a double market; a
market of consumption, and a market of supply. This
double market for millions with naval stores, you are
giving to your hereditary rival.

America has carried you through four wars, and
will now carry you to your death, if you do not take
things in time. In the sportsman's phrase, when you

have found yourselves at fault, you must try back. You have ransacked every corner of lower Saxony; but forty thousand German boors never can conquer ten times the number of British freemen. They may ravage; they cannot conquer. But you would conquer, you say! Why, what would you conquer? the map of America? I am ready to meet any general officer on the subject.

What will you do out of the protection of your fleet? In the winter, if together, they are starved; and if dispersed, they are taken off in detail. I am experienced in *spring* hopes and *vernal* promises. I know what ministers throw out; but at last will come your *equinoctial* disappointment. They tell you—what? That your army will be as strong as it was last year, when it was not strong enough. You have gained nothing in America but stations. You have been three years teaching them the art of war. They are apt scholars; and I will venture to tell your lordships, that the American gentry will make officers enough, fit to command the troops of all the European powers. What you have sent there, are too many to make peace, too few to make war.

If you conquer them, what then? You cannot make them respect you; you cannot make them wear your cloth. You will plant an invincible hatred in their breasts against you. Coming from the stock they do, they can never respect you. If ministers are founded in saying there is no sort of treaty with France, there is still a moment left; the point of honor is still safe. France must be as self-destroying as England, to make a treaty while you are giving her America, at the expense of twelve millions a year. The intercourse has produced every thing to France; and England, poor old England must pay for all.

I have at different times made different propositions, adapted to the circumstances in which they were offered. The plan contained in the former bill is now impracticable; the present motion will tell you where you are, and what you have now to depend upon. It may produce a respectable division in America, and unanimity at home. It will give America an option: she has yet made no option. You have said, Lay down your arms, and she has given you the Spartan answer, " Come and take them."

I will get out of my bed, on Monday, to move for an immediate redress of all their greivances, and for continuing to them the right of disposing of their own property. This will be the herald of peace; this will open the way for treaty; this will show that parliament is sincerely disposed. Yet still much must be left to treaty. Should you conquer this people; you conquer under the cannon of France; under a masked battery then ready to open. The moment a treaty with France appears, you must declare war, though you had only five ships of the line in England: but France will defer a treaty as long possible.

You are now at the mercy of every little German chancery; and the pretensions of France will increase daily, so as to become an avowed party in either peace or war. We have tried for unconditional submission; let us try what can be gained by unconditional redress. Less dignity will be lost in the repeal, than in submitting to the demands of German chanceries. We are the aggressors. We have invaded them. We have invaded them as much as the Spanish armada invaded England. Mercy cannot do harm; it will seat the king where he ought to be, throned on the hearts of the people; and millions at home and abroad, now employed in obloquy or revolt, would then pray for him.

ON THE DAY OF JUDGMENT.

AT midnight, when mankind are wrapp'd in peace,
　And worldly fancy feeds on golden dreams;
To give more dread to man's most dreadful hour;
At midnight, 'tis presum'd, this pomp will burst
From tenfold darkness; sudden as the spark
From smitten steel; from nitrous grain the blaze.
Man, starting from his couch, shall sleep no more!
The day is broke, which never more shall close!
Above, around, beneath, amazement all!
Terror and glory join'd in their extremes!
Our God in grandeur, and our world on fire!
All nature struggling in the pangs of death!
Dost thou not hear her? Dost thou not deplore
Her strong convulsions, and her final groan?
Where are we now? Ah me! the ground is gone,
On which we stood, LORENZO! while thou mayst,
Provide more firm support, or sink forever!
Where? how? from whence? vain hope! It is too late!
Where, *where*, for shelter, shall the *guilty* fly,
When consternation turns the good man pale?
　Great day! for which all other days were made;
For which earth rose from chaos, man from earth;
And an eternity, the date of gods,
Descended on poor earth-created man!
Great day of dread, decision, and despair!
At thought of thee, each sublunary wish
Lets go its eager grasp, and drops the world;
And catches at each reed of hope in heav'n.
At *thought* of thee! And art thou *absent* then,
LORENZO! no; 'tis here; it is begun;
Already is begun the grand assize,
In thee, in all. Deputed conscience scales
The dread tribunal, and forestals our doom:
Forestals; and by forestalling, proves it sure.
Why on himself should man *void* judgment pass?
T

Is idle nature laughing at her sons?
Who *conscience* sent, her sentence will support,
And God above assert *that* God in man?
   Thrice happy they, who enter now the court
Heav'n opens in their bosoms: but how rare!
Ah me! that magnanimity how rare!
What hero-like the man who stands himself;
Who dares to meet his naked heart alone;
Who hears, intrepid, the full charge it brings,
Resolv'd to silence future murmurs there?
The coward flies; and flying is undone.
(Art thou a coward? No.) The coward flies;
Thinks, but thinks slightly; asks, but fears to *know;*
Asks " What is truth?" with Pilate; and retires;
Dissolves the court, and mingles with the throng;
Asylum sad! from reason, hope, and heav'n!
   Shall all, but man, look out with ardent eye,
For that great day, which was ordain'd *for* man?
O day of consummation! Mark supreme
(If men are wise) of human thought! nor least,
Or in the sight of angels, or their King!
Angels, whose radiant circles, height o'er height,
Order o'er order rising, blaze o'er blaze,
As in a theatre, surround this scene,
Intent on man, and anxious for his fate:
Angels look out for thee; for thee, their Lord,
To vindicate his glory; and for thee,
Creation universal calls aloud,
To disinvolve the moral world, and give
To Nature's renovation brighter charms.

THE DISSIPATED OXFORD STUDENT; A DIALOGUE
BETWEEN A BROTHER, AND HIS TWO SISTERS.

LIONEL, LAVINIA, *and* CAMILLA.

Lionel. HOW do you do, girls, how do you do? I
am glad to see you, upon my soul I am.
[*Shaking them hard by the hand.*

Lavinia. I thought, brother, you had been at Dr.
Marchmont's!

Lion. All in good time, my dear; I shall certainly
visit the old gentleman before long.

Lav. Gracious, Lionel!—If my mother——

Lion. My dear little Lavinia, [*Chucking her under
the chin*] I have a mighty notion of making visits at
my own time and appointment, instead of my mamma's.

Lav. O Lionel! and can you just now——

Lion. Come, come, don't let us waste our precious
moments in this fulsome moralizing. If I had not
luckily been hard by, I should not have known the
coast was clear. Pray where are the old folks gone
tantivying.

Camilla. To Cleves.

Lion. To Cleves! What a happy escape! I was upon the point of going thither myself. Camilla, what is
the matter with thee, my little duck?

Cam. Nothing—I am only thinking—Pray when
do you go to Oxford?

Lion. Poh, poh, what do you talk of Oxford for?
you have grown quite stupid, girl. I believe you have
lived too long with that old maid of a Margland. Pray
how does that dear creature do? I am afraid she will
grow melancholy from not seeing me so long. Is she
as pretty as she used to be? I have some notion of
sending her a suitor.

Lav. O brother, is it possible you can have such
spirits?

Lion. O hang it; if one is not merry when one can, what is the world good for? Besides, I do assure you, I fretted so consumedly hard at first, that for the life of me I can fret no longer.

Cam. But why are you not at Dr. Marchmont's?

Lion. Because, my dear soul, you can't conceive how much pleasure these old doctors take in lecturing a youngster who is in any disgrace.

Cam. Disgrace!

Lav. At all events, I beseech you to be a little careful; I would not have my poor mother find you here for the world.

Lion. O, as to that, I defy her to desire the meeting less than I do. But come, let us talk of something else. How go on the classics? Is my old friend, Dr. Orkborne, as chatty and amusing as ever?

Cam. My dear Lionel, I am filled with apprehension and perplexity. Why should my mother wish not to see you? And why—and how is it possible you can wish not to see her?

Lion. What, don't you know it all?

Cam. I only know that something is wrong; but how, what, or which way, I have not heard.

Lion. Has not Lavinia told you, then?

Lav. No; I could be in no haste to give her so much pain.

Lion. You are a good girl enough. But how came you here, Camilla? and what is the reason you have not seen my mother yourself?

Cam. Not seen her! I have been with her this half hour.

Lion. What! and in all that time did she not tell you?

Cam. She did not name you.

Lion. Is it possible? Well, she is a noble creature, I must confess. I wonder how she could ever have such a son. And I am still less like my father than I am like her. I believe in my conscience, I was changed in the cradle. Will you own me, young ladies, if some villanous attorney or exciseman should claim me by and by?

Cam. Dear Lionel, do explain to me what has happened. You talk so wildly, that you make me think it important and trifling twenty times in a minute.

Lion. O, a horrid business! Lavinia must tell you. I'll withdraw till she has done. Don't despise me, Camilla. I am confounded sorry, I assure you. [*Going; and then immediately returning.*] Come, upon the whole, I had better tell it to you myself: for she'll make such a dismal ditty of it, that it won't be over this half year. The sooner we have done with it, the better. It will only put you out of spirits. You must know I was in rather a bad scrape at Oxford last year——

Cam. Last year! and you never told us of it before!

Lion. O, 'twas about something you would not understand; so I shall not mention particulars now. It is enough for you to know, that two or three of us wanted a little cash! Well, so——in short, I sent a letter—somewhat of a threatening sort—to old uncle Relvil; and—

Cam. O Lionel!

Lion. O, I did not sign it. It was only begging a little money, which he can afford to spare very well; and just telling him, if he did not send it to a certain place which I mentioned, he would have his brains blown out.

Cam. How horrible!

Lion. Poh, poh; he had only to send the money, you know, and then his brains might keep their place. Besides, you can't suppose there was gunpowder in the words; though, to be sure, the letter was charged with a few volleys of oaths. But, would you believe it! the poor old gull was fool enough actually to send the money where it was directed.

Lav. Hold, hold, Lionel! I cannot endure to hear you speak in such disgraceful terms of that worthy man. How could you treat that excellent uncle in such a cruel manner! How could you find a heart to swear at so meek, so benevolent, so indulgent——

Lion. My dear little chicken, don't be so precise and old maidish. Don't you know it is a relief to a man's mind to swear a few cutting oaths now and then, when he's in a passion? when all the time he would no more do harm to the people he swears at, than you would, who mince out all your words as if you were talking treason, and thought every man a spy that heard you. It is very innocent refreshment to a man's mind, my dear. But the difficulty is, you know nothing of the world.

Cam. Fie, brother! You know how sickly our uncle has always been, and how easily he might be alarmed.

Lion. Why, yes, Camilla; I really think it was a very wicked trick; and I would give half my little finger that I had not done it. But it's over now, you know; so what signifies making the worst of it?

Cam. And did he not discover you?

Lion. No; I gave him particular orders in my letter not to attempt any thing of that sort; assuring him there were spies about him to watch his proceedings. The good old simpleton took it all for gospel. So there the matter ended. However, as ill luck would have it, about three months ago we wanted another sum——

Lav. And could you again——

Lion. Why, my dear, it was only taking a little of my own fortune beforehand, for I am his heir; so we all agreed it was merely robbing myself; for we had several consultations about it; and one of us is to be a lawyer.

Cam. But you give me some pleasure here; for I had never heard that my uncle had made you his heir.

Lion. Neither had I, my deary; but I take it for granted. Besides, our little lawyer put it into my head. Well, we wrote again, and told the poor old soul, for which I assure you I am heartily penitent, that if he did not send me double the sum, in the same manner, without delay, his house was to be set on fire,

while he and all his family were in bed and asleep.
Now don't make faces and shruggings; for I promise
you, I think already I deserve to be hung for giving
him the fright; though I would not really hurt the
hair of his head for half his fortune. But who could
have guessed that the old codger would have *bitten*
so readily? The money, however, came; and we
thought the business all secure, and agreed to get
the same sum annually.

Cam. Annually! O horrible!

Lion. Yes, my darling. You have no conception
how convenient it would have been for our extra ex-
penses. But unluckily uncle grew worse, and went
abroad; and then consulted with some crab of a friend,
and that friend, with some demagogue of a magistrate,
and so all is now blown. However, we have managed
it so cleverly, that it cost them nearly three months to
find it out; owing, I must confess, to poor uncle's
cowardice, in not making his inquiries before the
money was carried off, and he himself beyond the
sea. The other particulars Lavinia must give you;
for I have talked of it now till I have made myself
quite sick. Do tell me some diverting story to drive
it a little out of my head. But, by the way, pray
what has carried the old folks to Cleves? Have they
gone to tell this sad tale to uncle Hugh, so that I
might lose him too?

Lav. No; your afflicted parents are determined not
to name it. They are striving that nobody else shall
know any thing of the matter except Dr. Marchmont.

Lion. Well, they are good souls, it must be acknowledged. I wish I deserved them better. I wish too it
was not such plaguy dull business to be good. I confess, girls, it wounds my conscience to think how I
have afflicted my parents, especially my poor mother,
who is not so well able to bear it. But when one is at
Oxford, or in London—your merry blades there, I
can't deny it, my dear sisters, your merry blades there,
are but sad fellows. Yet there is such fun, such spirit.

such genuine sport among them, I cannot, for my life, keep out of the way. Besides, you have no conception, young ladies, what a by-word you soon become among them, if they find you *flinching*. But this is little to the purpose; for you know nothing of life yet, poor things.

Lav. I would not for the world say any thing to pain you, my dear brother; but if this is what you call life, I wish we never might know any thing of it. I wish more, that you had been so happy as never to have known it. You pity our ignorance—we pity your folly. How strangely infatuated you are! But yet I will hope, that, in future, your first study will be to resist such dangerous examples, and to shun such unworthy friends. Pray reflect one moment on the distressing situation of your dear parents, who cannot endure your presence, through the poignancy of grief! What labours and hardships has your poor father encountered, to gain wherewithal to support you at the University! And what is your return! Such, my dear brother, as will soon bring down his gray hairs with sorrow to the grave. As for your poor mother, it is quite uncertain whether any of us ever see her again, as your injured uncle has sent for her over sea to attend him in his sickness; and to-morrow she sets out. She has left it in solemn charge with me, to deliver you a message from her, which, if you have any sensibility remaining, will cut you to the heart.

Lion. I know she can have said nothing worse than I expect, or than I merit. Probe me, then, Lavina, without delay. Keep me not in a moment's suspense. I feel a load of guilt upon me, and begin sincerely to repent. She is acting towards me like an angel; and if she were to command me to turn hermit, I know I ought to obey her.

Lav. Well, then, my mother says, my dear Lionel, that the fraud you have practised——

Lion. The fraud! what a horrid word! Why it was a mere trick! a joke! a frolic! just to make an old hunks open his purse-strings to his natural heir. I am astonished at my mother! I really don't care whether I hear another syllable.

Lav. Well, then, my dear Lionel, I will wait till you are calmer: my mother, I am sure, did not mean to irritate but to convince.

Lion. [*Striding about the room.*] My mother makes no allowances. She has no faults herself, and for that reason she thinks nobody else should have any. Besides, how should she know what it is to be a young man? and to want a little cash, and not to know how to get it?

Lav. But I am sure, if you wanted it for any proper purpose, my father would have denied himself every thing, in order to supply you.

Lion. Yes, yes; but suppose I want it for a purpose that is *not* proper, how am I to get it then?

Cam. Why, then, my dear Lionel, surely you must be sensible you ought to go without it.

Lion. Ay, that's as you girls say; who know nothing of the matter. If a young man, when he goes into the world, were to make such a speech as that, he would be pointed at. Besides, whom must he live with? You don't suppose he is to shut himself up, with a few musty books, sleeping over the fire, under pretence of study, all day long, do you? like young Melmond, who knows no more of the world than either of you?

Cam. Indeed, he seems to me an amiable and modest young man, though very romantic.

Lion. O, I dare say he does! I could have laid any wager of that. He's just a girl's man, just the very thing, all sentiment, and poetry, and heroics. But we, my little dear, we lads of spirit, hold all that amazingly cheap. I assure you, I would as soon be seen trying on a lady's cap at a glass, as poring over a crazy old author. I warrant you think, because one is at the University, one must be a book-worm!

Lav. Why, what else do you go there for but to study?

Lion. Every thing else in the world, my dear.

Cam. But are there not sometimes young men who are scholars without being book-worms? Is not Edgar Mandlebert such a one?

Lion. O yes, yes; an odd thing of that sort happens now and then. Mandlebert has spirit enough to carry it off pretty well, without being ridiculous; though he is as deep, for his time, as e'er an old fellow of a college. But then this is no rule for others. You must not expect an Edgar Mandlebert at every turn, my dear innocent creatures.

Lav. But Edgar has had an extraordinary education, as well as possessing extraordinary talents and goodness; you too, my dear Lionel, to fulfil what may be expected from you, should look back to your father, who was brought up at the same University, and is now considered as one of the first men it has produced. While he was respected by the learned for his application, he was loved even by the indolent for his candour and kindness of heart. And though his income, as you know, was very small, he never ran in debt; and by an exact but open economy, escaped all imputation of meanness.

Lion. Yes; but all this is nothing to the purpose. My father is no more like other men than if he had been born in another planet; and my attempting to resemble him would be as great a joke, as if you were to dress up in Indiana's flowers and feathers, and expect people to call you a beauty. I was born a bit of a buck; and have no manner of natural taste for study and poring, and expounding, and black-letter work. I am a light, airy spark, at your service, ladies; not quite so wise as I am merry. I am one of your eccentric geniuses; but let that pass. My father, you know, is firm as a rock. He minds neither wind nor weather, nor fleerer nor sneerer, nor joker nor jeerer; but his firmness he has kept all to himself; not a whit of it do I inherit. Every wind that blows veers me about, and gives me a new direction. But with all my father's firmness and knowledge, I very much doubt whether he knows any thing of real life. That is the main thing, my dear hearts. But, come, Lavinia, finish your message.

Lav. My mother says, the fraud you have practised, whether from wanton folly to give pain, or from rapacious discontent to get money, she will leave without comment; satisfied that if you have any feeling at all, its effects must bring remorse; since it has dangerously increased the infirmities of your uncle, driven him to a foreign land, and forced your mother to forsake her home and family in his pursuit, unless she were willing to see you punished by the entire disinheritance with which you are threatened. But——

Lion. O, no more! no more! I am ready to shoot myself already! My dear, excellent mother, what do I not owe you! I had never seen, never thought of the business in this solemn way before. I meant nothing at first but a silly joke; and all this mischief has followed unaccountably. I assure you, I had no notion at the beginning, he would have minded the letter; and afterwards, Jack Whiston persuaded me, that the money was as good as my own, and that it was nothing but a little cribbing from myself. I will never trust him again! I see the whole now, in its true and atrocious colours. I will devote all the means in my power to make amends to my dear incomparable mother. But proceed, Lavinia.

Lav. But since you are permitted, said my mother, to return home, by the forgiving temper of your father, who is himself, during the vacation, to be your tutor after he is sufficiently composed to admit you into his presence, you can repay his goodness only by the most intense application to those studies which you have, hitherto neglected, and of which your neglect has been the cause of your errors. She charges you also to ask yourself, upon what pretext you can justify the wasting of his valuable time, however little you may regard your own. Finally——

Lion. I never wasted his time! I never desired to have any instruction in the vacations. 'Tis the most deuced thing in life to be studying so incessantly. The waste of time is all his own affair, his own choice, not mine. Go on, however, and open the whole of the budget.

Lav. Finally, she adjures you to consider, that if you still persevere to consume your time in wilful negligence, to bury all thought in idle gaiety, and to act without either reflection or principle, the career of faults which begins but in unthinking folly, will terminate in shame, in guilt and in ruin! And though such a declension of all good must involve your family in your affliction, your disgrace will ultimately fall but where it ought; since your own want of personal sensibility will neither harden nor blind any human being beside yourself. This is all.

Lion. And enough too. I am a very wretch! I believe that, though I am sure I can't tell how I came so; for I never intend any harm, never think, never dream of hurting any mortal! But as to study, I must own to you, I hate it most deucedly. Any thing else; if my mother had but exacted any thing else, with what joy I would have shown my obedience! If she had ordered me to be horse-ponded, I do protest to you, I would not have demurred.

Cam. How you always run into the ridiculous!

Lion. I was never so serious in my life; not that I should like to be horse-ponded in the least, though I would submit to it by way of punishment, and out of duty: but then when it was done, it would be over. Now the deuce of study is, there is no end to it! And it does so little for one! one can go through life so well without it! there is but here and there an old codger who asks one question that can bring it into any play. And then, a turn upon one's heel, or looking at one's watch, or wondering at one's short memory, or happening to forget just that one single passage, carries off the whole in two minutes, as completely as if one had been working one's whole life to get ready for the assault. And pray now tell me, how can it be worth one's best days, one's gayest hours, the very flower of one's life, all to be sacrificed to plodding over musty grammars and lexicons, merely to cut a figure just for about two minutes, once or twice in a year?

Cam. Indeed, Lionel, you appear to me a striking example of what a hard thing it is to learn to do well, after one has been accustomed to do evil. How volatile! how totally void of all stability! One minute you exhibit appearances of repentance and reformation, and the next minute, all fair prospects vanish. How I lament that you were so early exposed to a vitious world, before you had gained sufficient strength of mind to withstand bad examples?

Lion. Forbear, Camilla. You hurt me too much. You excite those severe twinges of remorse, which I am obliged to own, I have never been wholly free from, since I joined my merry companions, and began to learn the world. Notwithstanding my gaiety, and my apparent contentment, I confess there is something within, which constantly admonishes me of my errors, and makes me feel unhappy: so that, if it were not for *fashion's* sake, I can truly say, I could wish I were in your recluse situation; here to remain, in my once pleasant abode, and never more mingle with the world.

Lav. Dear brother, I cannot leave you, without once more calling your attention to your parents, your family and your friends. Think of their present situation. If you have no regard for your own character, your present, or future happiness, I entreat you to have some pity for them. Let not the tyrant fashion bring you into abject slavery. Pardon me when I tell you, your pretended friends are your worst enemies. They have led you into a path which will carry you directly to inevitable ruin, unless you immediately forsake it. That knowledge of the world, of which you so vainly

U

boast, is infinitely worse than the ignorance which you so much despise. Believe me, my dear brother, it is a knowledge, which, by your own confession, never has produced you any happiness, nor will it ever; but will guide you to wretchedness and misery.

Lion. My dear sisters, I am convinced. Your words have pierced my very soul. I am now wretched, and I deserve to be so. I am determined from this moment to begin my reformation, and, with the assistance of Heaven, to complete it. Never more will I see my vile companions, who have enticed me to go such lengths in wickedness. What do I not owe to my amiable sisters for their friendly and seasonable advice! I will go directly to my father, and, like the prodigal son, fall on my knees before him, beg his forgiveness, and put myself entirely under his direction and instruction; and, so long as I live, I never will offend him again.

Lav. May heaven assist you in keeping your resolution!

----◆----

EXTRACT FROM A SPEECH IN CONGRESS, APRIL, 1796, ON THE SUBJECT OF THE TREATY WITH GREAT BRITAIN.

IF any, against all these proofs which have been offered, should maintain that the peace with the Indians will be stable without the Western Posts, to them I will urge another reply. From arguments calculated to produce conviction, I will appeal directly to the hearts of those who hear me, and ask whether it is not already planted there! I resort especially to the convictions of the Western gentlemen, whether, supposing no Posts and no Treaty, the settlers will remain in security? Can they take it upon them to say, that an Indian peace, under these circumstances, will prove firm? No, Sir, it will not be peace, but a sword; it will be no better than a lure to draw victims within the reach of the tomahawk.

On this theme, my emotions are unutterable. If I could find words for them, if my powers bore any proportion to my zeal, I would swell my voice to such a note of remonstrance, it should reach every log house beyond the mountains. I would say to the inhabitants, Wake from your false security! Your cruel dangers, your more cruel apprehensions are soon to be renewed. The wounds, yet unhealed, are to be torn open again. In the day time, your path through the woods will be ambushed. The darkness of midnight will glitter with the blaze of your dwellings. You are a father; the blood of your sons shall fatten your cornfield. You are a mother; the war-whoop shall wake the sleep of the cradle.

On this subject you need not suspect any deception on your feelings. It is a spectacle of horror which cannot be overdrawn. If you have nature in your hearts, they will speak a language compared with which, all I have said or can say, will be poor and frigid. Will it be whispered that the treaty has made me a new champion for the protection of the frontiers? It is known that my voice as well as vote have been uniformly given in conformity with the ideas I have expressed. Protection is the right of the frontiers; it is our duty to give it.

Who will accuse me of wandering out of the subject? Who will say that I exaggerate the tendencies of our measures? Will any one answer by a sneer, that all this is idle preaching? Will any one deny that we are bound, and I would hope to good purpose, by the most solemn sanctions of duty for the vote we give? Are despots alone to be reproached for unfeeling indifference to the tears and blood of their subjects? Are republicans unresponsible? Have the principles on which you ground the reproach upon cabinets and kings no practical influence, no binding force? Are they merely themes of idle declamation, introduced to decorate the morality of a newspaper essay, or to furnish pretty topics of harangue from the windows of that Statehouse?

I trust it is neither too presumptuous nor too late to ask, Can you put the dearest interests of society at risk, without guilt, and without remorse?

By rejecting the posts, we light the savage fires; we bind the victims. This day we undertake to render account to the widows and orphans whom our decision will make, to the wretches that will be roasted at the stake, to our country, and I do not deem it too serious to say, to conscience, and to God. We are answerable; and if duty be any thing more than a word of imposture; if conscience be not a bugbear, we are preparing to make ourselves as wretched as our country.

There is no mistake in this case; there can be none. Experience has already been the prophet of events, and the cries of our future victims have already reached us. The Western inhabitants are not a silent and uncomplaining sacrifice. The voice of humanity issues from the shade of the wilderness. It exclaims, that while one hand is held up to reject this treaty, the other grasps a tomahawk. It summons our imagination to the scenes that will open. It is no great effort of the imagination to conceive that events so near are already begun. I can fancy that I listen to the yells of savage vengeance and the shrieks of torture. Already they seem to sigh in the western wind; already they mingle with every echo from the mountains.

Let me cheer the mind, weary, no doubt, and ready to despond on this prospect, by presenting another, which is yet in our power to realize, Is it possible for a real American to look at the prosperity of this country without some desire for its continuance, without some respect for the measures, which, many will say, produced and all will confess, have preserved it? Will he not feel some dread that a change of system will reverse the scene? The well grounded fears of our citizens, in 1794, were removed by the treaty, but are not forgotten. Then they deemed war nearly inevitable; and would not this adjustment have been considered at that day as a happy escape from the calamity?

The great interest and the general desire of our people was to enjoy the advantages of neutrality. This instrument, however misrepresented, affords America that inestimable security. The causes of our disputes are either cut up by the roots, or referred to a new negotiation, after the end of the European war. This was gaining every thing, because it confirmed our neutrality, by which our citizens are gaining every thing. This alone would justify the engagements of the government. For, when the fiery vapors of the war lowered in the skirts of our horizon, all our wishes were concentered in this one, that we might escape the desolation of the storm. This treaty, like a rainbow on the edge of the cloud, marked to our eyes the space where it was raging, and afforded at the same time the sure prognostic of fair weather. If we reject it, the vivid colours will grow pale; it will be a baleful meteor portending tempest and war.

Let us not hesitate then to agree to the appropriation to carry it into faithful execution. Thus we shall save the faith of our nation, secure its peace, and diffuse the spirit of confidence and enterprise that will augment its prosperity. The progress of wealth and improvement is wonderful, and, some will think, too rapid. The field for exertion is fruitful and vast; and if peace and good government should be preserved, the acquisitions of our citizens are not so pleasing as the proofs of their industry, as the instruments of their future success. The rewards of exertion go to augment its power. Profit is every hour becoming capital. The vast crop of our neutrality is all seed wheat, and is sown again, to swell, almost beyond calculation, the future harvest of prosperity. And in this progress, what seems to be fiction is found to fall short of experience.

U 2

EXTRACT FROM AN ORATION, PRONOUNCED AT
WORCESTER, (MASS.) JULY 4, 1796; BY FRANCIS
BLAKE, ESQ.

IN viewing the causes which led to the event of this
joyous anniversary; in tracing the effects which
have resulted to America; in searching for the principles which impelled to the contest; in recalling the
feelings which supported us in the struggle, it cannot
fail to occur to us that the causes have not been confined to the limits of our continent; that the effects
have extended far beyond the boundaries of our nation; that the glorious example with electrical rapidity, has flashed across the Atlantic; that, guided by the
same principles, conducted by the same feelings, the
people, who so gallantly fought and bled for the security of our lives and our liberties, are now fighting
and bleeding in defence of their own.

On this day, therefore, religiously devoted to the
consecration of our independence, it becomes us, as the
votaries of freedom, as friends to the rights of man,
and bound to support them whenever invaded, to turn
our attention, with a grateful enthusiasm, to the
scenes of their sufferings, their revolt, and their victories. While exulting in the full enjoyment of peace
and tranquillity, shall not a tear for the unexampled
distresses of this magnanimous nation, check, for a
moment, the emotions of our joy?

They have sworn that they will live FREE or DIE!
They have solemnly sworn, that the sword, which has
been drawn in defence of their country, shall never be
returned to its scabbard, till it has secured to them victory and freedom. Let us then breathe forth a fervent
ejaculation to Heaven, that their vows may be remembered; that the cause of our former allies may not be

deserted, till they have scourged their invaders, till they have driven them back in confusion to the regions of terror, from whence they emerged.

While we remember with horror the continued effusion of blood, which darkened the morning of their revolution, let us not forget that their vengeance was roused by the champions of despotism, whose lives have since justly atoned for the crimes they committed. While we lament the sanguinary scenes, which clouded its progress, let it not be forgotten that they arose from the bloody manifesto of a band of tyrants, combined for the hellish purpose of again riveting the chains they had broken.

The league of Pilnitz, like the league of Satan and his angels, revolting against the Majesty of heaven, was professedly fabricated, to arrest forever the progress of freedom; to usurp the dominion of France, and divide the spoil among this band of royal plunderers. Have we not heard that the noble, the generous, the grateful monarch of the forest, that fawned at the feet of Androcles, when remembering his former friendship, will ever turn with fury on his pursuers; and when robbed of his whelps, rests not till his fangs are crimsoned in the blood of the aggressor?

Shall then the fervor of our friendship be abated, by remembering the transitory frenzy of a people distracted with the enthusiasm of freedom and irritated to madness by the dreadful prospect of losing what they had enjoyed but for a moment? Let it never be said of us, as of Rome and of Athens, that ingratitude is the common vice of republics. Was it to the crowned monarch, named Louis the Sixteenth, or to the people of France, that we were indebted, for the blood and treasure that were so profusely lavished in our cause? Shall then their services be forgotten, in the remembrance of their momentary excesses? or shall we refuse our most cordial concurrence in the feelings which impel them to the present contest with the ruffian potentates of Europe?

Can we doubt, for a moment, which is the cause we are bound to support with our sanction, when we behold the winds and the seas, those dreadful ministers of Heaven's vengeance, commissioned to advance their progress, and deluge their enemies? When we behold Ariel, with his attendant spirits, gently hovering over their navies, and wafting them to victory on the bosom of the ocean; while Neptune and Boreas have combined against the league of their oppressors, to overwhelm in the deep these deluded followers of Pharaoh! Have we not seen them fed, as with manna from heaven; the waters divided, and the walls of Jericho falling before them, while the fair prospect of liberty has led them in triumph through the wilderness, as a cloud by day, and a pillar of fire by night!

AMERICANS! Let us join in a fervent supplication, that the sacred charters of humanity, which we have once sealed with our blood, may be forever preserved from the deadly grasp of tyrants.

FRENCHMEN! Be firm; be undaunted in the struggle you have thus miraculously supported. Evince to the world, now gazing with admiration at your exploits in the field of battle, that you have virtue equal to your courage; that you are friends to the friends of humanity; that your arms are nerved only against the enemies of man. Let not the sacred name of LIBERTY be polluted by the frenzy of licentious passions; but may your present glorious constitution, while it protects your freedom from the unhallowed ravages of tyranny, remain an unshaken bulwark against the destructive fury of faction.

TYRANTS! Turn from the impious work of blood in which your hands are imbrued, and tremble at the desperation of your revolting subjects! Repent in sackcloth and ashes. For behold, ye, who have been exalted up to heaven, shall, ere long, be cast down to hell! The final period of your crimes is rapidly approaching. The grand POLITICAL MILLENNIUM is at hand;

when tyranny shall be buried in ruins; when all nations shall be united in ONE MIGHTY REPUBLIC! when the four angels, that stand on the four corners of the globe, shall, with one accord, lift up their voices to heaven; proclaiming PEACE ON EARTH, AND GOOD WILL TO ALL MEN.

GENERAL DESCRIPTION OF AMERICA.

EXTRACT FROM A POEM SPOKEN AT DARTMOUTH COLLEGE, ON COMMENCEMENT DAY, 1795.

FROM Patagonia's snow invested wilds,
  To Darien, where constant verdure smiles,
The Andes meet the morning's earliest ray,
O'erlook the clouds and check the flood of Day.
In copious torrents from their eastern side,
Flow the vast streams of Amazonia's tide,
Roll on majestic through her boundless plain,
And swell the surface of the neighbouring main.
Nor Plata less a broad, deep channel fills;
Danube and Wolga by his side were rills.
But leave, my muse, this wide extended clime,
By nature stamp'd with all she owns sublime.
Here she has wrought upon her largest plan,
But mourns in solitude the wrongs of man.
Here Guatemozin writh'd in flames of fire,
And slaughter'd millions round their prince expire.
Rise, sleeping vengeance! vindicate their cause;
And thou, stern justice, execute thy laws:
Ye Andes, strike Hesperian fraud with dread,
Burst thy volcanoes on the guilty head!
  Where Cancer's sun pours down his ardent blaze,
Draws the Monsoons, and lengthens out his days,
The spacious gulf of Mexic' rolls his tide,
And thronging fleets of various nations ride.
The fertile isles their rich luxuriance pour,
And western dainties crown the eastern shore.

But weep, humanity, the black disgrace,
And spread thy blushes o'er oppression's face!
Ye sons of mirth, your bowls, your richest food,
Is mingled with fraternal tears and blood.
Still groans the slave beneath his master's rod,
But nature, wrong'd, appeals to nature's GOD.
The sun frowns angry at th' inhuman sight;
The stars, offended, redden in the night:
In western skies, drear horror gathers round,
And waking vengeance murmurs under ground;
O'er all the gulf the dark'ning vapors rise,
And the black clouds sail awful round the skies.
From heaven to earth swift thunder-bolts are hurl'd,
And storm's dread demon shakes th' astonish'd world.
The rich plantation lies a barren waste,
And all the works of slavery are defac'd.
Ye tyrants, own the devastation just;
'Tis for your wrongs the fertile earth is curs'd.
    Columbia's States unfold their milder scenes,
And freedom's realms afford more pleasing themes.
From Georgia's plains, to Hudson's highest source,
The northern Andes range their varied course:
Rank above rank, they swell their growing size,
Rear their blue arches, and invade the skies.
Here spreads a forest; there a city shines;
Here swell the hills, and there a vale declines.
Here, through the meads, meand'ring rivers run;
There placid lakes reflect the full orb'd sun.
From mountain sides perennial fountains flow,
And streams majestic bend their course below.
Here rise the groves; there opes the fertile lawn,
Fresh fragrance breathes, and Ceres waves her corn.
Along the east, where the proud billows roar,
Capacious harbours grace the winding shore:
The nation's splendor and the merchant's pride
Wafts with each gale, and floats with ev'ry tide.
From Iroquois to vast Superior's strand,
Spread the wide lakes and insulate the land.

Here growing commerce shall unfold her sail,
Load the rich bark, and woo the inland gale.
Far to the west, where savage hordes reside, ⎫
Smooth Mississippi rolls his copious tide, ⎬
And fair Ohio weds his silver side. ⎭

  Hail, happy States! thine is the blissful seat,
Where nature's gifts and art's improvements meet.
Thy temp'rate air breathes health; thy fertile soil,
In copious plenty pays the labourer's toil.
Ask not for mountains of Peruvian ore,
Nor court the dust that shines on Afric' shore.
The plough explores for thee the richest mine;
Than autumn's fruit, no goodlier ore can shine.
O'er the wide plain and through the op'ning glade,
Flows the canal obsequious to the spade.
Commerce to wealth and knowledge turns the key,
Floats o'er the land and sails to ev'ry sea.
Thrice happy art! be thy white sail unfurl'd,
Not to corrupt, but socialize the world.

  The muse prophetic views the coming day,
When federal laws beyond the line shall sway.
Where Spanish indolence inactive lies.
And ev'ry art and ev'ry virtue dies;
Where pride and avarice their empire hold,
Ignobly great, and poor amid their gold,
Columbia's genius shall the mind inspire,
And fill each breast with patriotic fire.
Nor east nor western oceans shall confine
The gen'rous flame that dignifies the mind;
O'er all the earth shall freedom's banner wave,
The tyrant blast, and liberate the slave.
Plenty and peace shall spread from pole to pole,
Till earth's grand family possess one soul.

DIALOGUE BETWEEN A MASTER AND SLAVE.

Master. NOW, villian! what have you to say for this second attempt to run away? Is there any punishment that you do not deserve?

Slave. I well know that nothing I can say will avail. I submit to my fate.

Mast. But are you not a base fellow, a hardened and ungrateful rascal?

Slave. I am a slave. That is answer enough.

Mast. I am not content with that answer. I thought I discerned in you some tokens of a mind superior to your condition. I treated you accordingly. You have been comfortably fed and lodged, not overworked, and attended with the most humane care when you were sick. And is this the return?

Slave. Since you condescend to talk with me, as man to man, I will reply. What have you done, what can you do for me, that will compensate for the liberty which you have taken away?

Mast. I did not take it away. You were a slave when I fairly purchased you.

Slave. Did I give my consent to the purchase?

Mast. You had no consent to give. You had already lost the right of disposing of yourself.

Slave. I had lost the power, but how the right? I was treacherously kidnapped in my own country, when following an honest occupation. I was put in chains, sold to one of your countrymen, carried by force on board his ship, brought hither, and exposed to sale like a beast in the market, where you bought me. What step in all this progress of violence and injustice can give a *right?* Was it in the villain who stole me, in the slave-merchant who tempted him to do so, or in you who encouraged the slave-merchant to bring his cargo of human cattle to cultivate your lands?

Mast. It is in the order of Providence that one man should become subservient to another. It ever has been so, and ever will be. I found the custom, and did not make it.

Slave. You cannot but be sensible, that the robber who puts a pistol to your breast may make just the same plea. Providence gives him a power over your life and property; it gave my enemies a power over my liberty. But it has also given me legs to escape with; and what should prevent me from using them? Nay, what should restrain me from retaliating the wrongs I have suffered, if a favourable occasion should offer?

Mast. Gratitude! I repeat, gratitude! Have I not endeavoured ever since I possessed you to alleviate your misfortunes by kind treatment? and does that confer no obligation? Consider how much worse your condition might have been under another master.

Slave. You have done nothing for me more than for your working cattle. Are they not well fed and tended? Do you work them harder than your slaves? Is not the rule of treating both designed only for your own advantage? You treat both your men and beast slaves better than some of your neighbours, because you are more prudent and wealthy than they.

Mast. You might add, more humane too.

Slave. Humane! Does it deserve that appellation to keep your fellow men in forced subjection, deprived of all exercise of their free will, liable to all the injuries that your own caprice, or the brutality of your overseers, may heap on them, and devoted, soul and body, only to your pleasure and emolument? Can gratitude take place between creatures in such a state, and the tyrant who holds them in it? Look at these limbs; are they not those of a man? Think that I have the spirit of a man too.

Mast. But it was my intention not only to make your life tolerably comfortable at present, but to provide for you in your old age.

X

Slave. Alas! is a life like mine, torn from country, friends, and all I held dear, and compelled to toil under the burning sun for a master, worth thinking about for old age? No; the sooner it ends, the sooner I shall obtain that relief for which my soul pants.

Mast. Is it impossible, then, to hold you by any ties but those of constraint and severity?

Slave. It is impossible to make one, who has felt the value of freedom, acquiesce in being a slave.

Mast. Suppose I were to restore you to your liberty, would you reckon that a favour?

Slave. The greatest; for although it would only be undoing a wrong, I know too well how few among mankind are capable of sacrificing interest to justice, not to prize the exertion when it is made.

Mast. I do it, then; be free.

Slave. Now I am indeed your servant, though not your slave. And as the first return I can make for your kindness, I will tell you freely the condition in which you live. You are surrounded with implacable foes, who long for a safe opportunity to revenge upon you and the other planters all the miseries they have endured. The more generous their natures, the more indignant they feel against that cruel injustice which has dragged them hither, and doomed them to perpetual servitude. You can rely on no kindness on your part, to soften the obduracy of their resentment. You have reduced them to the state of brute beasts; and if they have not the stupidity of beasts of burden, they must have the ferocity of beasts of prey. Superior force alone can give you security. As soon as that fails, you are at the mercy of the merciless. Such is the social bond between master and slave!

Part of Mr. O'Connor's Speech in the Irish House of Commons, in Favour of the Bill for emancipating the Roman Catholics, 1795.

IF I were to judge from the dead silence with which my speech has been received, I should suspect that what I have said was not very palatable to some men in this House. But I have not risked connexions, endeared to me by every tie of blood and friendship, to support one set of men in preference to another. I have hazarded too much, by the part I have taken, to allow the breath of calumny to taint the objects I have had in view. Immutable principles, on which the happiness and liberty of my countrymen depend, convey to my mind the only substantial boon for which great sacrifices should be made.

And I here avow myself the zealous and earnest advocate for the most unqualified emancipation of my catholic countrymen, in the hope and conviction, that the monopoly of the rights and liberties of my country, which has hitherto effectually withstood the efforts of a part of the people, must yield to the unanimous will, to the decided interest, and to the general effort of a whole united people. It is from this conviction, and it is for that transcendently important object, that, while the noble Lord and the Right Honorable Secretary, are offering to risk their lives and fortunes in support of a system that militates against the liberty of my countrymen, I will risk every thing dear to me on earth.

It is for this great object I have, I fear, more than risked connexions dearer to me than life itself. But he must be a spiritless man, and this a spiritless nation, not to resent the baseness of a British Minister, who has raised our hopes in order to seduce a rival to share with him the disgrace of this accursed political crusade, and blast them afterwards, that he may degrade a competitor to the station of a dependent. And, that he may de-stroy friendship which his nature never knew, he has sported with the feelings of a whole nation. Raising the cup with one hand to the parched lip of expect-ancy, he has dashed it to the earth with the other, in all the wantonness of insult, and with all the aggrava-tion of contempt.

Does he imagine, that the people of this country, after he has tantalized them with the cheering hope of present alleviation, and of future prosperity, will tame-ly bear to be forced to a reendurance of their former sufferings, and to a reappointment of their former spoilers? Does he, from confidence of long success in debauching the human mind, exact from you, calling yourselves the representatives of the people of Ireland, to reject a bill, which has received the unanimous consent of your constituents? or does he mean to puzzle the versatile disposition of this House, on which he has made so many successful experiments already, by distracting you between obedience to his imperious mandates, and obedience to the will of the people you should represent?

Or does he flatter himself, that he shall now succeed, because he has succeeded in betraying his own country, into exchanging that peace, by which she might have retrieved her shattered finances, for a war, in which he has squandered twenty times a greater treasure, in the course of two years, than with all his famed economy, he had been able to save, in the course of ten? for a war in which the prime youth of the world have been offered up, victims to his ambition and his schemes, as boundless and presumptuous, as ill concerted and ill combined; for a war in which the plains of every na-tion in Europe have been crimsoned with oceans of blood; for a war in which his country has reaped nothing but disgrace, and which must ultimately prove her ruin?

Does he flatter himself, that he shall be enabled, Satan like, to end his political career by involving the whole empire in a civil war, from which nothing can accrue, but a doleful and barren conquest to the victor? I trust the people of England are too wise and too just to attempt to force measures upon us which they would themselves reject with disdain. I trust they have not themselves so soon forgotten the lesson they so recently learned from America, which should serve as a lasting example to nations, against employing force to subdue the spirit of a people, determined to be free!

But if they should be so weak, or so wicked, as to suffer themselves to be seduced by a man, to whose soul, duplicity and finesse are as congenial, as ingenuousness and fair dealing are a stranger, to become the instruments of supporting a few odious public characters in power and rapacity, against the interest and against the sense of a whole people; if we are to be dragooned into measures against our will, by a nation that would lose her last life, and expend her last guinea, in resenting a similar insult, if offered to herself, I trust she will find in the people of this country a spirit in nowise inferior to her own.

You are at this moment at the most awful period of your lives. The Minister of England has committed you with your country; and on this night your adoption or rejection of this bill, must determine, in the eyes of the Irish nation, which you represent, the Minister of England or the people of Ireland! And, although you are convinced, you do not represent the people of Ireland; although you are convinced, every man of you, that you are self-created, it does not alter the nature of the contest; it is still a contest between the Minister of England and the people of Ireland; and the weakness of your title should only make you the more circumspect in the exercise of your power.

Fortunately, the views of the British minister have been detected; fortunately, the people of this country see him in his true colors. Like the desperate gamester, who has lost his all, in the wildest schemes of aggrandizement, he looks round for some dupe to supply him with the further means of future projects; and in the crafty subtleness of his soul, he fondly imagines, he has found that easy dupe in the credulity of the Irish nation. After he has exhausted his own country in a crusade against that phantom, political opinion, he flatters himself he shall be enabled to resuscitate her at the expense of yours.

As you value the peace and happiness of your country; as you value the rights and liberties of the soil that has given you birth; and if you are not lost to every sense of feeling for your own consequence and importance as men, I call on you this night to make your stand. I call on you to rally round the independence of your country, whose existence has been so artfully assailed. Believe me, the British Minister will leave you in the lurch, when he sees that the people of this nation are too much in earnest to be tricked out of their rights, or the independence of their country.

What a display of legislation have we had on this night? Artificers who neither know the foundation on which they work, the instruments they ought to use, nor the materials required! Is it on the narrow basis of monopoly and exclusion you would erect a temple to the growing liberty of your country? If you will legislate; know, that on the broad basis of immutable justice only, you can raise a lasting, beauteous temple to the liberty of your island; whose ample base shall lodge, and whose roof shall shelter her united family from the rankling inclemency of rejection and exclusion. Know, that reason is that silken thread by which the lawgiver leads his people; and above all, know, that in the knowledge of the temper of the public mind, consists the skill and the wisdom of the legislator.

Do not imagine that the minds of your countrymen have been stationary, while that of all Europe has been rapidly progressive; for you must be blind not to perceive, that the whole European mind has undergone a revolution, neither confined to this nor to that country; but as general as the great causes which have given it birth, and still continue to feed its growth. In vain do these men, who subsist but on the abuses of the government under which they live, flatter themselves that what we have seen these last six years is but the fever of the moment, which will pass away as soon as the patient has been let blood enough.

As well may they attempt to alter the course of nature, without altering her laws. If they would effect a counter revolution in the European mind, they must destroy commerce and its effects; they must abolish every trace of the mariner's compass; they must consign every book to the flames; they must obliterate every vestige of the invention of the press; they must destroy the conduit of intelligence, by destroying the institution of the postoffice. Then, and not till then, they and their abuses may live on, in all the security which ignorance, superstition, and want of concert in the people can bestow.

But while I would overwhelm with despair those men who have been nursed in the lap of venality and prostitution; who have been educated in contempt and ridicule of a love for their country; and who have grown gray in scoffing at every thing like public spirit, let me congratulate every true friend to mankind, that that commerce, which has begotten so much independence, will continue to beget more; and let me congratulate every friend to the human species, that the press, which has sent such a mass of information into the world, will continue, with accelerated rapidity, to pour forth its treasures so beneficial to mankind.

It is to these great causes we are indebted, that the combination of priests and despots, which so long tyrannized over the civil and political liberty of Europe, has been dissolved. It is to these great causes we are indebted, that no priest, be his religion what it may, dares preach the doctrine which inculcates the necessity of sacrificing every right and every blessing this world can afford, as the only mean of obtaining eternal happiness in the life to come.

This was the doctrine by which the despotism of
Europe was so long supported; this was the doctrine
by which the political popery of Europe was supported;
but the doctrine and the despotism may now sleep in
the same grave, until the trumpet of ignorance, superstition, and bigotry, shall sound their resurrection.

SCENE FROM THE TRAGEDY OF TAMERLANE.

Enter OMAR *and* TAMERLANE.

Omar. HONOR and fame
[*Bowing.*] Forever wait the Emperor; may our
    Prophet
Give him ten thousand thousand days of life,
And every day like this. The captive sultan,
Fierce in his bonds, and at his fate repining,
Attends your sacred will.
 Tamerlane. Let him approach.
[*Enter* BAJAZET *and other Turkish Prisoners in*
 chains with a guard.]
When I survey the ruins of this field,
The wild destruction, which thy fierce ambition
Has dealt among mankind; (so many widows
And helpless orphans has thy battle made,
That half our eastern world this day are mourners;)
Well may I, in behalf of heaven and earth,
Demand from thee atonement for this wrong.
 Baj. Make thy demand of those that own thy
   power;
Know I am still beyond it; and though fortune
Has stript me of the train and pomp of greatness,
That outside of a king; yet still my soul,
Fix'd high, and of itself alone dependent,
Is ever free and royal; and even now,
As at the head of battle, does defy thee.
I know what power the chance of war has given,
And dare thee to the use on't. This vile speeching,
This after-game of words, is what most irks me;

Spare that, and for the rest 'tis equal all,
Be it as it may.

Tam. Well was it for the world,
When, on their borders, neighbouring princes met,
Frequent in friendly parle, by cool debates
Preventing wasteful war: such should our meeting
Have been, hadst thou but held in just regard
The sanctity of leagues so often sworn to.
Canst thou believe thy Prophet, or, what's more,
That power supreme, which made thee and thy Pro-
  phet,
Will, with impunity, let pass that breach
Of sacred faith given to the royal Greek?

Baj. Thou pedant talker! ha! art thou a king
Possess'd of sacred power, Heav'n's darling attribute?
And dost thou prate of leagues, and oaths and prophets?
I hate the Greek, (perdition on his name!)
As I do thee, and would have met you both,
As death does human nature, for destruction.

Tam. Causeless to hate, is not of human kind:
The savage brute that haunts in woods remote
And desert wilds, tears not the fearful traveller,
If hunger, or some injury, provoke not.

Baj. Can a king want a cause, when empire bids
Go on! What is he born for, but ambition?
It is his hunger, 'tis his call of nature,
The noble appetite which will be satisfy'd,
And, like the food of gods, makes him immortal.

Tam. Henceforth I will not wonder we were foes,
Since souls that differ so by nature, hate,
And strong antipathy forbids their union.

Baj. The noble fire, that warms me, does indeed
Transcend thy coldness. I am pleas'd we differ,
Nor think alike.

Tam. No: for I think like man,
Thou like a monster, from whose baleful presence
Nature starts back; and though she fix'd her stamp
On thy rough mass, and mark'd thee for a man,
Now, conscious of her error, she disclaims thee,
As form'd for her destruction.

'Tis true, I am a king, as thou hast been;
Honor and glory too have been my aim;
But though I dare face death, and all the dangers
Which furious war wears in its bloody front,
Yet would I choose to fix my name by peace,
By justice, and by mercy; and to raise
My trophies on the blessings of mankind;
Nor would I buy the empire of the world
With ruin of the people whom I sway,
On forfeit of my honor.

   Baj. Phrophet, I thank thee.
Confusion! couldst thou rob me of my glory
To dress up this tame king, this preaching dervise!
Unfit for war, thou shouldst have liv'd secure
In lazy peace, and with debating senates
Shar'd a precarious sceptre; sat tamely still,
And let bold factions canton out thy power
And wrangle for the spoils they robb'd thee of;
Whilst I (O blast the power that stops my ardour)
Would, like a tempest, rush amidst the nations,
Be greatly terrible, and deal, like Alha,
My angry thunder on the frighted world.

   Tam. The world! 'twould be too little for thy pride:
Thou wouldst scale heav'n.

   Baj. I would. Away! my soul
Disdains thy conference.

   Tam. Thou vain, rash thing,
That, with gigantic insolence, hast dar'd
To lift thy wretched self above the stars,
And mate with power almighty, thou art fall'n!

   Baj. 'Tis false! I am not fall'n from aught I have
             been!
At least my soul resolves to keep her state,
And scorns to make acquaintance with ill fortune.

   Tam. Almost beneath my pity art thou fall'n;
Since, while the avenging hand of heav'n is on thee,
And presses to the dust thy swelling soul,
Fool-hardy, with the stronger thou contendest.
To what vast heights had thy tumultuous temper

Been hurried, if success had crown'd thy wishes!
Say, what had I to expect, if thou hadst conquer'd?

Baj. Oh, glorious thought! Ye powers, I will enjoy it,
Though but in fancy; imagination shall
Make room to entertain the vast idea.
Oh! had I been the master but of yesterday,
The world, the world had felt me; and for thee,
I had us'd thee, as thou art to me, a dog,
The object of my scorn and mortal hatred.
I would have cag'd thee for the scorn of slaves.
I would have taught thy neck to know my weight,
And mounted from that footstool to the saddle:
Till thou hadst begg'd to die; and e'en that mercy
I had deny'd thee. Now thou know'st my mind,
And question me no farther.

Tam. Well dost thou teach me
What justice should exact from thee. Mankind,
With one consent cry out for vengeance on thee,
Loudly they call to cut off this league-breaker,
This wild destroyer, from the face of earth.

Baj. Do it, and rid thy shaking soul at once
Of its worst fear.

Tam. Why slept the thunder
That should have arm'd the idol deity,
And given thee power, ere yester sun was set,
To shake the soul of Tamerlane. Hadst thou an arm
To make thee fear'd, thou shoudst have prov'd it on me,
Amidst the sweat and blood of yonder field,
When, through the tumult of the war I sought thee,
Fenc'd in with nations.

Baj. Oh, blast the stars
That fated us to different scenes of slaughter!
Oh! could my sword have met thee!

Tam. Thou hadst then,
As now, been in my power, and held thy life
Dependent on my gift. Yes, Bajazet,
I bid thee live. So much my soul disdains
That thou shouldst think I can fear aught but Heaven.
Nay more; couldst thou forget thy brutal fierceness,

And form thyself to manhood, I would bid thee
Live and be still a king, that thou mayst learn
What man should be to man——
This royal tent, with such of thy domestics
As can be found, shall wait upon thy service;
Nor will I use my fortune to demand
Hard terms of peace; but such as thou mayest offer
With honor, I with honor may receive.

———

COLONEL BARRE's SPEECH IN THE BRITISH PAR-
LIAMENT, 1765, ON THE STAMP-ACT BILL.

ON the first reading of the bill, Mr. Townsend
spoke in its favour; and concluded with the following words: "And will these Americans, children
planted by our care, nourished up by our indulgence,
until they are grown to a degree of strength and opu-
lence; and protected by our arms; will they grudge
to contribute their mite, to relieve us from the heavy
weight of that burden which we lie under?"

On this Colonel Barre rose, and answered Mr.
Townsend in the following masterly manner.

"They planted by YOUR care!" No; your op-
pressions planted them in America. They fled from
your tyranny, to a then uncultivated and inhospitable
country, where they exposed themselves to almost all
the hardships to which human nature is liable; and
among others, to the cruelties of a savage foe, the
most subtle, and I will take upon me to say, the
most formidable of any people upon the face of the
earth; and yet, actuated by principles of true English
liberty, they met all hardships with pleasure, compared
with those they suffered in their own country, from the
hands of those who should have been their friends.

"They nourished up by YOUR indulgence!" They
grew by your neglect of them. As soon as you began
to care about them, that care was exercised in sending

persons, to rule them, in one department and another, who were, perhaps, the deputies of deputies to some members of this House, sent to spy out their liberties, to misrepresent their actions, and to prey upon them; men, whose behaviour, on many occasions, has caused the blood of those sons of liberty to recoil within them; men promoted to the highest seat of justice; some, who, to my knowledge, were glad, by going to a foreign country, to escape being brought to the bar of a court of justice in their own.

" They protected by YOUR arms!" They have nobly taken up arms in your defence; have exerted a valour, amidst their constant and laborious industry, for the defence of a country, whose frontier was drenched in blood, while its interior parts yielded all its little savings to your emoluments.

And, believe me; remember I this day told you so, that the same spirit of freedom, which actuated that people at first, will accompany them still. But prudence forbids me to explain myself further. Heaven knows, I do not at this time speak from motives of party heat; what I deliver are the genuine sentiments of my heart.

However superior to me in general knowledge and experience the respectable body of this House may be, yet I claim to know more of America than most of you, having seen and been conversant in that country. The people, I believe, are as truly loyal as any subjects the king has; but a people jealous of their liberties, and who will vindicate them, if ever they should be violated. But the subject is too delicate, I will say no more.

Y.

The Last Day.
Extract from a manuscript Poem.

THE day of Doom, the all-important day,
   I sing; that link extreme of time, which joins
The measur'd chain of days, and months, and years,
To one eternal, one effulgent day:
Day to the children of the day; but night,
Eternal night, to all the sons of darkness.
The time affixed by God's decree arrives.
Th' Almighty spake: heav'n open'd wide her gates,
The herald, Gabriel, far advanc'd in front,
Rais'd on seraphic wings, first issued forth.
Next the creation's Sire, veil'd in a cloud
Of awful gloom, from which red lightnings flash'd,
And rending thunders roar'd, pass'd through the gates.
At his right hand sat his eternal Son,
High rais'd upon a golden throne emboss'd
With gems, that sparkled through the cloud. Angels
And saints, the countless host of those, who hold
The realms of Bliss, next in procession mov'd:
Nor could the wide extended space from Aries
To the Scales, that poise the hemispheres,
Contain the army of the skies.
   The earth had never seen a larger host,
Than when the foe of Greece spread o'er the land
And sea from Hebrus to Thermopylæ;
But this was small compar'd with what the heavens
Now saw, as earth is small compar'd with heaven.
The numerous stars, that hold their course along
The milky-way, and in the neighb'ring skies,
No sooner saw their Maker cloth'd in storms,
And felt his thunder shake their solid spheres,
Than trembling they retire; as when some king
Enrag'd frowns on his slaves, who flee his face,
Till he commands them stand and hear his will.
So had the frighted stars fled off and left

The mundane space all void, had not the trump
Of Gabriel interpos'd, and with a voice
More loud, than ever yet creation heard,
Impress'd the mandates of all nature's God
Upon all nature's works. Ye stars! (said he)
Return, and hold your station in your orbs;
There stand and see what He on earth transacts
This day, and witness how He deals with man.
Thou sun! who from the birth of time hast roll'd
Thy chariot round the world, and shed thy beams
Alike on all mankind, look on and see
The equal justice of thy God to man
Outshine thy equal rays. Th' affrighted earth
Took the alarm of heav'n: the atmosphere
Assay'd to flee upon the wings of storm.
Fierce tempests beat the lofty mountains' sides,
Sweep forests down, and spread destruction o'er
The works of man. The troubled ocean heaves:
His surging billows mingle with the clouds:
His deepest caverns lie expos'd to view.
The earth, convuls'd from her deep centre, heaves.
Order forsook the world: discord spread wide.
The confus'd elements again had join'd
The listless empire of primeval chaos,
Had not harmonic sounds assuag'd their tumult.
    Spirit divine! thou soul of harmony
In heaven and earth, breathe through my lines and
            speak
The power of music's charms, when heavenly love
Warm'd every breast of angels, seraphim,
And doubly glow'd in the Almighty's Son;
Who, like a bridegroom clad in smiling youth
And robes of peace, prepar'd to meet his bride.
The lightning ceas'd; the thunders died, when he
Complacent smil'd. Gabriel, and all the choir
Of heaven, said he, hush the commoved world,
And wake the sleeping saints with sounds of peace
His words like melting music flow: his face,
More radiant than the vernal morn, that smiles
The earth to joy. The trump of Gabriel led

The choral song: unnumber'd harps of gold,
And voices sweet join'd the melodious sound.
Discord, that late had moved the elements
To war, and 'gan t' invade the spheres,
Was hush'd to sleep. Quick changed the scene,
From raging discord, universal storm,
To soothing sounds, and universal calm.
The sun, from blackest clouds, unveil'd his face,
And shone with double radiance on the earth.
The fixed stars had ceas'd to shed their beams,
And trembling, hid in sable darkness, stood;
But now, enraptur'd with symphonious sounds,
They dart their genial rays, and fill their orbs
With pleasing light, and soul-reviving warmth.
But thou, O Earth, most felt the pleasing change.
——Fierce storms were mute.
Old ocean heard, and smooth'd his tempest face;
And spring-like beauty smil'd on all the earth.
  Poets have sung of Orpheus' potent lyre;
Eurydice, forc'd from the bands of death,
Of bending trees and moving rocks obsequious
To the sound. But now whole worlds obey.
Death could not hold his victims in the tomb.
" Thou monarch of the grave, resign the just!
Awake! ye saints, from your long night of sleep.
Adorn'd with ever-blooming youth and robes
Of heav'nly innocence. Salute the morn
Of everlasting day." Thus sung the choir.
Death's dreary mansions heard with sad dismay.
In the mid regions of eternal night,
There sits the ghastly monarch on his throne.
Substantial darkness fills the broad domain:
Heart-chilling vapours rise from noxious lakes.
His servants, War, Intemp'rance, Plague, Revenge,
Consumption, wrinkled Age, groan discord round
His throne, and offer up their loathsome fumes
Of putrid corps, contagion, dead'ning blasts;
Sweet incense to their king; or run before
His grisly steed, when he rides o'er the earth.

And crops with chilling hand the bloom of life.
Here reigns the awful monarch of the dead;
When the full sounds spread thro' his darksome realms,
His heart appall'd, he trembles on his throne:
His iron nerves relax: his sceptre falls.
The saints releas'd, their dreary mansions leave:
But O how chang'd!
No cumb'rous load of grosser elements,
But pure aerial forms their souls possess;
Forms, like the glorious body of their Lord,
Glowing with beauty and immortal bloom.

A Dialogue on Loquacity.

Enter Stephen.

Stephen. LADIES and gentlemen, you have probably heard of Foote, the comedian: if not, it is out of my power to tell you any thing about him, except this; he had but one leg, and his name was Samuel. Or, to speak more poetically, one leg he had, and Samuel was his name. This Foote wrote a farce, called the Alderman; in which he attempted to ridicule a well-fed magistrate of the city of London. This last, hearing of the intended affront, called upon the player, and threatened him severely for his presumption. Sir, says Foote, it is my business to take off people. You shall see how well I can take myself off. So out of the room he went, as though to prepare. The Alderman sat waiting, and waiting, and waiting, and ———I have forgotten the rest of the story; but it ended very comically. So I must request of you, to muster up your wit, and each one end the story to his own liking. You are all wondering what this story leads to. Why, I'll tell you; Foote's farce was called the Alderman, ours is called the Medley; his was written according to rule, ours is composed at loose ends. Yet loose as it is, you will find it made up, like all other pieces, of nouns, pronouns, verbs, participles, adverbs, conjunctions, articles, adjectives, prepositions, and interjections. Now, words are very harmless things; though I confess that much depends upon the manner of putting them together. The only thing to be settled is, that, if you should dislike the arrangement, you will please to alter it, till it suits you.

Enter Truman.

Truman. What are you prating about, at such a rate?

Steph. I am speaking of Sam Foote, and prepositions, and adverbs, and many other great characters.

Tru. Now, don't you know that your unruly tongue will be the ruin of you? Did you ever see a man who was foaming and frothing at the mouth as you are, that ever said any thing to the purpose? You ought always to think before you speak, and to consider well to whom you speak, and the place and time of speaking.

Steph. Pray who taught you all this wordly wisdom?

Tru. My own experience, Sir; which is said to be the best school-master in the world, and ought to teach it to every man of common sense.

Steph. Then, do not imagine that you possess any great secret. " Keep your tongue between your teeth" is an old proverb, rusted and crusted over, till nobody can tell what it was first made of. Prudence, indeed, teaches the same. So prudence may teach a merchant to keep his vessels in port for fear of a storm at sea. But " nothing venture, nothing have" is my proverb. Now, suppose all the world should adopt this prudence, what a multitude of mutes we should have! There would be an end of news, law-suits, politics, and society. I tell you, Sir, that busy tongues are like main springs; they set every thing in motion.

Tru. But where's a man's dignity, all this time, while his tongue is running at random, without a single thought to guide it?

Steph. His dignity! that indeed! Out upon parole, where it ought to be. A man's dignity! as though we came into the world to support dignity, and by an affected distance, to make our friends feel their inferiority. I consider men like coins, which, because stamped with men's heads, pass for more than they are worth. And when the world is willing to treat a man better than he deserves, there is a meanness in endeavouring to extort more from them.

Tru. But shall a man speak without thinking? Did you ever read the old proverb, " Think twice, before you speak once?"

Steph. Yes, and a vile one it is. If a man speak from the impulse of the moment, he'll speak the meaning of his heart; and will probably speak the truth. But if he mind your musty proverb, there will be more pros and cons in his head, more hems and haws in his delivery, than there are letters in his sentences. To your sly, subtle, thinking fellows, we owe all the lies, cheating, hypocrisy, and double dealing there is in the world.

Tru. But you know that every subject has its sides; and we ought to examine, reflect, analyze, sift, consider, and determine, before we have a right to speak; for the world are entitled to the best of our thoughts. What would you think of a tradesmen, who should send home your coat, boots, or hat, half finished? You might think him a very honest-hearted fellow; but you'd never employ him again.

Steph. Now, was there any need of bringing in tailors, cobblers, and hatters, to help you out? They have nothing to do with this subject.

Tru. You don't understand me. I say, if you would never employ such workmen a second time, why should you justify a man for turning out his thoughts half finished? The mind labours as actually in thinking upon, and maturing a subject, as the body does in the field, or on the shop-board. And, if the farmer knows when his grain is ready for the sickle, and the mechanic, when his work is ready for his customer, the man, who is used to thinking, knows when he is master of his subject and the proper time to communicate his thoughts with ease to himself and advantage to others.

Steph. All this is escaping the subject. None of your figures, when the very original is before you. You talk about a man's mind, just as if it were a piece of ground, capable of bearing flax and hemp. You have fairly brought forward a shop-board, and mounted your tailor upon it. Now I have no notion of any cross-legged work in my inner man. In fact, I don't understand all this process of thinking. My knowledge upon all subjects is very near the root of my tongue, and I feel great relief, when it gets near the tip.

Tru. Depend on it that thousands have lost fame and even life by too great freedom of speech. Treasons, murders, and robberies, have been generally discovered by the imprudent boasting of the perpetrators.

Steph. Depend on it, that our world has suffered far more by silent, than by prattling knaves. Suppose every man were to speak all his thoughts, relate all his actions, declare all his purposes, would the world be in danger of crimes? No; be assured, that magistrates, bailiffs, thief-takers, prisons, halters, and gallows, all owe their dignity to the contrivance of your sly, plodding mutes.

Tru. You have let off from the tip of your tongue a picked company of dignified substantives; but take notice that my doctrine does not extend to the midnight silence of robbers; but to a due caution and reserve in conveying our thoughts to the world. And this I hope ever to observe. And if you determine on a different course, rest assured, that the consequence will not be very pleasant.   [*Exit.*

Steph. Consequences! That's counting chickens before they are hatched. Dignity of human nature! Pretty words! just fit to be ranked with the *honor* of thieves, and the *courage* of modern duellists.

AMERICAN SAGES.

SEE on yon dark'ning height bold Franklin tread,
Heav'ns awful thunders rolling o'er his head;
Convolving clouds the billowy skies deform,
And forky flames emblaze the black'ning storm.
See the descending streams around him burn,
Glance on his rod, and with his guidance turn;
He bids conflicting heav'ns their blast expire,
Curbs the fierce blaze, and holds th' imprison'd fire.
No more, when folding storms the vault o'erspread,
The lived glare shall strike thy face with dread;
Nor tow'rs nor temples, shudd'ring with the sound,
Sink in the flames, and spread destruction round.
His daring toils, the threat'ning blasts that wait,
Shall teach mankind to ward the bolts of fate;
The pointed steel o'er-top th' ascending spire,
And lead o'er trembling walls the harmless fire;
In his glad fame while distant worlds rejoice,
Far as the lightnings shine, or thunders raise their voice.
    See the sage Rittenhouse, with ardent eye,
Lift the long tube, and pierce the starry sky:
Clear in his view the circling systems roll,
And broader splendors gild the central pole.
He marks what laws th' eccentric wand'rers bind,
Copies creation in his forming mind,
And bids, beneath his hand, in semblance rise,
With mimic orbs, the labours of the skies.
There wond'ring crowds, with raptur'd eye, behold
The spangled heav'ns their mystic maze unfold;
While each glad sage his splendid hall shall grace,
With all the spheres that cleave th' etherial space.
    To guide the sailor in his wand'ring way,
See Godfrey's glass reverse the beams of day.
His lifted quadrant to the eye displays
From adverse skies the counteracting rays:
And marks, as devious sails bewilder'd roll,
Each nice gradation from the stedfast pole.

EXTRACT FROM MR. PITT'S SPEECH, NOV. 18, 1777, ON AMERICAN AFFAIRS.

I RISE, my lords, to declare my sentiments on this most solemn and serious subject. It has imposed a load upon my mind, which, I fear, nothing can remove; but which impels me to endeavour its alleviation, by a free and unreserved communication of my sentiments. In the first part of the address, I have the honor of heartily concurring with the noble Earl who moved it. No man feels sincerer joy than I do; none can offer more genuine congratulation on every accession of strength to the Protestant succession: I therefore join in every congratulation on the birth of another princess, and the happy recovery of her Majesty.

But I must stop here; my courtly complaisance will carry me no farther. I will not join in congratulation on misfortune and disgrace. I cannot concur in a blind and servile address, which approves, and endeavours to sanctify, the monstrous measures that have heaped disgrace and misfortune upon us; that have brought ruin to our doors. This, my lords, is a perilous and tremendous moment! It is not a time for adulation. The smoothness of flattery cannot now avail; cannot save us in this rugged and awful crisis. It is now necessary to instruct the throne in the language of truth. We must dispel the delusion and the darkness which envelop it; and display, in its full danger and true colours, the ruin that it has brought to our doors.

And *who* is the minister; *where* is the minister, who has dared to suggest to the throne the contrary, unconstitutional language, this day delivered from it? The accustomed language from the throne has been application to Parliament for advice, and a reliance on its constitutional advice and assistance. As it is the right of Parliament to give, so it is the duty of the crown to ask it. But on this day, and in this extreme momentous exigency, no reliance is reposed on our constitutional counsels! no advice is asked from the sober and enlightened care of Parliament! But the crown, from itself, and by itself, declares an unalterable determination to pursue measures. And what measures, my lords? The measures that have produced imminent perils that threaten us; the measures that have brought ruin to our doors.

Can the Minister of the day now presume to expect a continuance of support, in this ruinous infatuation? Can Parliament be so dead to its dignity and its duty, as to be thus deluded into the loss of the one, and the violation of the other? To give an unlimited credit and support for the perseverance in measures, which have reduced this late flourishing empire to ruin and contempt! " But yesterday, and England might have stood against the world: now none so poor to do her reverence." I use the words of a poet; but though it is poetry, it is no fiction. It is a shameful truth, that not only the power and strength of this country are wasting away and expiring; but her well earned glories, her true honors, and substantial dignity, are sacrificed.

France, my lords, has insulted you; she has encouraged and sustained America; and whether America be wrong or right, the dignity of this country ought to spurn at the officious insult of French interference. The ministers and ambassadors of those who are called rebels and enemies, are in Paris; in Paris they transact the reciprocal interests of America and France. Can there be a more mortifying insult? Can even our ministers sustain a more humiliating disgrace? Do they dare to resent it? Do they presume even to hint a vindication of their honor, and the dignity of the State, by requiring the dismissal of the plenipotentiaries of America? Such is the degradation to which they have reduced the glories of England!

The people, whom they affect to call contemptible rebels, but whose growing power has at last obtained the name of enemies; the people with whom they have engaged this country in war, and against whom they now command our implicit support in every measure of desperate hostility: this people, despised as rebels, are acknowledged as enemies, are abetted against you; supplied with every military store; their interests consulted, and their ambassadors entertained, by your inverate enemy! and our ministers dare not interpose with dignity or effect. Is this the honor of a great kingdom? Is this the indignant spirit of England, who but yesterday, gave law to the house of Bourbon? My lords, the dignity of nations demands a decisive conduct in a situation like this.

This ruinous and ignominious situation, where we cannot act with success, nor suffer with honor, calls upon us to remonstrate in the strongest and loudest language of truth, to rescue the ear of Majesty from the delusions which surround it. The desperate state of our arms abroad is in part known. No man thinks more highly of them than I do. I love and honor the English troops. I know they can achieve any thing except impossibilities: and I know that the conquest of English America is an impossibility. You cannot, I venture to say it, you CANNOT conquer America.

Your armies, last war, effected every thing that could be effected; and what was it? It cost a numerous army under the command of a most able general, now a noble lord in this House, a long and laborious campaign to expel five thousand Frenchmen from French America. My lords, you CANNOT conquer America. What is your present situation there? We do not know the worst; but we know, that in three campaigns we have done nothing, and suffered much. We shall soon know, and in any event, have reason to lament, what may have happened since.

As to conquest, therefore, my lords, I repeat, it is impossible. You may swell every expense, and every effort, still more extravagantly; pile and accumulate every assistance you can buy or borrow; traffic and

barter with every little pitiful German prince, who
sells his subjects to the shambles of a foreign power;
your efforts are forever vain and impotent; doubly so
from this mercenary aid on which you rely. For it
irritates to an incurable resentment, the minds of your
enemies, to overrun them with the mercenary sons of
rapine and plunder; devoting them and their possessions to the rapacity of hireling cruelty! If I were an
American, as I am an Englishman, while a foreign
troop remained in my country, I NEVER would
lay down my arms; NEVER, NEVER, NEVER.

SCENE FROM THE TRAGEDY OF CATO.

CATO, LUCIUS, *and* SEMPRONIUS.

Cato. FATHERS, we once again are met in council:
Cesar's approach has summon'd us together,
And Rome attends her fate from our resolves.
How shall we treat this bold, aspiring man?
Success still follows him, and backs his crimes:
Pharsalia gave him Rome, Egypt has since
Receiv'd his yoke, and the whole Nile is Cesar's.
Why should I mention Juba's overthrow,
And Scipio's death? Numidia's burning sands
Still smoke with blood. 'Tis time we should decree
What course to take. Our foe advances on us,
And envies us even Libya's sultry deserts.
Fathers, pronounce your thoughts; are they still fix'd
To hold it out, and fight it to the last?
Or are your hearts subdu'd at length, and wrought
By time and ill success to a submission?
Sempronius, speak.

    Sempronius. My voice is still for war.
Heav'ns! can a Roman senate long debate,
Which of the two to choose, slav'ry or death!
No; let us rise at once, gird on our swords,
And at the head of our remaining troops,

Z

Attack the foe, break through the thick array
Of his throng'd legions, and charge home upon him.
Perhaps some arm, more lucky than the rest,
May reach his heart, and free the world from bondage.
Rise, fathers, rise! 'tis Rome demands your help;
Rise, and revenge her slaughter'd citizens,
Or share their fate! The corpse of half her senate
Manure the fields of Thessaly, while we
Sit here delib'rating in cold debates,
If we should sacrifice our lives to honor,
Or wear them out in servitude and chains.
Rouse up, for shame! our brothers of Pharsalia
Point at their wounds, and cry aloud, To battle!
Great Pompey's shade complains that we are slow,
And Scipio's ghost stalks unreveng'd among us.

   Cato. Let not a torrent of impetuous zeal
Transport you thus beyond the bounds of reason.
True fortitude is seen in great exploits
That justice warrants, and that wisdom guides.
All else is tow'ring frenzy and distraction.
Are not the lives of those who draw the sword
In Rome's defence intrusted to our care?
Should we thus lead them to the field of slaughter,
Might not th' impartial world with reason say,
We lavish'd at our death the blood of thousands,
To grace our fall, and make our ruin glorious?
Lucius, we next would know what's your opinion?

   Luc. My thoughts, I must confess, are turn'd on
         peace.
Already have our quarrels fill'd the world
With widows, and with orphans. Scythia mourns
Our guilty wars, and earth's remotest regions
Lie half unpeopled by the feuds of Rome.
'Tis time to sheathe the sword, and spare mankind.
It is not Cesar, but the gods, my fathers;
The gods declare against us; repel
Our vain attempts. To urge the foe to battle,
Prompted by blind revenge, and wild despair,
Were to refuse th' awards of Providence,
And not to rest in Heav'n's determination.

Already have we shown our love to Rome;
Now let us show submission to the gods.
We took up arms, not to revenge ourselves,
But free the commonwealth; when this end fails,
Arms have no further use: our country's cause,
That drew our swords, now wrests them from our
    hands,
And bids us not delight in Roman blood,
Unprofitably shed. What men could do,
Is done already. Heav'n and earth will witness,
If Rome must fall, that we are innocent.

Cato. Let us appear nor rash nor diffident;
Immod'rate valour swells into a fault;
And fear, admitted into public councils,
Betrays like treason. Let us shun them both.
Fathers, I cannot see that our affairs
Are grown thus desp'rate: we have bulwarks round us:
Within our walls are troops inured to toil
In Africa's heats, and season'd to the sun:
Numidia's spacious kingdom lies behind us,
Ready to rise at its young prince's call.
While there is hope, do not distrust the gods;
But wait at least till Cesar's near approach
Force us to yield. 'Twill never be too late
To sue for chains and own a conqueror.
Why should Rome fall a moment ere her time?
No, let us draw our term of freedom out
In its full length, and spin it to the last;
So shall we gain still one day's liberty:
And let me perish, but in Cato's judgment,
A day, an hour of virtuous liberty,
Is worth a whole eternity in bondage.

EXTRACT FROM AN ORATION, DELIVERED AT BOSTON, JULY 4, 1794, IN COMMEMORATION OF AMERICAN INDEPENDENCE.

AMERICANS! you have a country vast in extent, and embracing all the varieties of the most salubrious climes: held not by charters wrested from unwilling kings, but the bountiful gift of the Author of nature. The exuberance of your population is daily divesting the gloomy wilderness of its rude attire, and splendid cities rise to cheer the dreary desert. You have a government deservedly celebrated as " giving the sanctions of law to the precepts of reason;" presenting, instead of the rank luxuriance of natural licentiousness, the corrected sweets of civil liberty. You have fought the battles of freedom, and inkindled that sacred flame which now glows with vivid fervour through the greatest empire in Europe.

We indulge the sanguine hope, that her equal laws and virtuous conduct will hereafter afford examples of imitation to all surrounding nations. That the blissful period will soon arrive when man shall be elevated to his primitive character; when illuminated reason and regulated liberty shall once more exhibit him in the image of his Maker; when all the inhabitants of the globe shall be freemen and fellow-citizens, and patriotism itself be lost in universal philanthropy. Then shall volumes of incense incessantly roll from altars inscribed to liberty. Then shall the innumerable varieties of the human race unitedly " worship in her sacred temple, whose pillars shall rest on the remotest corners of the earth, and whose arch will be the vault of heaven."

DIALOGUE BETWEEN A WHITE INHABITANT OF THE
UNITED STATES AND AN INDIAN.

White Man. YOUR friends, the inhabitants of the
United States, wish to bury the
Tomahawk, and live in peace with the Indian tribes.

Indian. Justice is the parent of peace. The Indians
love war only as they love justice. Let us enjoy our
rights, and be content with yours, and we will hang
the tomakawk and scalping knife upon the tree of
peace, and sit down together under its branches.

W. Man. This is what we desire, and what is your
interest as well as ours to promote. We have often
made leagues with you; they have been as often broken. If justice were your guide, and peace your desire, they would be better regarded.

Ind. The White Men are robbers. We do not
choose to be at peace with robbers; it is more to our
honor to be at war with them.

W. Man. It is in our power to punish the aggressors; we have more warriors than the Indians; but we
choose to employ arguments rather than force.

Ind. I have heard the arguments of White Men:
they are a fair bait; but their intentions are a bearded
hook. You call us brothers, but you treat us like
beasts; you wish to trade with us, that you may cheat
us; you would give us peace, but you would take our
lands, and leave us nothing worth fighting for.

W. Man. The white men want your lands; but
they are willing to pay for them. The great Parent
has given the earth to all men in common to improve
for their sustenance. He delights in the numbers of
his children. If any have a superior claim, it must be
those, who, by their arts and industry, can support the
greatest number on the smallest territory.

Ind. This is the way you talk; you act differently.
You have good on your tongue, but bad in your heart.

Z 2

I have been among White Men. I know as much about them as you do about Red Men. What would your people say, if poor men should go to a rich man, and tell him the great Parent has given the earth to all men in common; we have not land enough; you have more than you need; he delights in the number of his children; your great farm supports but few; by our superior arts and industry, it would support many; you may move to one corner of your land; that is sufficient for you; we will take the rest. We will live together as brothers, if you will be at peace with us; if not, we have more warriors than you; it is in our power to punish the aggressors. Should you call this just? No! no!

W. Man. Surely not.

Ind. Then justice among White Men and Red Men is different: will you show me the difference? I thought justice was our friend as well as yours.

W. Man. We are governed by laws that protect our property, and punish the disturbers of peace.

Ind. Then by what law do you encroach upon our property, and disturb our peace? If you consider us as your brothers, your laws ought to protect us as well as yourselves.

W. Man. Our ways of living are different from yours. We have many employments and much property: your manners are simple, your possessions small; our laws, of course, will not apply to your circumstances.

Ind. I know you have many laws on paper, and some that ought to make the paper blush. We have but few; they are founded in justice and written on the heart. They teach us to treat a stranger as our friend; to open our doors, and spread our tables to the needy. If a white man come among us, our heart is in our hand; all we have is his; yet you call us savages! But that must mean something better than civilized, if you are civilized.

W. Man. We do not impeach your hospitality, nor censure your humanity in many instances; but how can you justify your promiscuous slaughter of the innocent and guilty, your cruel massacres of helpless wives and children, who never injured you?

Ind. If a man provoke me to fight with him, I will break his head if I can: if he is stronger than I, then I must be content to break his arm or his finger. When the war-whoop is sounded, and we take up the tomahawk, our hearts are one; our cause is common; the wives and children of our enemies are our enemies also; they have the same blood, and we have the same thirst for it. If you wish your wives and children should escape our vengeance, be honest and friendly in your dealings with us; if they have ruffians for their protectors, they must not expect safety.

W. Man. We have both the same claim from each other; friendship and justice are all we require. Our ideas on these subjects are different; perhaps they will never agree. On one side, ferocity will not be dictated by humanity, nor stubbornness by reason; on the other, knowledge is not disposed to be advised by ignorance, nor power to stoop to weakness.

Ind. I believe we shall not make peace by our talks. If the contention is, who has the most humanity, let him who made us judge. We have no pretensions to superior knowledge; we ask, Who knows best how to use what they have? If we contend for power, our arms must decide: the leaves must wither on the tree of peace; we shall cut it down with the battle-ax, and stain the green grass that grows under it with your blood.

W. Man You know the blessings of peace, and the calamities of war. If you wish to live secure in your wigwams, and to rove the forest unmolested, cultivate our friendship. Break not into our houses in the defenceless hours of sleep. Let no more of our innocent friends be dragged from their protectors, and driven into the inhospitable wilderness; or what is still more inhuman, fall victims to your unrelenting barbarity! If you prefer war, we shall drive its horrors into your own settlements. The sword shall destroy your friends, and the fire comsume your dwellings.

Ind. We love peace; we love our friends; we love all men, as much as you. When your fathers came over the big water, we treated them as brothers: they had nothing: peace and plenty were among us. All the land was ours, from the east to the west water; from the mountains of snow in the north, to the burning path of the sun in the south. They were made welcome to our land and to all we possessed. To talk like White Men, they were beggars, and we their benefactors: they were tenants at will, and we their landlords. But we nourished a viper in our bosoms. You have poisoned us by your luxury; spread contention among us by your subtlety, and death by your treachery. The Indians have but two predominant passions, friendship and revenge. Deal with us as friends, and you may fish in our rivers or hunt in our forests. Treat us not like servants; we shall never own you as masters. If you provoke us, our vengeance shall pursue you. We shall drink your blood; you may spill ours. We had rather die in honorable war, than live in dishonorable peace.

EXTRACT FROM AN ORATION PRONOUNCED AT BOSTON, JULY 4, 1796.

THAT the best way for a great empire to tax her colonies is to confer benefits upon them, and, that no rulers have a right to levy contributions upon the property, or expect the services of their subjects, without their own or the consent of their immediate representatives, were principles never recognised by the ministry and parliament of Great-Britain. Fatally enamoured of their selfish systems of policy, and obstinately determined to effect the execution of their nefarious purposes, they were deaf to the suggestions of reason and the demands of justice. The frantic, though transient energy of intoxicated rage was exhibited in their every act, and blackened and distorted the features of their national character.

On the contrary, Americans had but one object in view, for in Independence are concentrated and condensed every blessing that makes life desirable, every right and every privilege which can tend to the happiness or secure the native dignity of man. In the attainment of Independence were all their passions, their desires, and their powers engaged. The intrepidity and magnanimity of their armies; the wisdom and inflexible firmness of their Congress; the ardency of their patriotism; their unrepining patience, when assailed by dangers and perplexed with aggravated misfortunes, have long and deservedly employed the pen of panegyric and the tongue of eulogy.

Through the whole revolutionary conflict, a consistency and systematic regularity were preserved, equally honorable as extraordinary. The unity of design and classically correct arrangement of the series of incidents, which completed the Epic story of American Independence, were so wonderful, so well wrought, that political Hypercriticism was abashed at the mighty production, and forced to join her sister Envy, in applauding the glorious composition.

It is my pleasing duty, my fellow-citizens, to felicitate you on the establishment of our national sovereignty; and among the various subjects for congratulation and rejoicing, this is not the most unimportant, that Heaven has spared so many veterans in the art of war; so many sages, who are versed in the best politics of peace; men, who were able to instruct and to govern, and whose faithful services, whose unremitted exertions to promote the public prosperity, entitle them to our firmest confidence and warmest gratitude. Uniting in the celebration of this anniversary, I am happy to behold many of the illustrious remnant of that band of patriots, who, despising danger and death, determined to be free, or gloriously perish in the cause. Their counte-

nances beam inexpressible delight! our joys are increased by their presence; our raptures are heightened by
their participation. The feelings, which inspired them
in the "times which tried men's souls," are communi-
cated to our bosoms. We catch the divine spirit which
impelled them to bid defiance to the congregated host
of despots. We swear to preserve the blessings they
toiled to gain, which they obtained by the incessant
labours of eight distressful years; to transmit to our
posterity, our rights undiminished, our honour untar-
nished, and our freedom unimpaired.

On the last page of Fate's eventful volume, with the
raptured ken of prophecy, I behold Columbia's name
recorded; her future honours and happiness inscribed.
In the same important book the approaching end of
Tyranny and the triumph of Right and Justice are
written in indelible characters. The struggle will soon
be over; the tottering thrones of despots will quickly
fall, and bury their proud incumbents in their massy
ruins!

Then peace on earth shall hold her easy sway,
And man forget his brother man to slay.
To martial arts, shall milder arts succeed;
Who blesses most, shall gain th' immortal meed.
The eye of pity shall be pain'd no more,
With vict'ry's crimson banners stained with gore.
Thou glorious era, come! Hail, blessed time!
When full-orb'd Freedom shall unclouded shine;
When the chaste Muses, cherish'd by her rays,
In olive groves shall tune their sweetest lays;
When bounteous Ceres shall direct her car,
O'er fields now blasted with the fires of war;
And angels view, with joy and wonder join'd,
The golden age return'd to bless mankind!

DIALOGUE BETWEEN EDWARD AND HARRY.

[EDWARD, *alone, reading.*]

Enter HARRY, *with an important air.*

Harry. HOW are you, Ned?

Edward. What, is it you, brother Harry? Were it not for the small part of your face, that appears between your fore-top and your cravat, I should never know you.

Har. My appearance is a little altered, to be sure; but I hope you will allow it is for the better.

Edw. I wish I could. I perceive, that, some how or other, you are completely metamorphosed from a plain country lad, to a Boston buck, beau, or fop: which is the current word in your varying town dialect, to express such a thing as yourself?

Har. Ah, either of them will do. The young ladies sometimes call me *Tippy Harry;* that suits my ear the best.

Edw. That, I suppose, means a little fop, or, as I should express it, a *foppee,* who is obliged to stand tip-toe to reach a lady her fan.

Har. One of your clownish blunders, Ned. It means an airy young gentleman, dressed out in complete bon ton from head to foot, like myself.

Edw. " An airy young gentleman, dressed out in complete *bon ton,* &c. &c." This definition may be of service to me; I will try to remember it. You always possessed one quality of a gentleman, a large share of good humour: I hope you will not be angry, brother, if I am a little inquisitive.

Har. Do, Ned, leave off using that oldfashioned word. I had rather you would do any thing to me than *brother,* me at this rate. If you should come to Boston, dressed as you are now, with your clumsy shoes, coarse stockings, great small-clothes, home-spun coat, and your old rusty go-to-mill hat, and shake hands with me, in your awkward way; and then, to complete the whole, should call me *brother*, I should be thunderstruck! For my credit's sake, I should swear it was some crazy straggler, I had seen in the country, and given a few coppers to keep him from starving. I would hide behind the counter, or lie rolled up in a piece of broadcloth a week, rather than be caught in such a scrape.

Edw. An airy young gentleman, indeed! would swear to half a dozen lies, hide behind the counter, and roll yourself up in a piece of broadcloth like a silkworm, to save your credit! You have improved much beyond my expectations, *Tippy* Harry! This sounds better in your refined ear than brother Harry, I suppose.

Har. Yes it does, Ned, I'll assure you: that's your sort! You begin to come on a little. Now I'll tell you how it is, Ned; if you would take your old musty library here, and lay it all on the fire together, and burn all your old-fashioned clothes with it, and then go to Boston—

Edw. What, without any clothes, Harry?

Har. Why, I think I should about as lief be seen with you stark naked, as with your coarse, narrow-backed, short-waisted coat. But as I was saying before, then put yourself under the care of a tailor, barber, shoemaker, and dancing master; keep a store of English goods about three months, go to the Theatre a dozen nights, chat with our Boston Tippies, have a few high goes, and freeze and thaw two or three times, for you are monstrously stiff; I say after all this; I believe, Ned, you would make a very clever fellow.

Edw. The freezing and thawing is a kind of discipline I should not so readily comply with. I have heard of several of your *clever fellows*, and ladies of *your sort*, who were found frozen in old barns, and behind board fences; but I never knew they were so fortunate as to thaw again. Now, Harry, I will be serious with you. Your airy young gentleman, in my opinion is a very insipid character; far beneath my ambition. A few materials from behind the counter, the tailor's needle and shears, the barber's puff and pomatum, a little sheep-skin modified by the shoe-maker, and what is the most insignificant of all, a little supple, puny machine, that in plain English, I should call a naked fool; to strut about the streets with all this finery; carry it to the theatre, or dancing school; and teach it to say a few pretty things by rote; these make the gentleman of *your sort*. Mine is composed of quite different materials.

Har. Pray let me know what they are? homespun, I dare say. I am superfine, you see, from head to foot.

Edw. Yes, Harry, you have blundered into one just observation. In the first place, I would lay up a good store of knowledge, *home-spun* from my own reflections, reading and observations; not the second-handed smattering of the most ignorant of all beings who use a tongue. The tailor's, barber's, and dancing-master's bill should not show an inventory of *all* I possessed. They may make my clothes, dress my hair, and teach me how to bow; but there must be something more to command the bow of respect from people of sense, the judges of real merit. In short, I would be a gentleman farmer; too well informed to be influenced by your railing newspaper politics; too much delighted with the bleating and playing of the flocks in my own pasture, to read the head of *Theatricals*, or be amused with any drove of stage players, that have invested our country from Charleston to Portsmouth. And I should be much more proud of raising one likely calf, than as many of the most insipid of all animals, called *Tippies*, as could stand in every ...ill.

DAVID AND GOLIATH.

Goliath. WHERE is the mighty man of war,
    who dares
Accept the challenge of Philistia's chief?
What victor-king, what general drench'd in blood,
Claims this high privilege? What are his rights?
What proud credentials does the boaster bring,
To prove his claim? What cities laid in ashes,
What ruin'd provinces, what slaughter'd realms,
What heads of heroes, and what hearts of kings,
In battle kill'd, or at his altars slain,
Has he to boast? Is his bright armory
Thick set with spears, and swords, and coats of mail,
Of vanquish'd nations, by his single arm
Subdu'd? Where is the mortal man so bold,
So much a wretch, so out of love with life,
To dare the weight of this uplifted spear,
Which never fell innoxious? Yet I swear,
I grudge the glory to his parting soul
To fall by this right hand. 'Twill sweeten death,
To know he had the honour to contend
With the dread son of Anak. Latest time
From blank oblivion shall retrieve his name,
Who dar'd to perish in unequal fight
With Gath's triumphant champion. Come, advance!
Philistia's gods to Israel's. Sound, my herald,
Sound for the battle straight!

   David. Behold thy foe!

   Gol. I see him not.

   Dav. Behold him here!

   Gol. Say, where?
Direct my sight. I do not war with boys.

   Dav. I stand prepar'd thy single arm to mine

   Gol. Why, this is mockery, minion'
To cost thee dear. Sport not with
But tell me who, of all this num'

Expects his death from me? Which is the man,
Whom Israel sends to meet my bold defiance?

Dav. The election of my sov'reign falls on me.

Gol. On thee! on thee! by Dagon, 'tis too much.
Thou curled minion! thou a nation's champion!
'Twould move my mirth at any other time;
But trifling's out of tune. Begone, light boy!
And tempt me not too far.

Dav. I do defy thee,
Thou foul idolater! Hast thou not scorn'd
The armies of the living God I serve?
By me he will avenge upon thy head
Thy nation's sins and thine. Arm'd with his name,
Unshrinking, I dare meet the stoutest foe
That ever bath'd his hostile spear in blood.

Gol. Indeed! 'tis wondrous well! Now, by my gods,
The stripling plays the orator! Vain boy!
Keep close to that same bloodless war of words,
And thou shalt still be safe. Tongue-valiant warrior
Where is thy sylvan crook, with garlands hung,
Of idle field flowers? Where thy wanton harp,
Thou dainty-finger'd hero? Better strike
Its note lascivious; or, the lulling lute
Touch softly, than provoke the tempest's rage.
I will not stain the honor of my spear
With thy inglorious blood. Shall that fair cheek
Be scarr'd with wounds unseemly? Rather go,
And hold fond dalliance with the Syrian maids;
To wanton measures dance; and let them braid
The bright luxuriance of thy golden hair;
They, for their lost Adonis, may mistake
Thy dainty form.

Dav. Peace, thou unhallow'd railer!
O tell it not in Gath, nor let the sound
Reach Askelon, how once your slaughter'd lords,
By mighty Samson found one common grave:
When his broad shoulder the firm pillars heav'd,
And to its base the tott'ring fabric shook.

Gol. Insulting boy; perhaps thou hast not heard
The infamy of that inglorious day,
When your weak hosts at Eben-ezer pitch'd
Their quick-abandon'd tents. Then, when your ark,
Your talisman, your charm, your boasted pledge
Of safety and success, was tamely lost!
And yet not tamely, since by me 'twas won.
When with this good right-arm, I thinn'd your ranks,
And bravely crush'd, beneath a single blow,
The chosen guardians of this vaunted shrine,
Hophni and Phineas. The fam'd ark itself,
I bore to Ashdod.

Dav. I remember too,
Since thou provok'st th' unwelcome truth, how all
Your blushing priests beheld their idol's shame;
When prostrate Dagon fell before the ark,
And your frail god was shiver'd. Then Philistia,
Idolatrous Philistia flew for succour
To Israel's help, and all her smitten nobles
Confess'd the Lord was. God, and the blest ark,
Gladly, with reverential awe restor'd!

Gol. By Ashdod's fame thou ly'st. Now will I
            meet thee,
Thou insect warrior! since thou dar'st me thus!
Already I behold thy mangled limbs,
Dissever'd each from each, ere long to feed
The fierce blood-snuffing vulture. Mark me well!
Around my spear I'll twist thy shining locks,
And toss in air thy head all gash'd with wounds;
Thy lips, yet quiv'ring with the dire convulsion
Of recent death! Art thou not terrified?

Dav. No.
True courage is not mov'd by breath of words;
But the rash bravery of boiling blood,
Impetuous, knows no settled principle.
A feverish tide, it has its ebbs and flows,
As spirits rise or fall, as wine inflames,
Or circumstances change. But inborn courage,
The gen'rous child of fortitude and faith,

Holds its firm empire in the constant soul;
And, like the stedfast pole star, never once
From the same fix'd and faithful point declines.

Gol. The curses of Philistia's gods be on thee!
This fine drawn speech is meant to lengthen out
That little life thy words pretend to scorn.

   Dav. Ha! say'st thou so? Come on then! Mark us
      well.
Thou com'st to me with sword, and spear, and shield!
In the dread name of Israel's God, I come;
The living Lord of Hosts, whom thou defy'st!
Yet though no shield I bring; no arms, except
These five smooth stones I gather'd from the brook,
With such a simple sling as shepherds use;
Yet all exposed, defenceless as I am,
The God I serve shall give thee up a prey
To my victorious arm. This day I mean
To make th' uncircumcised tribes confess
There is a God in Israel. I will give thee,
Spite of thy vaunted strength and giant bulk,
To glut the carrion kites. Nor thee alone;
The mangled carcasses of your thick hosts
Shall spread the plains of Elah; till Philistia,
Through all her trembling tents and flying bands,
Shall own that Judah's God is God indeed!
I dare thee to the trial!

   Gol. Follow me.
In this good spear I trust.

   Dav. I trust in Heaven!
The God of battles stimulates my arm,
And fires my soul with ardour, not its own.

————*+*————

AN ORATION ON THE POWERS OF ELOQUENCE,
WRITTEN FOR AN EXHIBITION OF A SCHOOL IN
BOSTON, 1794.

AMIDST the profusion of interesting and brilliant
objects in this assembly, should the speaker be able

to engage the attention of a few eyes, and a few ears, he will esteem his reception flattering. To another is allotted the pleasing task of closing the evening, with remarks on Female Education.* It is mine to recommend the POWERS OF ELOQUENCE, and to show the influence which it justly challenges, over the senses, passions and understandings of mankind.

Eloquence consists in a capacity of expressing, by the voice, attitude, gesture, and countenance, the emotions of the heart. To this art, Demosthenes and Cicero owe their immortality; by this, the late earl of Chatham gained his celebrity; and to this, are the great politicians, now in Europe, indebted for their distinction. Eloquent men begin to be heard with attention in our Congress; pulpit orators gain crowds, and eloquent lawyers gain causes.

When the enlightened Statesman is discussing the interests of a country, on which are grafted his fortune, fame and life, he *must* be eloquent. When the general harangues a brave soldiery, at the eve of a battle, on which depend their liberties and lives, he *must* be eloquent. When the compassionate lawyer, without hope of reward, advocates the cause of the suffering widow, or injured orphan, he *must* be eloquent.

But when true eloquence is introduced into the sacred desk, how elevated is the subject of the passion on the cross! With what animating zeal can the preacher call on his hearers, to " open a highway for their God!" With what rapture can he burst from the gloom of types and figures, into the brightness of that everlasting Gospel which brought " life and immortality to light!" With what heaven-taught joy can he hail the star in the East! and with what semblance of reality may he lead the imaginations of his audience to a sight of the babe in the manger! If he *feel* such subjects he must be eloquent and irresistible.

May we now look back and trace the progress and influence of Eloquence on different subjects, and at

* See American Preceptor, p. 47.

various periods? How do we feel its power, when we hear David expressing the appearing of the Highest! " He bowed the heavens also, and came down, and darkness was under his feet; he rode upon a cherub, and did fly, and he was seen upon the wings of the wind."

Who can hear, without emotion, the sublime eloquence of the prophet Isaiah, when he announces the future glory of the Church? " Violence shall no more be heard in thy land; wasting nor destruction within thy borders: but thou shalt call thy walls Salvation, and thy gates, Praise."

But in what language has the prophet Habakkuk described the majesty of the Creator? " Before him went the pestilence, and burning coals went forth at his feet: he stood, and measured the earth: he beheld, and drove asunder the nations: the everlasting mountains were scattered: the perpetual hills did bow: his ways are everlasting." Let us pass in respectful silence the eloquence of Him, who " spake, as never man spake."

But our attention is immediately arrested by the defence of Paul before Agrippa; in which he describes a light from heaven, above the brightness of the mid-day sun; when he declares his conversion, and commission to be a minister, and a witness of those things, which he had seen, and of those things, in which the Saviour would appear unto him. " Whereupon," says he, " O king Agrippa, I was not disobedient unto the heavenly vision."

Nor can we fail to mention that eloquence, which made Felix tremble on his throne. Nor can we read, unmoved, Paul's solemn account of the resurrection; when, " in a moment, in the twinkling of an eye, the dead shall be raised, and we shall be changed." But when we come to the vision on the isle of Patmos, where the glory of heaven was unveiled to a man of God, we are lost in the majesty and sublimity of the description of things, which must be hereafter; and must close the sacred scriptures, convinced of the irresistible Powers of Eloquence when employed upon divine subjects.

Among themes less interesting, is there *one*, on which these powers have been unsuccessfully employed? we read how the eloquence of one man governed all hearts in Greece, and how astonishing was its effect from the immortal orator at Rome. All civilized nations can furnish facts and arguments on this subject. Wherever arts and sciences have found a residence, oratory has been a sure attendant.

I am obliged to pass, with regret, the characters of D'Espremenil, Mirabeau, Burke, Fox, Flood, and Grattan, who, within our own days, have made the Senates of three different kingdoms ring with their eloquence. With greater reluctance must I pass the memorable time, when all the senses, passions, and almost breath of five thousand people were suspended at the admirable eloquence of Sheridan, while he described the cruelties of Hastings on the banks of the Ganges; when with unfeeling madness that despot reddened the waters with the blood of mothers and their infants, and made even the river blush for the honor of the British name.

With pleasure I bring my subject to the scenes of my native country; and here could, with the enthusiasm of Columbus in his vision, present before you the lofty Andes, the majestic Mississippi, the beautful Ohio, the falls of Niagara, and the lakes of the north. I might take a view of this country, extending through the five zones, comprehending all the climates, and producing all the varieties of the earth.

Our ears have heard what wonders have been wrought in United America. Our eyes see its present happy situation. After many toils and convulsions, we at length find ourselves safe on the top of Nebo and our Moses yet alive at the head of our rulers. Hence we look forward to the flattering prospects of futurity. Our orators and poets have announced blessed things in the latter days. Our prophets have taught us to expect the reality of golden dreams. The leaves of our future history are gilded, and the pages are left to be filled up, with the actions of a long list of *unambitious* Cesars.

We are told, that on this our native spot of earth, slavish government and slavish hierarchies shall cease; that here, the old prophecies shall be verified; that here shall be the last universal empire on earth, the empire of reason and virtue; under which the gospel of peace shall have free course and be glorified; that here " the wolf shall dwell with the lamb, and the leopard with the kid, and that nation shall no more lift up sword against nation."

When the philosopher of the East foresaw the beauty and excellence of this Western Continent, its immense rivers, lakes, and mountains; cities rising from the midst of desolation; " men like trees walking," where once were the haunts of savage beasts; arts and manners improving; the rose budding in the desert, and the flowers of the garden in the solitary place, rich indeed was the prospect. But *his* visions have become *our* realities. We live to enjoy blessings, more numerous than Columbus could count.

We see schools, academies, and colleges, opening their treasures to every family; and are taught, that religion, liberty and science, are constellations in the heavens, which, amidst the revolution of empires, visit in succession, all the kingdoms and people of the earth. We see one half of the world involved in darkness, and oblivious sleep; while the other is enjoying the blessings of day, and of vigilant industry.

The day of American glory has at length dawned. No more shall meteors of the air, and insects with gilded wings, lead astray the benighted traveller, nor the bleaking buzzards of the night triumph over the bird of Jove. Prejudice, ignorance, and tyranny, are flying on the wings of the wind. While this day is ours, let us be up and doing.

May I now introduce my subject within these walls? And here, how extensive is the theme for my feeble powers of Eloquence! yet may I employ them, in suggesting the motives which your sons and daughters have to cultivate their minds. Gratitude to their parents; your patronage; their own ambition; their prospects of future profit, usefulness, and honest fame, are among the first.

But highly important is rendered this morning of life and privilege to us, from a consideration, that we are born in the best of countries, at the best of times. While some of the human race are suffering the extreme heats of burning zones, and others are freezing beyond the influence of benignant rays, we live in a climate, temperate, salubrious, and healthful. While some inherit from their parents poverty and slavery, we are the heirs of private, public, and social benefits.

Our eyes have been opened in a country, where the Father of mercies has been pleased to condense his blessings. On us beams the sun of Science: ours is the hemisphere of Freedom: here are enjoyed THE RIGHTS OF MAN; and upon us shine, with ceaseless splendor, the rays of the STAR OF BETHLEHEM.

Blest in the dispensations of nature, providence, and grace, on us depends a faithful improvement of our numerous talents. Early taught the shortness and value of life, and the importance of improving each hour of youth, while we have leisure, and the assistance of instructers, we early learn to be diligent. Observing, that with our parents, the shadows of the evening begin to lengthen, and that soon the wheel will cease to turn round at the cistern; that soon they must leave us, and that we must fill their places, we learn to be ambitious and emulous to excel. But beyond these, we have with all other children of the universe, an argument still higher to improve these precious days. We live not only for ourselves, for our parents, friends, and country; but for the Giver of life: we live for immortality. Young as we are, and just entered the bark of being; yet like you, we are on a boundless ocean, and an eternal voyage.

As ELOQUENCE is my theme, perhaps I may be indulged in dwelling for the few remaining moments, on this last most interesting subject. While enjoying the blessings of health, and the festivities of youth, we stand on this bridge of life, careless of the rapid currents of yesterdays and to-morrows; yet reflection teaches that the hour is rapidly hastening, when " the cloud-capt towers; the gorgeous palaces; the solemn temples; yea, the great globe itself, with all which it inherits, shall dissolve, and like the baseless fabric of a vision, leave not a wreck behind." We shall survive.

Though the loss of parents and friends; though the frequent infirmities and vicissitudes of life, teach us gloomily to reflect, that " An angel's arm can't snatch us from the grave;" yet a sure prospect of a resurrection to ceaseless life, bids us say with triumph, " Legions of angels can't confine us there." We look back on the ages which have passed, and see the millions of men, who since the days of Adam, have been laid in the dust. We see nine hundred and fifty millions of rational beings, now in full life, who must, in a few years, be cold and in death; and in every day of our lives, no less than eighty-six thousand of the human race, are laid in the grave. What oceans of tears have been shed by surviving friends!

How have mourning, lamentation, and woe been heard not only in Rama, but throughout every quarter of the inhabited earth! We contemplate the time, when these bodies of ours, now full of life and motion, shall be cold. We elevate our thoughts to that scene, when the elements shall melt with fervent heat; when the sun shall be darkened, and the moon no more give light: when the stars of heaven shall fall from their places, and all nature be tumbling into ruins.

Then the trump of God shall sound; then shall he who once said, " Lazarus, come forth," descend from heaven with a mighty shout. Then, shall the dead hear the voice of the Son of God; then shall they burst the bands of death, and rise, never to sleep again. Then shall this mortal put on immortality, and death be swallowed up of life.

We shall be present at this august resurrection! Soon shall we cease to see the blue canopy of the day, and the starred curtain of the night; to hear the rolling of the thunder, or see the lightning of the heavens; scenes, which now impress us with awe and delight. We look round creation, and see all living nature, below our rank, dissolving to dust; never to revive. We see the flowers of spring die, and the leaves of autumn fade; never to resume their beauty and verdure. But contemplating the soul of man, we are led to the language of the poet,

" See truth, love, and mercy in triumph descending,
    And nature all glowing in Eden's first bloom,
On the cold cheek of death smiles and roses are blend-
        ing,
    And beauty immortal awakes from the tomb."

This subject, itself so full of Eloquence, is also full of instruction and argument. Whatever elevates the dignity of our natures, and extends our views, teaches us to live; daily to improve our minds; daily to better our hearts. May ELOQUENCE ever be improved in the cause of learning and virtue; ever employed in addressing important truths to the mind, in a most forcible and expressive manner.

May the daughters of America wear their charms, as attendants on their virtue, the satellites of their innocence, and the ornament of their sex. May her sons early learn the principles of honor, honesty, diligence, and patriotism; and when called to leave these happy seats, where care is a stranger, and where learning is a free gift, be prepared for the burden and heat of the day, and ever prove as a munition of rocks to their country.

A Dialogue between a City Gentleman of the Ton, and a Country Farmer.

Gentleman. HALLOO! there, Master? What have you got in your wallet?

Farmer. Fowls, Sir, at your service.

Gent. And what do you ask a pair?

Farm. Fifty cents a pair for ducks, and seventy-five cents a piece for geese and turkeys.

Gent. What is the fellow talking about? I inquired the price of fowls; not of geese and turkeys.

Farm. And pray, Mister, what is the difference between a fowl and a goose? My bible teaches me, that all the feathered tribe are ranged under the general name of fowl.

Gent. Why, you numskull! don't quote scripture to me, to prove such palpable absurdities. I can teach you, that a goose, or turkey, is no more like a fowl, than a human being is like one of the animal creation!

Farm. I crave your pardon, Mister. I begin to see that I never was larn'd the right use of language; for, since I come among these fine gentlefolks, I don't understand one half that's said to me.

Gent. So it seems. However, you have now entered a good school to learn *civilization.* What I wanted, was, a pair of those creatchures that lay eggs, wulgarly called hens.

Farm. Why, begging your pardon, Sir, and hoping no offence, I should suppose, that, at least, *one* of the sorts I have in my wallet lays eggs, from the multitude of *goslins* I see about your streets.

Gent. Why, you fool; where were you bred? I should imagine you come fifty miles off, where they tell me the people are almost savages; and that you were never in market before.

Farm. It is true, I live more than fifty miles off, and never was in this great city before; and in fact, I

2 B

begin to think I never shall desire to be again; for I have hitherto met with pretty rough handling, I assure you.

Gent. No wonder that such ignorance should expose you to insults. A man like you, who has been brung up among savages, and not able to speak intelligibly, must expect to receive severe discipline, when he first visits a land of *civilization.*

Farm. I begin to see what a sad thing it is, especially in such a place as this, to be so destitute as I am of the right kind of larning. I confess, that, so far from *civilization,* I have never received but little more than *christianization.* But I should think, even *that* ought to entitle an honest, well-meaning man to better treatment than I have met with this morning.

Gent. You have no right to complain. Such a blundering blockhead as you are ought to think himself forchunate, if he is suffered to pass the streets without having his head broke.

Farm. Indeed I have hardly escaped that. I have been accosted a hundred and fifty times since I entered the big town by all sorts and sizes of folks, both male and female. Which, at first, indeed, appeared civil enough; for not a child in the street but what *master'd* me, as mannerly as though I had teach'd school all my days. But whenever I approached them, it was old daddy, old man, old fellow, and so on; rising by degrees to such genteel language as your Worship seems to be master of. I hope no offence, Sir. The first time I had the honour to be noticed, a fine gentlewoman called to me from her window. So I civilly entered her door; when she squalled out " You filthy brute! Have you the impudence to come in at my front door?" Did you not call me, madam? replied I. Yes, truly, says she; but I thought you had more *civilization,* than to set your ugly, square-toed shoes upon my carpet. I craved her ladyship's pardon; told her I hoped I should learn *civilization* from such good example; and got off as well as I could.

Gent. It is evident you know nothing of the world.

Farm. How should I, since I live an hundred miles off, and never read scarcely any thing but my bible and psalm book?

Gent. Ay, sure enough. You are much to be pitied. Why, according to the rules of *civilization*, you offended the lady insufferably.

Farm. So I perceive; though, at first, I could not conceive, for the life of me, what harm there could be in entering the front door, since there was no other in the house; nor how my shoes could give offence, inasmuch as they were perfectly clean.

Gent. Why, did not you just acknowledge they where 'unfashionable?

Farm. Ay, right. And mayhap she discovered the nails in the heels; though I could have assured her they would not scratch; for they were well drove, and the heads smooth. Well, as I was saying, soon after I escaped from her ladyship's civilities, I was stopped by a squire-looking gentleman, whose palate was set for the same dainty that yours was, fowls. I told him I had as fine ones as ever were hatched. So I showed him the whole contents af my wallet; when, after examining it critically, he exclaimed, " You insulting puppy! I have a mind in my conscience to cane you. What, sirrah! tell me you have fowls to sell, when you have nothing but a parcel of poultry!" So, giving me a kick or two, he tells me to go and learn *civilization.*

Gent. And served you right enough too.

Farm. So as I proceeded peaceably through the street, I met a stripling, in his soldier's coat, making the same use of his sword as I did of my staff. Having a heavy load, and tripping my foot a little, I unfortunately jostled this beardless hero. " What do you mean, you dirty scoundrel!" he instantly exclaimed; lifting up his sword at the same time. " Have you no more *civilization* than to treat an officer of the navy in such a rude manner?" I beg pardon, says I. It was ·

purely an accident." If you were not beneath my notice, says he, swearing a big oath, which I dare not
repeat; if you were not beneath the notice of a gentleman, I say, I would soon lay you upon your beam
ends, you fresh water lobster! You are as destitute of
civilization, as if you never had been out of sight of
land in all your life."

Gent. You will learn in time to keep at a respectful distance from gentlemen of the sword. It is fort-
chunate for you, that the officer did not make day-
light shine through you.

Farm. I believe it dangerous, I confess, to venture very near *gentlemen*, if these may be called such.
Well, the next person I met, I took, from his brogue,
to be a "wild Irishman." At any rate, he was a fun-
ny fellow, and discovered some marks of *civilization*.
Maister, says he, have you any wery good weal in
your vallet? I do not understand Irish, Mister, replied
I. Irish! Irish! old mutton-head, said he; nor I neither.
It is enough for me, that I am able to speak good
English. I ax'd you what you had to sell. I am fit-
ting out a wessel for Wenice; loading her with warious
keinds of prowisions, and wittualling her for a long
woyage; and I want several hundred weight of weal,
wenison, &c. with a planty of inyons and vinegar, for
the preserwation of ealth. I assured him I did not
comprehend his meaning. It is wary natchural, replied he, to suppose it, as you are but a poor country
man and want *civilization*. So he peaceably withdrew.
And now, good Mister, ('*squire*, perhaps I ought to
say; for, before you stopped me, I heard you admin-
istering oaths;) I say, good 'Squire, as you have con-
descended to give me some useful instruction, pray
be so kind as to tell me, to what species of animals a
creature would belong, which should be, in every respect, exactly like yourself, excepting the addition of a
pair of long ears?

Gent. I will not disgrace myself by keeping your
company any longer.   [*Exit.*]

Farm. [*alone*] What a strange run of luck I have had to-day! If this is *civilization*, I desire to return to my savage haunt again. However, I don't despair yet of meeting with people of *real* civilization; for I have always been told that this place is not without its share. Yet I fear they have greatly degenerated from the simple manners of their forefathers. Their placing mere civility above Christianity is a plain proof of it. The ancestors of this people were anxious mainly to teach their posterity Christianity, not doubting but civility would naturally attend it. What vexes me most is, that I can't understand their language. For my part, I think they have but little reason to laugh at my pronunciation, This is the first time I ever heard that turkeys, geese, and ducks, were not fowls. They might as well tell me, that oxen, bulls, and cows are not cattle. I take this last chap to be of the race of coxcombs; and I think it is sometimes best, to indulge them in their own exalted opinion of themselves, till experience teaches them their folly. I know I am but a plain man; and no one feels want of larning more than I do. But I am certain I cannot appear more contemptible in this coxcomb's eyes, than he does in mine.

EXTRACT FROM A DISCOURSE DELIVERED BEFORE THE NEW-YORK SOCIETY FOR PROMOTING THE MANUMISSION OF SLAVES, APRIL 12, 1797. BY REV. SAMUEL MILLER.

I HAVE hitherto confined myself to the consideration of slavery as it exists among ourselves, and of that unjust domination which is exercised over the Africans and their descendants, who are already in our country. It is with a regret and indignation which I am unable to express, that I call your attention to the conduct of some among us, who, instead of diminishing, strive to increase the evil in question.

While the friends of humanity, in Europe and America, are weeping over their injured fellow-creatures, and directing their ingenuity and their labors to the removal of so disgraceful a monument of cruelty and avarice, there are not wanting men, who claim the title, and enjoy the privileges of American citizens who still employ themselves in the odious traffic of human flesh.

Yes, in direct opposition to public sentiment, and a law of the land, there are ships fitted out, every year, in the ports of the United States, to transport the inhabitants of Africa, from their native shores, and consign them to all the torments of West-India oppression.

Fellow citizens! is Justice asleep? Is Humanity discouraged and silent, on account of the many injuries she has sustained? Were not this the case, methinks the pursuit of the beasts of the forest would be forgotten, and such monsters of wickedness would, in their stead, be hunted from the abodes of men.

Oh Africa! unhappy, ill-fated region! how long shall thy savage inhabitants have reason to utter complaints, and to imprecate the vengeance of Heaven against civilization and Christianity? Is it not enough that nature's God has consigned thee to arid plains, to noxious vapours, to devouring beasts of prey, and to all the scorching influences of the torrid zone? Must rapine and violence, captivity and slavery, be superadded to thy torments; and be inflicted too by men, who wear the garb of justice and humanity, who boast the principles of a sublime morality; and who hypocritically adopt the accents of the benevolent religion of Jesus?

Oh Africa! thou loud proclaimer of the rapacity, the treachery, and cruelty of civilized man! Thou everlasting monument of European and American disgrace! " Remember not against us our offences, nor the offences of our forefathers; be tender in the great day of inquiry; and show a Christian world, that thou canst suffer, and forgive!"

A Forensic Dispute on the Question, Are the Anglo-Americans endowed with Capacity and Genius equal to Europeans?

A. MY opinion is decidedly on the affirmative of this question. In this opinion I am confirmed by sound argument and undeniable facts.

If nature has lavished her favours on some countries, and dealt them out with a sparing hand in others, the Western world is far from being the scene of her parsimony. From a geographical survey of our country, directly the reverse will appear.

This continent, extending through all the different climates of the earth, exhibiting on its immense surface the largest rivers and lakes, and the loftiest mountains in the known world, shows us that nature has wrought on her largest scale on this side the Atlantic.

The soil is neither so luxuriant as to indulge in sloth, nor so barren, as not to afford sufficient leisure from its own culture, to attend to that of the mind. These are facts, which existed before the migration of our ancestors from Europe. The argument I shall deduce from them, to me appears conclusive.

The soil and climate of every country is in some measure characteristic of the genius of its inhabitants. Nature is uniform in her works. Where she has stinted the productions of the earth, she also cramps her animal productions; and even the mind of man. Where she has clothed the earth with plenty, there is no deficiency in the animate creation, and man arrives to his full vigour.

In the application of these physical causes to our nature, there is an effect produced on the mind, as well as the body. The mind receives it tincture from the objects which it contemplates. This we find confirmed by the opposite sensations we feel, when viewing a beautiful and variegated landscape, and plodding our course over a craggy way, or uniform, barren plain. In these contrasted situations, it may almost be said, that we possess two different souls, and are not the same beings.

Those objects, which constantly surround us, must have a more permanent effect. Where man is doomed constantly to view the imperfect sketches and caricature paintings of nature, he forms a corresponding part of the group; when placed amidst her most beautiful and magnificent works, we find him elevated in thought and complete in corporeal stature.

These arguments may seem far-fetched; but when it is admitted that Chimborazo is higher than Teneriffe; the Amazon and La Plata superior to the largest rivers in the old world; and that America abounds with all the productions of nature in as great plenty as any country in Europe, premises will then be established, from which, by my reasoning, we shall draw the conclusion that if the Aborigines of this country are inferior to the savages of other parts of the world, nature must have contradicted her own first principles.

But the contrary must appear to every unprejudiced mind, both from reason and observation. It being granted that the savages on this continent possess genius and capacity, equal to those on the other, my argument is ended; the affirmative of the question is established; unless those who differ from me should be able to show, that, by some process or rather paradox of nature, the mental powers of our forefathers were degenerated by being transplanted to a soil, at least as congenial and fertile, as that which gave them birth.

Should it be any longer contended against me, I should still appeal to facts, and rely on the philosophical discoveries and miscellaneous writings of a Franklin, the heroic valour and sagacious prudence of a Washington, the political researches of an Adams, the numerous productions in polite literature, inventions and improvements in the useful arts; and especially that spirit of enterprise, which distinguishes our nation.

On these I should rely to vindicate the honor of my country, and to combat that prejudice, which would degrade the capacity and genius of Americans.

B. I have heard your argument with patience, and shall answer it with candour. It is readily granted, that there are as large rivers, extensive lakes, and lofty mountains, in America, as in any other part of the world; but I am totally unacquainted with the art of measuring the capacity and genius of men, by the height of the mountains they gaze upon, or the breadth of the river, whose margin they chance to inhabit.

Whether the savages of our deserts possess mental powers equal to those of other countries, is as foreign to my purpose, as the Chimborazo, Amazon, or La Plata. I shall admit your premises, and look for the materials of my argument on a ground you have slightly passed over, to confute the conclusion you have drawn from them.

The question is, whether the capacity and genius of Americans is equal to that of Europeans?

Let us adopt an unexceptionable rule; " Judge the tree by its fruit." If the literary productions and works of genius of our countrymen are found superior to those of Europeans, the affirmative of the question must be true; if inferior, the negative, without argument, is supported by fact.

Here the balance evidently turns in my favour. Europe can boast its masters in each of the sciences, and its models of perfection in the polite arts. Few Americans pursue the path of science; none have progressed, even so far as those bold and persevering geniuses of other countries, who have removed the obstacles and smoothed the way before them.

If there chance to spring up among us one whose inclination attaches him to the fine arts, the beggar's pittance, instead of fame and profit, becomes his portion. He is an exotic plant, that must be removed to some more congenial soil, or perish at home for want of culture.

It is far from my intentions to say any thing in

derogation of those respectable characters, on whom you rely to vindicate the literary honor of our country. But what will be the result of a comparison between a few correct authors, the miscellaneous productions, and casual discoveries, which we boast of as our own, within a century past; and the long and brilliant catalogue of profound scholars, celebrated writers, and those exquisite specimens of taste and genius in the fine arts, which have adorned almost every country of Europe, within the same period?

This comparison would be disgraceful indeed to America. It is granted, that her sons are industrious, brave, and enterprising; but, if prudent, they will certainly decline the contest with most European nations, when the palm of genius is the object of dispute.

C. Different climates undoubtedly have a different effect on the bodies and minds of those who inhabit them; and local causes, in the same climate, may be favourable, or adverse to the intellectual powers.

A pure, temperate atmosphere, and romantic scenery, are productive of clear intellects and brilliant imagination. America is far from being deficient in these advantages. The oratory, councils, and sagacity of its natives, prove that their conceptions are by no means cramped by physical causes.

This being granted, which cannot be denied, it will be extremely difficult to show a reason, why the mental powers of our ancestors, or their descendants, should suffer a decay in this country, so favourable by nature to sound judgment and brilliancy of thought.

Instead of forcing ourselves into such an absurd conclusion, we shall make an obvious distinction, which will lead to a conclusion, not derogatory to the American character; a distinction between natural genius, and its improvement by art. One depends on natural causes; the other, on the state of society.

With a well supported claim to the former, it is no dishonor to acknowledge ourselves inferior to the elder nations of Europe in the latter. Considering the in-

fant state of our country, and the nature of our government, we have more reason to boast, than be
ashamed of our progress in the fine arts.

If not equal in this respect, to our mother country,
we have made more rapid improvement than any other
nation in the world. Our government and habits are
republican; they cherish equal rights and tend to an
equal distribution of property. Our mode of education
has the same tendency to promote an equal distribution of knowledge, and to make us emphatically a " republic of letters:" I would not be understood, adepts
in the fine arts, but participants of useful knowledge.

In the monarchical and aristocratic governments of
Europe, the case is far different. A few privileged orders monopolize not only the wealth and honors, but
the knowledge of their country. They produce a few
profound scholars, who make study the business of
their lives; we acquire a portion of science, as a necessary instrument of livelihood, and deem it absurd to
devote our whole lives to the acquisition of imple-
ments, without having it in our power to make them
useful to ourselves or others.

They have their thousands who are totally ignorant
of letters; we have but very few, who are not instructed in the rudiments of science. They may boast a
small number of masters in the fine arts; we are all
scholars in the useful; and employed in improving the
works of nature, rather than imitating them.

So strong is our propensity to useful employments,
and so sure the reward of those who pursue them, that
necessity, " the mother of invention," has reared but
few professional poets, painters, or musicians among
us. Those, who have occasionally pursued the imitative
arts, from natural inclination, have given sufficient
proof, that even in them, our capacity and genius are
not inferior to those of Europeans; but the encouragement they have met shows that the spirit of our
habits and government tend rather to general improvement in the useful, than partial perfection in the amusing arts.

EXTRACT FROM AN ORATION, DELIVERED AT BOS-
TON, MARCH 5th, 1780; BY JONATHAN MASON,
JUN. ESQ.

THE rising glory of this western hemisphere is already announced; and she is summoned to her
seat among the nations of the earth. We have pub-
licly declared ourselves convinced of the destructive
tendency of standing armies. We have acknowledged
the necessity of public spirit and the love of virtue, to
the happiness of any people; and we profess to be sensible of the great blessings that flow from them. Let
us not then act unworthily of the reputable character
we now sustain. Let integrity of heart, the spirit of
freedom, and rigid virtue be seen to actuate every
member of the commonwealth.

The trial of our patriotism is yet before us; and we
have reason to thank Heaven, that its principles are
so well known and diffused. Exercise towards each
other the benevolent feelings of friendship; and let
that unity of sentiment, which has shone in the field,
be equally animating in our councils. Remember that
prosperity is dangerous; that though successful, we
are not infallible.

Let this sacred maxim receive the deepest impression
upon our minds, that if avarice, if extortion, if luxury,
and political corruption, are suffered to become popular among us, civil discord, and the ruin of our country will be the speedy consequence of such fatal vices.
But while patriotism is the leading principle, and our
laws are contrived with wisdom, and executed with
vigour; while industry, frugality, and temperance,
are held in estimation, and we depend upon public,
spirit and the love of virtue for our social happiness,
peace and affluence will throw their smiles upon the
brow of individuals; our commonwealth will flourish;
our land will become a land of Liberty, and AME-
RICA an asylum for the oppressed.

END.

Printed in the USA
CPSIA information can be obtained
at www.ICGtesting.com
LVHW082153130823
755087LV00008B/413